Sailors and Seababies

The Fairy Tales of Charles Kingsley

Edited and Annotated
by
Anne E. White

Sailors and Seababies: The Fairy Tales of Charles Kingsley
Copyright © 2024 by Anne E. White

Cover photo by Anne E. White. Cover design by Bryan White.

All rights reserved. No part of this publication may be reproduced, stored in a retrieval system or transmitted in any form by any means, electronic, mechanical, photocopy, recording or otherwise, without the prior permission of the publisher, except as provided by Canadian copyright law.

ISBN: 978-1-990258-24-4

Table of Contents

Preface: The Landscape of Charles Kingsley i

Book I: The Heroes 1

    A First Look At *The Heroes* 2

    Lesson #1 (Perseus) 6

    Lesson #2 10

    Lesson #3 14

    Lesson #4 18

    Lesson #5 22

    Lesson #6 24

    Lesson #7 26

    Lesson #8 31

    Lesson #9 35

    Examination Questions for Perseus 41

    Lesson #10 (Jason) 42

    Lesson #11 46

    Lesson #12 49

    Lesson #13 52

    Lesson #14 56

    Lesson #15 59

 Lesson #16 63

 Lesson #17...70

 Lesson #18 74

 Lesson #19 79

 Lesson #20 84

 Lesson #21 88

 Examination Questions for Jason and the Argonauts......................92

 Lesson #22 (Theseus)...93

 Lesson #23 97

 Lesson #24 101

 Lesson #25 103

 Lesson #26 107

 Lesson #27 110

 Lesson #28 112

 Lesson #29 115

 Lesson #30 121

 Examination Questions for Theseus 124

Book II: The Water-Babies 125

 Introduction: Swimming With *The Water-Babies*.......................... 126

Poetic Interlude #1 133

 Reading #1 134

 Reading #2 141

 Reading #3 146

- Poetic Interlude #2 154
  - Reading #4 155
  - Reading #5 160
  - Reading #6 163
  - Reading #7 168
- Poetic Interlude #3 174
  - Reading #8 175
  - Reading #9 179
  - Reading #10 183
  - Reading #11 188
  - Reading #12 190
- Poetic Interlude #4 194
  - Reading #13 195
  - Reading #14 198
  - Reading #15 203
- Poetic Interlude #5 211
  - Reading #16 212
  - Reading #17 216
  - Reading #18 220
  - Reading #19 224
- Poetic Interlude #6 228
  - Reading #20 229
  - Reading #21 232

Reading #22 236
Poetic Interlude #7 242
Reading #23 243
Reading #24 246
Reading #25 250
Reading #26 254
Poetic Interlude #8 260
Reading #27 261
Reading #28 264
Reading #29 267
Reading #30 272
Reading #31 277
Entirely Optional Exam Questions for *The Water-Babies* 281
Bibliography 282

Preface: The Landscape of Charles Kingsley

Why fairy tales?

When I first thought of calling this volume *The Fairy Tales of Charles Kingsley*, I was thinking of Kingsley's insistence that *The Water-Babies* was "just a fairy tale." I thought, like the character Professor Ptthmllnsprts, that it was quite clever of me to notice that Kingsley was doing much the same thing with his book of mythology. But I had forgotten that the subtitle of *The Heroes* was actually *Greek Fairy Tales For My Children*. So Kingsley beat me to it.

> Perhaps we might secure at least a hundred lovely landscapes too,— sunsets, cloudscapes, starlight nights. At any rate he should go forth well furnished... (Charlotte Mason, *A Philosophy of Education*)

In her book *Much May Be Done With Sparrows*, Karen Glass writes that, out of those "hundred lovely landscapes" recommended by Mason, the most endangered is the "landscape beyond." While I don't think we've gone completely beyond needing visual art (and music, and poetry, and all the rest), I agree with her that one of the saddest features of childhood today is its updated map stating "Here be no dragons."

Anthony Esolen writes,

> It has been a great victory for the crushers of imagination to label such figures "stereotypes," and add a sneer to it, as if people who used them in their stories were not very imaginative—or, sometimes, as if they were downright narrow-minded and wicked. (*Ten Ways to Destroy the Imagination of Your Child*, p. 96)

But even in Kingsley's day, there were many like Professor Ptthmllnsprts, who refused to see beyond the "concatenations of atoms." In this story, at least, the professor is punished for his stubbornness.

> So [the fairy] filled his head with things as they are not, to try if he would like them better... (*The Water-Babies*)

Choose door number one, "water-babies," Kingsley is saying. And golden fleeces, sea-toffees, and balls of string; Gairfowls, centaurs, and ships that can take you to the land of Colchis or St. Brendan's Isle. Because, truly, there are much more frightening things in this world, and in worlds beyond that.

Charlotte Mason warned of the ways that many adults, though well-meaning, nevertheless offend, despise, and hinder little ones (*Home Education*). She hinted that one of those ways is to keep them from the "landscape beyond."

> Once more, we know that there is a storehouse of thought wherein we may find all the great ideas that have moved the world. We are

> above all things anxious to give the child the key to this storehouse. The education of the day, it is said, does not produce reading people. We are determined that the children shall love books, therefore we do not interpose ourselves between the book and the child. We read him his *Tanglewood Tales*, and when he is a little older his Plutarch, not trying to break up or water down, but leaving the child's mind to deal with the matter as it can. (Charlotte Mason, *Parents and Children*)

So, these stories are "door number one," a beginning, a first gift to children living in a world that tells them (and their parents and teachers) not only to ignore the "storehouse," but that it doesn't exist at all.

In his introduction to *The Heroes* (not included here), Kingsley wrote to his child readers,

> Come hither, children, at this blessed Christmas time, when all God's creatures should rejoice together, and bless Him who redeemed them all. Come and see old friends of mine, whom I knew long ere you were born. They are come to visit us at Christmas, out of the world where all live to God; and to tell you some of their old fairy tales, which they loved when they were young like you…there are [few] fairy tales like these old Greek ones, for beauty, and wisdom, and truth, and for making children love noble deeds, and trust in God to help them through.

(Fun fact: Nathaniel Hawthorne's *A Wonder-Book* and *Tanglewood Tales* were published only a couple of years before Kingsley's *The Heroes*.)

Why should Christians read these books?

> The Secondary World of storytellers, artists, and poets renews the Primary World of the day-to-day. In reading great literature, especially high fantasy and mythology, we see once again the drama of our world as we might have seen it when the world was young, and each event was marvellous in its newness. (Andrew Buckley, "Coffee With Keats")

Learning our fairy tales from a safe childhood place can help us to tell the good and true from the evil and deceitful.

> One of the ways I like to illustrate how Beauty fits into this is with the Greek mythology of the Muses and the Sirens: The Muses are the daughters of Zeus who inspire Beauty and Truth, while the Sirens are water nymphs that lure sailors to their death through their bewitching songs. Both involve what appears to be Beauty, but with very different outcomes: one leads to life, while the other leads to death… Beauty awakens love; false beauty elicits lust. Truth attracts,

lies seduce. (Steven R. Turley, *Beauty Matters*)

Charles Kingsley wrote his own response to this question:

> For you must not fancy, children, that because these old Greeks were heathens, therefore God did not care for them, and taught them nothing. The Bible tells us that it was not so, but that God's mercy is over all His works, and that He understands the hearts of all people, and fashions all their works ...

> For Jesus Christ, remember, is the Light who lights every man who comes into the world. And no one can think a right thought, or feel a right feeling, or understand the real truth of anything in earth and heaven, unless the good Lord Jesus teaches him by His Spirit, which gives man understanding. (Introduction to *The Heroes*)

Kingsley notes that the Greeks, later in their history, "forgot what God had taught them."

> But, at the time of which this little book speaks, they had not fallen as low as that. They worshipped no idols, as far as I can find; and they still believed in the last six of the ten commandments, and knew well what was right and what was wrong. And they believed (and that was what gave them courage) that the gods loved men, and taught them, and that without the gods men were sure to come to ruin. And in that they were right enough, as we know—more right even than they thought; for without God we can do nothing, and all wisdom comes from Him. (Introduction to *The Heroes*)

A Concluding Thought from Kingsley

> The stories are not all true, of course, nor half of them; you are not simple enough to fancy that; but the meaning of them is true, and true for ever, and that is—Do right, and God will help you. (Introduction to *The Heroes*)

Book I: The Heroes

Sailors and Seababies

A First Look At *The Heroes*

What is a hero?

Let's begin with a message from Charles Kingsley to his young readers (in particular, his children Rose, Maurice, and Mary):

> Now, why have I called this book 'The Heroes'? Because that was the name which the Hellenes gave to men who were brave and skillful, and dared do more than other men. At first, I think, that was all it meant: but after a time it came to mean something more; it came to mean men who helped their country… and therefore after they were dead, were honoured, because they had left their country better than they found it. (Introduction to *The Heroes*)

There are three parts to the book, with several chapters each about Perseus, Jason, and Theseus. All three of these characters appear near each other in Bulfinch's *Age of Fable*, after the general descriptions of gods, but before the Trojan War. By comparison, in Edith Hamilton's *Mythology*, Perseus and Theseus are labelled (along with Hercules and Atalanta) as "The Great Heroes before the Trojan War." Jason's story, "The Quest of the Golden Fleece," is part of a larger section called "Stories of Love and Adventure."

When the goddess Athena first speaks to Perseus (**Lesson #2**), she tells him that there are people with "souls of clay," and others with "souls of fire," who are born to take unusual risks and will be "[driven] forth by strange paths…[to] fight the Titans and the monsters, the enemies of gods and men." Will these brave souls succeed, become famous, or even survive? Athena makes no promises, but she asks Perseus one question: would you rather be a hero, or live your life like a trailing gourd vine that doesn't even offer the world a bit of shade from the sun? Perseus doesn't have to think long about his response.

Perseus, Jason, and Theseus can all be considered "Heroes," both in Athena's sense of the word but also using a more general definition. But each of these three had companions, and each was helped by various people along the way. So, while you think about the main "heroes" of these tales, look for the small ones as well, and also for those that behave "heroically" in one situation (though perhaps not in another).

Where do these stories take place?

> Now you must remember one thing—that 'Greeks' was not their real name. They called themselves always 'Hellenes,' but the Romans miscalled them Greeks; and we have taken that wrong name from the Romans—it would take a long time to tell you why. They were made up of many tribes and many small separate states; and when you hear in this book of Minyae, and Athenians, and other such

names, you must remember that they were all different tribes and
peoples of the one great Hellene race, who lived in what we now call
Greece...And if you are puzzled by the names of places in this book,
you must take the maps and find them out. It will be a pleasanter
way of learning geography than out of a dull lesson-book. (Kingsley,
Introduction to *The Heroes*)

The trouble with "taking the maps and finding them out," is that, often, real places and imaginary ones have gotten mixed in the telling of the tales. However, it is not an impossible feat to map the journeys (even the mythical ones). Online searches (especially image searches) for "map Jason Argonauts journey" or "map of journey of Theseus to Athens" will turn up a variety of helpful resources; the website www.igreekmythology.com is one place to look, as is www.argonauts-book.com. Perhaps the best use of such maps is not to verify each stop on a journey, but just to get a sense of a ship, say, sailing down the coast of Italy and then crossing the Mediterranean.

While keeping that bigger picture in mind, I have tried to give notes for the places named, especially those which will be helpful in future history and geography studies.

Let's talk about Medea

Medea is a powerful and dangerous woman (she is referred to as "the witch-maiden").
She is sometimes a helpful woman.
She is often an angry woman.
She appears in both the Jason and the Theseus stories, which may cause some confusion. Of course there are different versions and details of her story than those presented by Kingsley. But the following is what we know of her in *The Heroes*: Medea is the daughter of King Aietes, and (according to this story) the sister of Chalciope, the widow of Phrixus (a cousin of Jason). She has supernatural relatives including Circe, someone that students will remember from *Tanglewood Tales*.

When Jason arrives at her father's palace (**Lesson #16**), Medea thinks to herself, 'I could show him how to win the [golden] fleece.' And she does: she tells him how to tame the bulls, sow the serpents' teeth, and so on. She also gives him magic ointment to keep him from harm. Jason carries out all the required tasks so successfully that Aietes becomes suspicious that Medea has helped Jason, so she runs to Jason and the crew for protection. They make a deal: Medea will help the Argonauts to get the fleece, and Jason will marry Medea, and they will "rule over the rich princes of the Minyae, in Iolcos by the sea." Happy ending for everybody? Medea has a bad feeling about this, but she agrees, and they go off to get the fleece.

In a following lesson, Medea, realizing her father's ships are close behind them, murders her young brother and throws him overboard, as a distraction. However, this crime enrages not only her father, but Zeus, and his anger is directed not only against Medea but against all the Argonauts; that makes it impossible to carry on with their quest. They visit Circe on her island, asking to be cleansed from their sin. Soon afterwards, they are tempted by the singing Sirens, but Medea shows them how to get past safely.

In **Lesson #19**, the crew and Medea arrive at the palace of King Alcinous and Queen Arete. Medea asks them for refuge, especially against the men she has recognized there from her father's court. The queen takes her side, but the king is not so sure. He says to the queen, "The minstrel's song has charmed you: but I must remember what is right." Arete continues to try to persuade him, but King Aietes' men demand the return of Medea. Jason warns the king that if he crosses Medea, he might be risking her "thousand plans and wiles." In the end, Medea and Jason go off to set up housekeeping together, and she helps the Argonauts kill a giant along the way. The last we hear of Medea is that "Jason could not love her, after all her cruel deeds." Obviously Jason has forgotten his own advice to Aietes.

The story we are missing, in between Jason and Theseus, is that Medea goes to Athens and marries King Aegeus (who happens to be the long-lost father of Theseus). Medea has a son, Medus, with King Aegeus, and she plans for Medus to inherit the kingdom. When Theseus arrives, she knows that he is the true heir, and so attempts to poison him with wine. Theseus may not know who Medea is, but he does realize that she has "the eyes of a snake," so he tries to force her to drink first. After smashing the cup and ruining the flooring, she disappears in a dragon chariot, "and no man saw her more." (Another version of the story has Aegeus himself knocking the cup from her hand, and embracing Theseus as his son.)

Where did Medea go in her chariot? The legends vary. Some say that she returned to her own kingdom and helped restore her father to his throne. Others say that she and her son flew to a place far away and lived among a people who eventually changed their name to the Medes.

But your guess is as good as anyone else's.

Using this book study, Charlotte Mason-style

The Heroes is set as literature reading for AO Year Three (or Form IC). That means several things: that it is meant to be read over the course of one school year, as scheduled on the AO website; that it might be read by some third-graders alone, but that it would just as likely be read aloud by a parent/teacher to children of between six and eight years old; and that some of these children would have heard or read a bit of Greek mythology in previous years. (*A Wonder Book* and *Tanglewood Tales* are suggested as extra reading in Year Two; and some children will also be familiar with *D'Aulaires' Book of Greek Myths*). There may be a bit of overlap between this book and previous readings, e.g. *A Wonder Book* and *The Heroes* both tell the story of "The Gorgon's Head."

Another assumption made here is that the parent/teacher is acquainted with Charlotte Mason's educational practices such as narration. The simplest way to present these lessons is with a short bit of introduction, such as remembering what happened in the last reading, and with a word or two about a place or object that might be unfamiliar to the listeners; then one reading of the text, followed by narration (although younger children, especially, can benefit by having more frequent breaks); and then, perhaps, a few words of discussion and summary. The narration will most likely be oral (rather than written), but it can also be done in creative formats such as dramatization or drawing a picture. The original PNEU term examinations sometimes asked children to draw (or paint) "A picture (with name) of a story you have read in your Tales."

The book can also be used for copywork or dictation, following the instructions on the AO website or in Karen Glass's book *Know and Tell*.

Pronunciation and Spelling of Greek Names

In other study guides, such as those in the *Plutarch Project*, the notes on **People** are always followed by a date or a word of explanation. The lists here, however, are more focused on pronunciation. Those of you who know more Greek than I do may quite rightfully take issue with the quick-and-easy pronunciation guides; but still it seems that a little bit of help is better than none, and it may keep a few students from speaking of "Per-sa-phone."

There are a few spelling changes for names and places, and these are noted.

Abridgement and General Updates

Although Kingsley is someone who could often have used an editor, *The Heroes* is one book where he pretty much "stuck to the script," so the text has not been changed significantly. There are, however, a few omissions and updated words.

Please note that Kingsley's dialogue was originally written using single quotation marks, and we have not changed this.

Using the three sets of examination questions

The questions included for *The Heroes* are from original PNEU programmes.

As term lengths and reading speed can vary, it was hard to know where students might land in *The Heroes* at examination time; so there are separate examination questions for each of the three sections. These can be used in any combination. For example, if you do one lesson every week, you will get to the end of Term One having done all of Perseus and a bit of Jason; so you might ask one question about each of those, or decide to stick to Perseus and save the Jason questions for next term.

Lesson #1 (Perseus)

Introduction

In her book *Mythology*, Edith Hamilton says, "[Perseus] is the only myth in which magic plays a decisive part, and it seems to have been a great favorite in Greece."

Charles Kingsley lets us know very quickly here that we are travelling in a world outside of the everyday, even if the story seems to be set in a real place.

Vocabulary

kindred: family, relatives

Danae bore a son: Kingsley does not explain how this could be possible if Danae had been imprisoned by her father. However, other sources say that **Zeus**, the highest of the Greek gods, fathered the child through enchantment.

the song which she sang: The Greek poet Simonides of Ceos (c. 556-468 B.C.) wrote a lullaby for Danae, of which we have now only a fragment. One of the verses, translated into English, goes like this:

> Wrapt in thy little cloak, my child,
> Thou heed'st not the waters wild,
>   As o'er thy long dark hair they sweep;
>   My love, my life! if thou couldst see
>   Thy hapless mother's misery,
>   Those slumb'ring eyes would learn to weep.

headland: a high point of land dropping down into a body of water

billows, breakers: waves

frieze: coarse woolen cloth

trident: three-pronged spear

whence: where do you come from

eat the bread of idleness: Kingsley is quoting from Proverbs 31:27.

People

Acrisius (Ah-KREESS-ius)

Proetus (PREE-tus)

Cyclopes (sy-KLOH-peez)

The Heroes

Danae (**DA-nay** or **DA-nee**)

Alcyone (**Al-kee-oh-nee** or **Al-see-oh-nee**), Ceyx (**SAY-ix**): mythological characters who were turned into seabirds (as explained in the text)

Immortals: divine beings, gods

Polydectes (**PAH-lee-dec-teez**): ruler of **Seriphos**

Dictys (**DIK-tiss**)

Places

Argos (**AR-goss**) a city in **Argolis**, in the southern part of **Greece** which is called the **Peloponnese**. It is believed to be one of the oldest continuously inhabited cities in the world; but in this story it seems to be more of a village.

Hellas (Hellenes): Greece

Tiryns: a hill fort and town in the **Argolis** region

Reading

Part One

Once upon a time there were two princes who were twins. Their names were **Acrisius** and **Proetus**, and they lived in the pleasant vale of **Argos**, far away in **Hellas**. They had fruitful meadows and vineyards, sheep and oxen, great herds of horses *[omission]*, and all that men could need to make them blest; and yet they were wretched, because they were jealous of each other. From the moment they were born they began to quarrel; and when they grew up each tried to take away the other's share of the kingdom, and keep all for himself.

So first Acrisius drove out Proetus; and he [Proetus] went across the seas, and brought home a foreign princess for his wife, and foreign warriors to help him, who were called **Cyclopes**; and drove out Acrisius in his turn; and then they fought a long while up and down the land, till the quarrel was settled, and Acrisius took Argos and one half the land, and Proetus took **Tiryns** and the other half. And Proetus and his Cyclopes built around Tiryns great walls of unhewn stone, which are standing to this day.

But there came a prophet to that hard-hearted Acrisius, and prophesied against him, and said, 'Because you have risen up against your own blood, your own blood shall rise up against you; because you have sinned against your **kindred**, by your kindred you shall be punished. Your daughter **Danae** shall bear a son, and by that son's hands you shall die. So the gods have ordained, and it will surely come to pass.'

At that Acrisius was very much afraid; but he did not mend his ways. He had been cruel to his own family, and, instead of repenting and being kind to them, he went on to be more cruel than ever; for he shut up his fair daughter Danae in a cavern underground, lined with brass, that no one might come near her. So he fancied himself more cunning than the gods; but you will see presently whether he was able to escape them.

Part Two

Now it came to pass that in time **Danae bore a son**; so beautiful a babe that any but King Acrisius would have had pity on it. But he had no pity; for he took Danae and her babe down to the seashore, and put them into a great chest and thrust them out to sea, for the winds and the waves to carry them whithersoever they would. The northwest wind blew freshly out of the blue mountains, and down the pleasant vale of Argos, and away and out to sea. And away and out to sea before it floated the mother and her babe, while all who watched them wept, save that cruel father, King Acrisius.

So they floated on and on, and the chest danced up and down upon the **billows**, and the baby slept upon its mother's breast; but the poor mother could not sleep, but watched and wept, and she sang to her baby as they floated; and **the song which she sang** you shall learn yourselves someday.

And now they are past the last blue **headland**, and in the open sea; and there is nothing round them but the waves, and the sky, and the wind. But the waves are gentle, and the sky is clear, and the breeze is tender and low; for these are the days when **Alcyone** and **Ceyx** build their nests, and no storms ever ruffle the pleasant summer sea. And who were Alcyone and Ceyx? You shall hear while the chest floats on. Alcyone was a fairy maiden, the daughter of the beach and of the wind. And she loved a sailor-boy, and married him; and none on earth were so happy as they. But at last Ceyx was wrecked; and before he could swim to the shore the billows swallowed him up. And Alcyone saw him drowning, and leapt into the sea to him; but in vain. Then the **Immortals** took pity on them both, and changed them into two fair seabirds; and now they build a floating nest every year, and sail up and down happily forever upon the pleasant seas of Greece.

So a night passed, and a day, and a long day it was for Danae; and another night and day beside, till Danae was faint with hunger and weeping, and yet no land appeared. And all the while the babe slept quietly; and at last poor Danae drooped her head and fell asleep likewise with her cheek against the babe's.

Part Three

After a while she was awakened suddenly; for the chest was jarring and grinding, and the air was full of sound. She looked up, and over her head were mighty cliffs, all red in the setting sun, and around her rocks and **breakers**, and flying flakes of foam. She clasped her hands together, and shrieked aloud for help. And when she cried, help met her: for now there came over the rocks a tall and stately man, and looked down wondering upon poor Danae tossing about in the chest among the waves.

He wore a rough cloak of **frieze**, and on his head a broad hat to shade his face. In his hand he carried a **trident** for spearing fish, and over his shoulder was a casting-net; but Danae could see that he was no common man by his stature, and his walk, and his flowing golden hair and beard; and by the two servants who came behind him, carrying baskets for his fish. But she had hardly time to look at him, before he had laid aside his trident and leapt down the rocks, and thrown his casting-net so surely over Danae and the chest, that he drew it, and her, and the baby, safe upon a ledge of rock.

Then the fisherman took Danae by the hand, and lifted her out of the chest, and said— 'O beautiful damsel, what strange chance has brought you to this island in so frail a ship? Who are you, and **whence**? Surely you are some king's daughter; and this boy is somewhat more than mortal.'

And as he spoke he pointed to the babe; for its face shone like the morning star.

But Danae only held down her head, and sobbed out— 'Tell me to what land I have come, unhappy that I am; and among what men I have fallen!'

And he said, 'This isle is called **Seriphos**, and I am a **Hellene**, and dwell in it. I am the brother of **Polydectes** the king; and men call me **Dictys** the netter, because I catch the fish of the shore.'

Then Danae fell down at his feet, and embraced his knees, and cried— 'Oh, sir, have pity upon a stranger, whom a cruel doom has driven to your land; and let me live in your house as a servant; but treat me honourably, for I was once a king's daughter, and this my boy (as you have truly said) is of no common race. I will not be a charge to you, or **eat the bread of idleness**; for I am more skillful in weaving and embroidery than all the maidens of my land.'

And she was going on; but Dictys stopped her, and raised her up, and said— 'My daughter, I am old, and my hairs are growing grey; while I have no children to make my home cheerful. Come with me then, and you shall be a daughter to me and to my wife, and this babe shall be our grandchild. For I fear the gods and show hospitality to all strangers; knowing that good deeds, like evil ones, always return to those who do them.'

So Danae was comforted, and went home with Dictys the good fisherman, and was a daughter to him and to his wife, till fifteen years were past.

Narration and Discussion

As you can probably guess, the child's name is Perseus (**PER-see-us**). Imagine a day, a few years later, when Perseus asks his mother, or Dictys, or Mrs. Dictys, who he is and how they came there. How might they answer? (If you have a group of students, this could be acted out.)

Do you know any stories about little babies who had to be hidden or sent away because they were in danger?

For further thought: Why might King Acrisius have chosen not to kill his grandson, but to set him and his mother afloat instead?

For even further thought: Kingsley says that Danae "shrieked aloud for help." Who might Danae have been hoping would help her? If you were in such a situation, to whom might you call for help? (Think of Matthew 8:23-27.)

Lesson #2

Introduction

Perseus, now a young man, has a life-changing encounter with the goddess Athena. Maybe it was just a dream, says Kingsley. But in any case, Perseus begins to discover his own "soul of fire."

Vocabulary

> **merchandise:** things to buy and sell
>
> **quoit:** quoits is a game like horseshoes; but it appears that what Kingsley means here is the **discus**, a heavy disk thrown in competitions
>
> **javelin:** a lightweight spear; in athletic competitions, the aim was to throw it the furthest
>
> **lading:** being loaded
>
> **turf:** grassy area
>
> **a mighty shield of brass:** Usually vocabulary notes suggest easier words, not more complicated ones. However, it is worth knowing that Athena's shield is also called her **aegis**, and this word is now used in the English language to mean "protection."
>
> **manhood:** physical and character qualities such as strength and courage. Athena refers to those having these qualities as those with **souls of fire**, and particularly those she calls the **Heroes**, those who will be given unusual powers to do exceptional tasks.
>
> **baseness:** the opposite of "manhood"; dishonesty, cowardice. Athena says that such people have **souls of clay**.
>
> **gourd:** a trailing or climbing, fruit-bearing plant (similar to a melon)
>
> **hell:** We need to be cautious about the use of this word in ancient times. Space does not allow us to discuss early Greek beliefs about the afterlife and the "underworld," but they were quite different from later beliefs, especially those of Christians. In any case, it is clear that Athene is saying such people go into an unhappy afterlife.

unrenowned: unremembered, unknown

brazen: made of brass

viper: snake

brood: family of young ones

mastiff: large dog

boar: wild pig

cunning: cleverness, trickery

People

Pallas Athena (PAL-lass Ah-THEE-nah): also called Athena; the Greek goddess of wisdom, warfare, and handicrafts; the city of Athens is named for her. (Kingsley spells her name Pallas Athene.)

Titans: the generation of Greek gods who ruled before those on Olympus, and had been banished (so did not have a good relationship with gods such as **Athena**)

Medusa (Meh-DIU-sah)

Places

Samos: a **Greek** island in the **Aegean Sea**, off the west coast of present-day **Turkey**

Reading

Part One

Fifteen years were past and gone, and the babe was now grown to be a tall lad and a sailor, and went [on] many voyages after **merchandise** to the islands round. His mother called him Perseus; but all the people in Seriphos said that he was not the son of mortal man, and called him "the son of Zeus," the king of the Immortals. For though he was but fifteen, he was taller by a head than any man in the island; and he was the most skillful of all in running and wrestling and boxing, and in throwing the **quoit** and the **javelin**, and in rowing with the oar, and in playing on the harp, and in all which befits a man. And he was brave and truthful, gentle and courteous, for good old Dictys had trained him well; and well it was for Perseus that he had done so. For now Danae and her son fell into great danger, and Perseus had need of all his wit to defend his mother and himself.

I said that Dictys' brother was Polydectes, king of the island. He was not a righteous man, like Dictys; but greedy, and cunning, and cruel. And when he saw fair Danae, he

Sailors and Seababies

wanted to marry her. But she would not; for she did not love him, and cared for no one but her boy, and her boy's father, whom she never hoped to see again. At last Polydectes became furious; and while Perseus was away at sea he took poor Danae away from Dictys, saying, 'If you will not be my wife, you shall be my slave.' So Danae was made a slave, and had to fetch water from the well, and grind in the mill *[omission]*, because she would not marry that cruel king. But Perseus was far away over the seas in the isle of **Samos**, little thinking how his mother was languishing in grief.

Now one day at Samos, while the ship was **lading**, Perseus wandered into a pleasant wood to get out of the sun, and sat down on the **turf** and fell asleep. And as he slept a strange dream came to him—the strangest dream which he had ever had in his life.

There came a lady to him through the wood, taller than he, or any mortal man; but beautiful exceedingly, with great grey eyes, clear and piercing, but strangely soft and mild. On her head was a helmet, and in her hand a spear. And over her shoulder, above her long blue robes, hung a goatskin, which bore up **a mighty shield of brass**, polished like a mirror. She stood and looked at him with her clear grey eyes; and Perseus saw that her eyelids never moved, nor her eyeballs, but looked straight through and through him, and into his very heart, as if she could see all the secrets of his soul, and knew all that he had ever thought or longed for since the day that he was born. And Perseus dropped his eyes, trembling and blushing, as the wonderful lady spoke.

'Perseus, you must do an errand for me.'

'Who are you, lady? And how do you know my name?'

'I am **Pallas Athena**; and I know the thoughts of all men's hearts, and discern their **manhood** or their **baseness**. And from the **souls of clay** I turn away, and they are blessed, but not by me. They fatten at ease, like sheep in the pasture, and eat what they did not sow, like oxen in the stall. They grow and spread, like the **gourd** along the ground; but, like the gourd, they give no shade to the traveler, and when they are ripe Death gathers them, and they go down unloved into **hell**, and their name vanishes out of the land.

'But to the **souls of fire** I give more fire, and to those who are manful I give a might more than man's. These are the Heroes, the sons of the Immortals, who are blessed, but not like the souls of clay. For I drive them forth by strange paths, Perseus, that they may fight the **Titans** and the monsters, the enemies of gods and men. Through doubt and need, danger and battle, I drive them; and some of them are slain in the flower of youth, no man knows when or where; and some of them win noble names, and a fair and green old age; but what will be their latter end I know not, and none, save Zeus, the father of gods and men. Tell me now, Perseus, which of these two sorts of men seem to you more blessed?'

Then Perseus answered boldly: 'Better to die in the flower of youth, on the chance of winning a noble name, than to live at ease like the sheep, and die unloved and **unrenowned**.'

Then that strange lady laughed, and held up her **brazen** shield, and cried: 'See here, Perseus; dare you face such a monster as this, and slay it, that I may place its head upon this shield?' And in the mirror of the shield there appeared a face, and as Perseus looked on it his blood ran cold. It was the face of a beautiful woman; but her cheeks were pale as death, and her brows were knit with everlasting pain, and her lips were thin and bitter like a snake's; and instead of hair, **vipers** wreathed about her temples, and shot out their forked tongues; while round her head were folded wings like an eagle's, and [instead of hands she had] claws of brass.

And Perseus looked awhile, and then said: 'If there is anything so fierce and foul on earth, it were a noble deed to kill it. Where can I find the monster?'

Then the strange lady smiled again, and said: 'Not yet; you are too young, and too unskilled; for this is **Medusa** the Gorgon, the mother of a monstrous **brood**. Return to your home, and do the work which waits there for you. You must play the man in that before I can think you worthy to go in search of the Gorgon.'

Then Perseus would have spoken, but the strange lady vanished, and he awoke; and behold, it was a dream. But day and night Perseus saw before him the face of that dreadful woman, with the vipers writhing round her head.

Part Two

So he returned home; and when he came to Seriphos, the first thing which he heard was that his mother was a slave in the house of Polydectes.

Grinding his teeth with rage, he went out, and away to the king's palace, and through the men's rooms, and the women's rooms, and so through all the house (for no one dared stop him, so terrible and fair was he), till he found his mother sitting on the floor, turning the stone hand-mill, and weeping as she turned it. And he lifted her up, and kissed her, and bade her follow him forth.

But before they could pass out of the room Polydectes came in, raging. And when Perseus saw him, he flew upon him as the **mastiff** flies on the **boar**. 'Villain and tyrant!' he cried; 'is this your respect for the gods, and thy mercy to strangers and widows? You shall die!' And because he had no sword he caught up the stone hand-mill, and lifted it to dash out Polydectes' brains.

But his mother clung to him, shrieking, 'Oh, my son, we are strangers and helpless in the land; and if you kill the king, all the people will fall on us, and we shall both die.'

Good Dictys, too, who had come in, entreated him. 'Remember that he is my brother. Remember how I have brought you up, and trained you as my own son, and spare him for my sake.'

Then Perseus lowered his hand; and Polydectes, who had been trembling all this while like a coward, because he knew that he was in the wrong, let Perseus and his mother pass. Perseus took his mother to the temple of Athena, and there the priestess made her one of the temple-sweepers; for there they knew she would be safe, and not even Polydectes would dare to drag her away from the altar. And there Perseus, and the good Dictys, and his wife, came to visit her every day; while Polydectes, not being able to get what he wanted by force, cast about in his wicked heart how he might get it by **cunning**.

Narration and Discussion

According to Athena, some people have souls of fire, but others have souls of clay. Does she mean that some people are virtuous (good), and others are evil or just not-as-good? Or is she speaking of something different, that those with souls of clay are the everyday people, and the souls of fire are something much rarer?

How is Perseus is already showing his "soul of fire?"

Describe one person in the story who definitely seems to have a "soul of clay."

Lesson #3

Introduction

Perseus, getting a bit hot-headed at Polydectes' party, brags that he can bring back the head of the Gorgon. "Right! Off you go then," says Polydectes. "And don't hurry back." But, unknown to the king, help is about to come to Perseus.

Vocabulary

    a great feast: Some sources say it was a wedding feast; Lang's *Tales of Troy and Greece* calls it his birthday party.

    do him homage: honour him

    foundling: orphan

    jeering: mocking, teasing

    light-limbed: nimble, agile

    stag: male deer

    scimitar: a short sword with a curved blade. We will soon hear more about this sword.

    condescension: In this context, this word means "mercy" and "courtesy"

    nymph: a spirit in the form of a beautiful maiden, usually inhabiting rivers or woods.

    venom: poison

    Touch them not, for they are immortal: Perseus would not be able to kill the other two sisters with the sword

renown: fame

gird them on: put them on

lest your heart relent: in case you change your mind

People

Three Grey Sisters: Also called the Graeae.

Echidna (E-KID-nah): the mother of many fabled monsters

Geryon (JEER-ee-un)

Stheno (there are various ways to say this, but **STEH-no** will do**)**

Eurale (YOO-ri-ale) (Kingsley spells it Euryte)

Hermes: the messenger of the gods. Pronunciation varies depending on the language of the speaker, but one acceptable way is to say "Hermies," to rhyme with "germies."

Argus: a hundred-eyed giant killed by Hermes

Places

Olympus: Mount Olympus, located in **Thessaly**, which was believed to be the home of the twelve major Greek gods

Reading

Part One

Now [Polydectes] was sure that he could never get back Danae as long as Perseus was in the island; so he made a plot to rid himself of him. And first he pretended to have forgiven Perseus, and to have forgotten Danae; so that, for a while, all went as smoothly as ever.

Next he proclaimed **a great feast**, and invited to it all the chiefs, and landowners, and the young men of the island, and among them Perseus, that they might all **do him homage** as their king, and eat of his banquet in his hall.

On the appointed day they all came; and as the custom was then, each guest brought his present with him to the king. One brought a horse, another a shawl, or a ring, or a sword; and those who had nothing better brought a basket of grapes, or of game; but Perseus brought nothing, for he had nothing to bring, being but a poor sailor-lad.

He was ashamed, however, to go into the king's presence without his gift; and he was too proud to ask Dictys to lend him one. So he stood at the door sorrowfully, watching the rich men go in; and his face grew very red as they pointed at him, and smiled, and whispered, 'What has that **foundling** to give?'

Now this was what Polydectes wanted; and as soon as he heard that Perseus stood without, he bade them bring him in, and asked him scornfully before them all, 'Am I not your king, Perseus, and have I not invited you to my feast? Where is your present, then?'

Perseus blushed and stammered, while all the proud men round laughed, and some of them began **jeering** him openly. 'This fellow was thrown ashore here like a piece of weed or driftwood, and yet he is too proud to bring a gift to the king.'

'And though he does not know who his father is, he is vain enough to let the old women call him the son of Zeus.'

And so forth, till poor Perseus grew mad with shame, and hardly knowing what he said, cried out,— 'A present! who are you who talk of presents? See if I do not bring a nobler one than all of yours together!' So he said, boasting; and yet he felt in his heart that he was braver than all those scoffers, and more able to do some glorious deed.

'Hear him! Hear the boaster! What is it to be?' cried they all, laughing louder than ever.

Then his dream at Samos came into his mind, and he cried aloud, 'The head of the Gorgon.' He was half afraid, after he had said the words, for all laughed louder than ever, and Polydectes loudest of all.

'You have promised to bring me the Gorgon's head? Then never appear again in this island without it. Go!' Perseus ground his teeth with rage, for he saw that he had fallen into a trap; but his promise lay upon him, and he went out without a word.

Part Two

Down to the cliffs he went, and looked across the broad blue sea; and he wondered if his dream were true, and prayed in the bitterness of his soul: 'Pallas Athena, was my dream true? and shall I slay the Gorgon? If thou didst really show me her face, let me not come to shame as a liar and boastful. Rashly and angrily I promised; but cunningly and patiently will I perform.'

But there was no answer, nor sign; neither thunder nor any appearance; not even a cloud in the sky. And three times Perseus called weeping, 'Rashly and angrily I promised; but cunningly and patiently will I perform.'

Then he saw afar off above the sea a small white cloud, as bright as silver. And it came on, nearer and nearer, till its brightness dazzled his eyes.

Perseus wondered at that strange cloud, for there was no other cloud all round the sky; and he trembled as it touched the cliff below. And as it touched, it broke, and parted, and within it appeared Pallas Athena, as he had seen her at Samos in his dream, and beside her a young man more **light-limbed** than the stag, whose eyes were like sparks of fire. By his side was a **scimitar** of diamond, all of one clear precious stone, and on his feet were golden sandals, from the heels of which grew living wings.

They looked upon Perseus keenly, and yet they never moved their eyes; and they came up the cliffs towards him more swiftly than the seagull, and yet they never moved their feet, nor did the breeze stir the robes about their limbs; only the wings of the youth's sandals quivered, like a hawk's when he hangs above the cliff. And Perseus fell down and worshipped, for he knew that they were more than man.

But Athena stood before him and spoke gently, and bid him have no fear.

Part Three

Then— 'Perseus,' she said, 'he who overcomes in one trial merits thereby a sharper trial still. You have braved Polydectes, and done manfully. Dare you brave Medusa the Gorgon?'

And Perseus said, 'Try me; for since you spoke to me in Samos a new soul has come into my breast, and I should be ashamed not to dare anything which I can do. Show me, then, how I can do this!'

'Perseus,' said Athena, 'think well before you attempt; for this deed requires a seven years' journey, in which you cannot repent or turn back nor escape; but if your heart fails you, you must die in the Unshapen Land, where no man will ever find your bones.'

'Better so than live here, useless and despised,' said Perseus. 'Tell me, then, oh tell me, fair and wise goddess, of your great kindness and **condescension**, how I can do but this one thing, and then, if need be, die!'

Then Athena smiled and said—

'Be patient, and listen; for if you forget my words, you will indeed die. You must go northward *[omission]* till you find the Three Grey Sisters, who have but one eye and one tooth between them. You must ask them the way to the **nymphs**, the daughters of the Evening Star *[omission]*. They will tell you the way to the Gorgon, that you may slay her, my enemy, the mother of monstrous beasts. Once she was a maiden as beautiful as morn, till in her pride she sinned a sin at which the sun hid his face; and from that day her hair was turned to vipers, and her hands to eagle's claws; and her heart was filled with shame and rage, and her lips with bitter **venom**; and her eyes became so terrible that whosoever looks on them is turned to stone; and her children are the winged horse and the giant of the golden sword; and her grandchildren are **Echidna** the witch-adder, and **Geryon** the [three-headed giant]. So she became the sister of the Gorgons, **Stheno** and **Euryale** the Abhorred, the daughters of the Queen of the Sea. **Touch them not, for they are immortal**; but bring me only Medusa's head.'

'And I will bring it!' said Perseus; 'but how am I to escape her eyes? Will she not freeze me too into stone?'

'You shall take this polished shield,' said Athena, 'and when you come near her look not at her herself, but at her image in the brass; so you may strike her safely. And when you have struck off her head, wrap it, with your face turned away, in the folds of the goatskin on which the shield hangs *[omission]*. So you will bring it safely back to me, and win to yourself **renown**, and a place among the heroes who feast with the Immortals upon the peak where no winds blow.'

Then Perseus said, 'I will go, though I die in going. But how shall I cross the seas without a ship? And who will show me my way? And when I find her, how shall I slay her, if her scales be iron and brass?'

Then the young man spoke: 'These sandals of mine will bear you across the seas, and over hill and dale like a bird, as they bear me all day long; for I am **Hermes**, the far-famed **Argus**-slayer, the messenger of the Immortals who dwell on **Olympus**.'

Then Perseus fell down and worshipped.

Part Four

The young man spoke again: 'The sandals themselves will guide you on the road, for they are divine and cannot stray; and this sword itself, the Argus-slayer, will kill her, for it is divine, and needs no second stroke. Arise, and **gird them on**, and go forth.' So Perseus arose, and girded on the sandals and the sword.

And Athena cried, 'Now leap from the cliff and be gone.'

But Perseus lingered. 'May I not bid farewell to my mother and to Dictys? And may I not offer burnt offerings to you, and to Hermes the far-famed Argus-slayer, and to Father Zeus above?'

'You shall not bid farewell to your mother, **lest your heart relent** at her weeping. I will comfort her and Dictys until you return in peace. Nor shall you offer burnt offerings to the Olympians; for your offering shall be Medusa's head. Leap, and trust in the armour of the Immortals.'

Then Perseus looked down the cliff and shuddered; but he was ashamed to show his dread. Then he thought of Medusa and the renown before him, and he leaped into the empty air. And behold, instead of falling he floated, and stood, and ran along the sky. He looked back, but Athena had vanished, and Hermes; and the sandals led him on northward ever *[omission]*.

Narration and Discussion

In this reading, Perseus goes from being called "a piece of driftwood" to floating through the sky in a pair of magic sandals. Explain how he got there.

Should Perseus have managed his temper better at the party? Why or why not?

Creative narration: Write (or draw) a to-do list for Perseus.

Lesson #4

Introduction

Perseus travels north to get information from the Grey Sisters, and then heads south, hoping to find Atlas and his daughters.

Vocabulary

going dry-shod: keeping his feet dry

moors: wild upland areas

fens: boggy places

the air was full of feathers: it was snowing

venerable: deserving respect because of age

insolent: rude, cheeky

gamboled: jumped about playfully

People

Atlas the Giant: one of the Titans, who was forced by Zeus to bear the weight of the earth on his shoulders

Hesperides: three nymphs, nieces (in this story anyway) of Atlas

Tritons: Triton is a god of the sea, but **Tritons** (plural) refers to mer-men.

Galatea: the beautiful Nereid Galatea. See **Reading #15** in *The Water-Babies*.

Places

Cythnus…Thessalian plains: all parts of Greece

Thracian mountains: Thrace was a region) in southeastern Europe, between the **Balkan Mountains**, the **Aegean Sea**, and the **Black Sea**.

Ister stream: the Dniester, a river in Eastern Europe

Scythian plains: present-day Ukraine (more or less)

Unshapen Land: the unpleasant frozen place where the Three Grey Sisters live

Reading

Part One

So Perseus started on his journey, **going dry-shod** over land and sea; and his heart was high and joyful, for the winged sandals bore him each day a seven days' journey.

And he went by **Cythnus**, and by **Ceos**, and the pleasant **Cyclades** to **Attica**; and past **Athens** and **Thebes**, and the **Copaic lake**, and up the **vale of Cephissus**, and past the peaks of **Oeta** and **Pindus**, and over the rich **Thessalian plains**, till the sunny hills of Greece were behind him, and before him were the wilds of the north. Then he passed the **Thracian mountains**, and many a barbarous tribe, Paeons and Dardans and Triballi, till he came to the **Ister stream**, and the dreary **Scythian plains**. And he walked across the Ister, dry-shod; and away through the **moors** and **fens**, day and night toward the bleak north-west, turning neither to the right hand nor the left, till he came to the **Unshapen Land**, and the place which has no name.

And seven days he walked through it, on a path which few can tell; for those who have trodden it like least to speak of it, and those who go there again in dreams are glad enough when they awake; till he came to the edge of the everlasting night, where **the air was full of feathers**, and the soil was hard with ice; and there at last he found the three Grey Sisters, by the shore of the freezing sea, nodding upon a white log of drift-wood, beneath the cold white winter moon; and they chanted a low song together, 'Why the old times were better than the new.'

Part Two

There was no living thing around them, not a fly, not a moss upon the rocks. Neither seal nor sea-gull dare come near, lest the ice should clutch them in its claws. The surge broke up in foam, but it fell again in flakes of snow; and it frosted the hair of the Three Grey Sisters, and the bones in the ice-cliff above their heads.

They passed the eye from one to the other, but for all that they could not see; and they passed the tooth from one to the other, but for all that they could not eat; and they sat in the full glare of the moon, but they were none the warmer for her beams. And Perseus pitied the Three Grey Sisters; but they did not pity themselves.

So he said, 'Oh, **venerable** mothers, wisdom is the daughter of old age. You therefore should know many things. Tell me, if you can, the path to the Gorgon.'

Then one cried, 'Who is this who reproaches us with old age?'

And another, 'This is the voice of one of the children of men.'

[Perseus said], 'I do not reproach, but honour your old age, and I am one of the sons of men and of the Heroes. The rulers of Olympus have sent me to you to ask the way to the Gorgon.'

Then one said, 'There are new rulers in Olympus, and all new things are bad.'

And another, 'We hate your rulers, and the Heroes, and all the children of men. We are the kindred of the Titans, and the Giants, and the Gorgons, and the ancient monsters of the deep.'

And another, 'Who is this rash and **insolent** man who pushes unbidden into our world?'

And the first, 'There never was such a world as ours, nor will be; if we let him see it, he will spoil it all.'

Then one cried, 'Give me the eye, that I may see him'; and another, 'Give me the tooth, that I may bite him.'

But Perseus, when he saw that they were foolish and proud, and did not love the children of men, left off pitying them, and said to himself, 'Hungry men must needs be hasty; if I stay making many words here, I shall be starved.' Then he stepped close to them, and watched till they passed the eye from hand to hand. And as they groped about between themselves, he held out his own hand gently, till one of them put the eye into it, fancying that it was the hand of her sister. Then he sprang back, and laughed, and cried—

'Cruel and proud old women, I have your eye; and I will throw it into the sea, unless you tell me the path to the Gorgon, and swear to me that you tell me right.'

Part Three

Then they wept, and chattered, and scolded; but in vain. They were forced to tell the truth, though, when they told it, Perseus could hardly make out the road.

'You must go,' they said, 'foolish boy, to the southward, into the ugly glare of the sun, till you come to **Atlas the Giant**, who holds the heaven and the earth apart. And you must ask his daughters, the **Hesperides**, who are young and foolish like yourself. And now give us back our eye, for we have forgotten all the rest.'

So Perseus gave them back their eye; but instead of using it, they nodded and fell fast asleep, and were turned into blocks of ice, till the tide came up and washed them all away. And now they float up and down like icebergs forever, weeping whenever they meet the sunshine, and the fruitful summer and the warm south wind, which fill young hearts with joy.

But Perseus leaped away to the southward, leaving the snow and the ice behind: past the isle of the Hyperboreans, and the tin isles, and the long Iberian shore, while the sun rose higher day by day upon a bright blue summer sea. And the terns and the seagulls swept laughing round his head, and called to him to stop and play, and the dolphins **gamboled** up as he passed, and offered to carry him on their backs. And all night long the sea-nymphs sang sweetly, and the **Tritons** blew upon their conchs, as they played round **Galatea** their queen, in her car of pearled shells.

Day by day the sun rose higher, and leaped more swiftly into the sea at night, and more swiftly out of the sea at dawn; while Perseus skimmed over the billows like a seagull, and his feet were never wetted; and leapt on from wave to wave, and his limbs were never weary, till he saw far away a mighty mountain, all rose-red in the setting sun. Its feet were wrapped in forests, and its head in wreaths of cloud; and Perseus knew that it was Atlas, who holds the heavens and the earth apart.

Narration and Discussion

Pretend you are Perseus giving a news interview, OR writing a postcard home. What have been the best and worst parts of the journey so far?

For those who want to know more: Do you know the story of how Atlas was forced to hold up the heavens? It can be found in many books of Greek myths.

Lesson #5

Introduction

Perseus finds the Nymphs, who want him to stay for a while—but duty calls.

Vocabulary

glen: narrow valley

People

Heracles (HAIR-a-kleez) the mighty, who will come to rob our garden: One of the Labours of Heracles was to steal golden apples from the Garden of the Hesperides.

Hades (HAY-deez): Greek god of the underworld, brother of Zeus and Poseidon (the god of the sea).

Reading

Part One

[Perseus] came to the mountain, and leapt on shore, and wandered upward, among pleasant valleys and waterfalls, and tall trees and strange ferns and flowers; but there was no smoke rising from any **glen**, nor house, nor sign of man. At last he heard sweet voices singing; and he guessed that he was come to the garden of the Nymphs, the daughters of the Evening Star.

They sang like nightingales among the thickets, and Perseus stopped to hear their song; but the words which they spoke he could not understand; no, nor no man after him for many a hundred years. So he stepped forward and saw them dancing, hand in hand around the charmed tree, which bent under its golden fruit; and round the tree-foot was coiled the dragon Ladon, the sleepless snake, who lies there forever, listening to the song of the maidens, blinking and watching with dry bright eyes.

Then Perseus stopped, not because he feared the dragon, but because he was bashful before those fair maids; but when they saw him, they too stopped, and called to him with trembling voices— 'Who are you? Are you **Heracles the mighty, who will come to rob our garden**, and carry off our golden fruit?'

And he answered— 'I am not Heracles the mighty, and I want none of your golden fruit. Tell me, fair Nymphs, the way which leads to the Gorgon, that I may go on my way and slay her.'

'Not yet, not yet, fair boy; come dance with us around the tree in the garden which knows no winter, the home of the south wind and the sun. Come hither and play with us awhile; we have danced alone here for a thousand years, and our hearts are weary with longing for a playfellow. So come, come, come!'

'I cannot dance with you, fair maidens; for I must do the errand of the Immortals. So tell me the way to the Gorgon, lest I wander and perish in the waves.'

Then they sighed and wept; and answered— 'The Gorgon! she will freeze you into stone.'

'It is better to die like a hero than to live like an ox in a stall. The Immortals have lent me weapons, and they will give me wit to use them.'

Then they sighed again and answered, 'Fair boy, if you are bent on your own ruin, be it so. We know not the way to the Gorgon; but we will ask the giant Atlas, above upon the mountain peak, the brother of our father, the silver Evening Star. He sits aloft and sees across the ocean, and far away into the Unshapen Land.'

Part Two

So they went up the mountain *[omission]*, and Perseus went up with them. And they found the giant kneeling, as he held the heavens and the earth apart. They asked him, and he answered mildly, pointing to the sea-board with his mighty hand, 'I can see the Gorgons lying on an island far away, but this youth can never come near them, unless he has the hat of darkness, which whosoever wears cannot be seen.'

Then cried Perseus, 'Where is that hat, that I may find it?'

But the giant smiled. 'No living mortal can find that hat, for it lies in the depths of **Hades**, in the regions of the dead. But my nieces are immortal, and they shall fetch it for you, if you will promise me one thing and keep your faith.'

Then Perseus promised; and the giant said, 'When you come back with the head of Medusa, you shall show me the beautiful horror, that I may lose my feeling and my breathing, and become a stone for ever; for it is weary labour for me to hold the heavens and the earth apart.'

Then Perseus promised, and the eldest of the Nymphs went down, and into a dark cavern among the cliffs, out of which came smoke and thunder *[omission]*. And Perseus and the Nymphs sat down seven days, and waited trembling, till the Nymph came up again; and her face was pale, and her eyes dazzled with the light, for she had been long in the dreary darkness; but in her hand was the magic hat. Then all the Nymphs kissed Perseus, and wept over him a long while; but he was only impatient to be gone. And at last they put the hat upon his head, and he vanished out of their sight.

Narration and Discussion

Was it a hard choice for Perseus to leave the garden of the nymphs? What reason did he give for continuing on the journey?

Creative narration: What would you do if you had a hat that made you invisible?

Lesson #6

Introduction

Armed with the "hat of darkness," Perseus travels through the Unshapen Land, searching for Medusa and her sisters.

Vocabulary

talons: claws

venomous: full of poison

Harpe (HAR-peh): the weapon belonging to Hermes, said to be a cross between a sickle and a sword. Not to be confused with the Harpies, who we will hear about in the story of Jason.

Reading

Part One

But Perseus went on boldly, past many an ugly sight, far away into the heart of the Unshapen Land *[omission]*, to the isles where no ship cruises, where is neither night nor day, where nothing is in its right place, and nothing has a name; till he heard the rustle of the Gorgons' wings and saw the glitter of their brazen **talons**; and then he knew that it was time to halt, lest Medusa should freeze him into stone.

He thought awhile with himself, and remembered Athena's words. He rose aloft into the air, and held the mirror of the shield above his head, and looked up into it that he might see all that was below him.

And he saw the three Gorgons sleeping, as huge as elephants. He knew that they could not see him, because the hat of darkness hid him; and yet he trembled as he sank down near them, so terrible were those brazen claws.

Two of the Gorgons were foul as swine, and lay sleeping heavily, as swine sleep, with their mighty wings outspread; but Medusa tossed to and fro restlessly, and as she tossed Perseus pitied her, she looked so fair and sad. Her plumage was like the rainbow, and her face was like the face of a nymph, only her eyebrows were knit, and her lips clenched, with everlasting care and pain; and her long neck gleamed so white in the mirror that Perseus had not the heart to strike, and said, 'Ah, that it had been either of her sisters!'

But as he looked, from among her tresses the vipers' heads awoke, and peeped up with their bright dry eyes, and showed their fangs, and hissed; and Medusa, as she tossed, threw back her wings and showed her brazen claws; and Perseus saw that, for all her beauty, she was as foul and **venomous** as the rest.

Then he came down and stepped to her boldly, and looked steadfastly on his mirror, and struck with the **Harpe** stoutly once; and he did not need to strike again.

Part Two

Then he wrapped the head in the goatskin, turning away his eyes, and sprang into the air aloft, faster than he ever sprang before. For Medusa's wings and talons rattled as she sank dead upon the rocks; and her two foul sisters woke, and saw her lying dead. Into the air they sprang yelling and looked for him who had done the deed. Thrice they swung round and round, like hawks who beat for a partridge; and thrice they snuffed round and round, like hounds who draw upon a deer. At last they struck upon the scent of the blood, and they checked for a moment to make sure; and then on they rushed with a fearful howl, while the wind rattled hoarse in their wings.

On they rushed, sweeping and flapping, like eagles after a hare; and Perseus' blood ran cold, for all his courage, as he saw them come howling on his track; and he cried, 'Bear me well now, brave sandals, for the hounds of Death are at my heels!'

And well the brave sandals bore him, aloft through cloud and sunshine, across the shoreless sea; and fast followed the hounds of Death, as the roar of their wings came down the wind. But the roar came down fainter and fainter, and the howl of their voices died away; for the sandals were too swift even for Gorgons; and by nightfall they were far behind, two black specks in the southern sky, till the sun sank and he saw them no more.

Part Three

Then he came again to Atlas, and the garden of the Nymphs; and when the giant heard him coming he groaned, and said, 'Fulfil thy promise to me.'

Then Perseus held up to him the Gorgon's head, and he had rest from all his toil; for he became a crag of stone, which sleeps forever far above the clouds.

[Perseus asked the Nymphs], 'By what road shall I go homeward again, for I wandered far round in coming hither?'

And they wept and cried, 'Go home no more, but stay and play with us, the lonely maidens, who dwell forever far away from gods and men.'

But he refused, and they told him his road, and said, 'Take with you this magic fruit, which, if you eat once, you will not hunger for seven days. For you must go eastward and eastward ever." *[omission]*

Narration and Discussion

Why did Perseus feel a little bit sorry for having to kill Medusa?

Why did Atlas want Perseus to turn him to stone?

Creative narration: This story lends itself well to dramatization, illustration, or other creative narration formats.

Lesson #7

Introduction

Stuck in the desert! This isn't exactly what Perseus signed up for, and he begins to worry a bit about how he will get back to Greece. However, after journeying through Egypt, he makes a new friend.

Vocabulary

asps and adders: snakes

prevail: succeed

gale: storm

clove: stuck

oases: plural of **oasis**, a place of water in the desert, where trees and other plants can grow

timbrels: frame drums

cubit: a unit of length based on the length from the elbow to the tip of the middle finger

barbarians: The word "barbarian" mostly meant "foreigners"; the word was not used as a judgement on behaviour.

tresses: hair

hyacinth: a type of flowering plant

fetters: chains

devoted as a victim to the sea-gods: she is to be drowned as a sacrifice

flax: a flowering plant which is the source of linen

People

Psylli: a tribe of ancient Libya (also called Seli)

dwarfs who fought with cranes: This refers to an imaginary race of tiny people who are mentioned by Homer and also by later Greek writers. You can find "The Pygmies" in Bulfinch's *Age of Fable*, and another version of it in *Tanglewood Tales*. So how does this help pin down the location of Perseus? The "pygmies" are said to have lived somewhere near the source of the Nile River; and, as we will see, Perseus is working his way towards Egypt, so the geography does start to make sense.

Eos: the goddess of the dawn

Places

Mediterranean: the sea surrounding Greece (and other countries)

Egypt: a country bridging the northwest corner of Africa and the Sinai Peninsula in the southwest corner of Asia; bordered by the **Red Sea** to the east, and watered by the **Nile River.**

Chemmis: the Greek name for the Egyptian city of **Akhmim**, on the east bank of the **Nile**

Mount Casius: Ras Kasaroun; a small mountain between Egypt and Syria

the vast Serbonian bog: Lake Bardawil, on the north coast of the Sinai Peninsula

at the water's edge, under a black rock: The spot where Perseus met the girl is believed to be the port of **Jaffa** (or **Joppa**), now part of Tel Aviv-Yafo, Israel. This is probably why Kingsley says (in the next reading) that her father is the king of "Iopa," although he seems to be conflating that with "Aethiopia."

Reading

Part One

So Perseus flitted onward *[omission]* across the desert: over rock-ledges, and banks of shingle, and level wastes of sand, and shell-drifts bleaching in the sunshine, and the skeletons of great sea-monsters, and dead bones of ancient giants, strewn up and down upon the old sea-floor. And as he went the blood-drops fell to the earth from the Gorgon's head, and became poisonous **asps and adders**, which breed in the desert to this day.

Over the sands he went,—he never knew how far or how long, feeding on the fruit which the Nymphs had given him, till he saw the hills of the **Psylli**, and the **dwarfs who fought with cranes**. Their spears were of reeds and rushes, and their houses of the eggshells of the cranes; and Perseus laughed, and went his way to the north-east, hoping all day long to see the blue **Mediterranean** sparkling, that he might fly across it to his home.

But now came down a mighty wind, and swept him back southward toward the desert. All day long he strove against it; but even the winged sandals could not **prevail**. So he was forced to float down the wind all night; and when the morning dawned there was nothing to be seen, save the same old hateful waste of sand.

And out of the north the sandstorms rushed upon him, blood-red pillars and wreaths, blotting out the noonday sun; and Perseus fled before them, lest he should be choked by the burning dust. At last the **gale** fell calm, and he tried to go northward again; but again came down the sandstorms, and swept him back into the waste, and then all was calm and cloudless as before. Seven days he strove against the storms, and seven days he was driven back, till he was spent with thirst and hunger, and his tongue **clove** to the roof of his mouth. Here and there he fancied that he saw a fair lake, and the sunbeams shining on the water; but when he came to it, it vanished at his feet, and there was nought but burning sand. And if he had not been of the race of the Immortals, he would have perished in the waste; but his life was strong within him, because it was more than man's.

Part Two

Then he cried to Athena, and said— 'Oh, fair and pure, if thou hearest me, wilt thou leave me here to die of drought? I have brought thee the Gorgon's head at thy bidding, and hitherto thou hast prospered my journey; dost thou desert me at the last? Else why will not these immortal sandals prevail, even against the desert storms? Shall I never see my mother more, and the blue ripple round Seriphos, and the sunny hills of Hellas?' So he prayed; and after he had prayed there was a great silence.

The heaven was still above his head, and the sand was still beneath his feet; and Perseus looked up, but there was nothing but the blinding sun in the blinding blue; and round him, but there was nothing but the blinding sand.

And Perseus stood still awhile, and waited, and said, 'Surely I am not here without the will of the Immortals, for Athena will not lie. Were not these sandals to lead me in the right road? Then the road in which I have tried to go must be a wrong road.'

Then suddenly his ears were opened, and he heard the sound of running water.

And at that his heart was lifted up, though he scarcely dare believe his ears; and weary as he was, he hurried forward, though he could scarcely stand upright; and within a bowshot of him was a glen in the sand, and marble rocks, and date-trees, and a lawn of [omission] green grass. And through the lawn a streamlet sparkled and wandered out beyond the trees, and vanished in the sand.

The water trickled among the rocks, and a pleasant breeze rustled in the dry date-branches and Perseus laughed for joy, and leapt down the cliff, and drank of the cool water, and ate of the dates, and slept upon the turf, and leapt up and went forward again: but not toward the north this time; for he said, 'Surely Athena hath sent me hither, and will not have me go homeward yet. What if there be another noble deed to be done, before I see the sunny hills of Hellas?'

Part Three

So he went east, and east forever, by fresh **oases** and fountains, date-palms, and lawns of grass, till he saw before him a mighty mountain-wall, all rose-red in the setting sun. Then he towered in the air like an eagle, for his limbs were strong again; and he flew all night across the mountain till the day began to dawn, and rosy-fingered **Eos** came blushing up the sky.

And then, behold, beneath him was the long green garden of **Egypt** and the shining stream of [the] **Nile**. And he saw cities walled up to heaven, and temples, and obelisks, and pyramids, and giant gods of stone. And he came down amid fields of barley, and flax, and millet, and clambering gourds; and saw the people coming out of the gates of a great city, and setting to work, each in his place, among the watercourses, parting the streams among the plants cunningly with their feet, according to the wisdom of the Egyptians. But when they saw him they all stopped their work, and gathered round him, and cried—

'Who art thou, fair youth? and what bearest thou beneath thy goatskin there? Surely thou art one of the Immortals; for thy skin is white like ivory, and ours is red like clay. Thy hair is like threads of gold, and ours is black and curled. Surely thou art one of the Immortals;' and they would have worshipped him then and there.

But Perseus said— 'I am not one of the Immortals; but I am a Hero of the Hellenes. And I have slain the Gorgon in the wilderness, and bear her head with me. Give me food, therefore, that I may go forward and finish my work.'

Then they gave him food, and fruit, and wine; but they would not let him go. And when the news came into the city that the Gorgon was slain, the priests came out to meet him, and the maidens, with songs and dances, and **timbrels** and harps; and they would have brought him to their temple and to their king; but Perseus put on the hat of darkness, and vanished away out of their sight.

Therefore the Egyptians looked long for his return, but in vain, and worshipped him as a hero, and made a statue of him in **Chemmis**, which stood for many a hundred years; and they said that he appeared to them at times, with sandals a **cubit** long; and that whenever he appeared the season was fruitful; and the Nile rose high that year.

Part Four

Then Perseus went to the eastward, along the **Red Sea** shore; and then, because he was afraid to go into the Arabian deserts, he turned northward once more, and this time no storm hindered him.

He went past *[omission]* **Mount Casius**, and **the vast Serbonian bog**, and [up the coast of the great sea] *[omission]*. But the lowlands were all drowned by floods, and the highlands blasted by fire, and the hills heaved like a babbling cauldron before the wrath of King Poseidon, the shaker of the earth. And Perseus feared to go inland, but flew along the shore above the sea; and he went on all the day, and the sky was black with smoke; and he went on all the night, and the sky was red with flame.

And at the dawn of day he looked toward the cliffs; and **at the water's edge, under a black rock**, he saw a white image stand. 'This,' thought he, 'must surely be the statue of some sea-god; I will go near and see what kind of gods these **barbarians** worship.'

So he came near; but when he came, it was no statue, but a maiden of flesh and blood; for he could see her **tresses** streaming in the breeze; and as he came closer still, he could see how she shrank and shivered when the waves sprinkled her with cold salt spray. Her arms were spread above her head, and fastened to the rock with chains of brass; and her head drooped *[omission]* with sleep, or weariness, or grief. But now and then she looked up and wailed, and called her mother; yet she did not see Perseus, for the cap of darkness was on his head.

Full of pity and indignation, Perseus drew near and looked upon the maid. Her cheeks were darker than his were, and her hair was blue-black like a **hyacinth** *[omission]*. Perseus thought, 'I have never seen so beautiful a maiden; no, not in all our isles. Surely she is a king's daughter. Do barbarians treat their kings' daughters thus? She is too fair, at least, to have done any wrong I will speak to her.'

And, lifting the hat from his head, he flashed into her sight. She shrieked with terror, and tried to hide her face with her hair, for she could not with her hands; but Perseus cried— 'Do not fear me, fair one; I am a Hellene, and no barbarian. What cruel men have bound you? But first I will set you free.'

And he tore at the **fetters**, but they were too strong for him; while the maiden cried— 'Touch me not; I am accursed, **devoted as a victim to the sea-gods**. They will slay you, if you dare to set me free.'

'Let them try,' said Perseus; and drawing the Harpe from his thigh, he cut through the brass as if it had been **flax**.

'Now,' he said, 'you belong to me, and not to these sea-gods, whosoever they may be!' *[omission]* And he clasped her in his arms, and cried, 'Where are these sea-gods, cruel and unjust, who doom fair maids to death? I carry the weapons of Immortals. Let them measure their strength against mine."

Narration and Discussion

The maiden has not yet told her story; but how might Perseus tell her his?

Do you think Perseus is going to have to fight something or someone because of his actions here?

For further thought: When Perseus was most desperate, he thought, "Surely I am not here without the will of the Immortals, for Athena will not lie. Were not these sandals to lead me in the right road? Then the road in which I have tried to go must be a wrong road." Have you ever been lost, or stuck in a difficult situation where you didn't know what to do next? What did you do?

Though he was a calm and resourceful person, Oliver was only six years old after all. So the next move seemed to be to cry. He stumbled and banged along the street, sobbing quietly and wiping his nose on his sleeve, wishing with all his heart that he was at home with Cuffy, and that he had never heard of hot dogs or cotton candy. Dimly he was aware of a clopping of hoofs on pavement but he was too miserable to look up until he heard a voice say:

"Whatsa matter, sonny?"

(Elizabeth Enright, The Saturdays [AO Free Reading, Year Three])

Lesson #8

Introduction

Who is the mysterious girl, and can Perseus save her from the sea monster that is about to eat her?

Vocabulary

hapless: unfortunate, unlucky

ere: before

galley: ship

at their bleaching: probably washing clothes

in sackcloth and ashes: in mourning clothes

betrothed to my son: Some versions say that Andromeda was betrothed to Phineus himself.

People

Cepheus (SEE-fee-us, or **SEH-fee-us):** ruler of Aethiopia

Cassiopeia (Kass-ee-oh-pee-ah): wife of **Cepheus.** (Kingsley spells it **Cassiopoeia.**)

Andromeda (An-DRAH-meh-da, or **An-DROH-meh-da)** their daughter

the daughters of Nereus (NEARY-yoos): Kingsley names a different goddess, but we are going to go with a more common version of the story

Phineus (FIN-ni-us): uncle of Andromeda

Places

Aethiopia: usually refers to the Upper Nile region of Sudan

Reading

Part One

[Then Perseus said], 'But tell me, maiden, who you are, and what dark fate brought you here.'

And she answered, weeping— 'I am the daughter of **Cepheus**, King of **Aethiopia**, and my mother is **Cassiopoeia** of the beautiful tresses, and they called me **Andromeda**, as long as life was mine. And I stand bound here, **hapless** that I am, for the sea-monster's food, to atone for my mother's sin. For she boasted of me once that I was fairer than [**the daughters of Nereus**]; so [Poseidon] sent earthquakes, and wasted all the land [with floods], and after the floods [he sent] a monster bred of the slime, who devours all living things. And now he must devour me, guiltless though I am—me who never harmed a living thing, nor saw a fish upon the shore but I gave it life, and threw it back into the sea *[omission]*. Yet the priests say that nothing but my blood can atone for a sin which I never committed.'

But Perseus laughed, and said, 'A sea-monster? I have fought with worse than him: I would have faced Immortals for your sake; how much more a beast of the sea?'

Then Andromeda looked up at him, and [began to feel] hope *[omission]*, so proud and fair did he stand, with one hand round her, and in the other the glittering sword. But she only sighed, and wept the more, and cried— 'Why will you die, young as you are? Is there not death and sorrow enough in the world already? It is noble for me to die, that I may save the lives of a whole people; but you, better than them all, why should I slay you too? Go you your way; I must go mine.'

But Perseus cried, 'Not so; for the Lords of Olympus, whom I serve, are the friends of the heroes, and help them on to noble deeds. Led by them, I slew the Gorgon, the beautiful horror; and not without them do I come hither, to slay this monster with that same Gorgon's head. Yet hide your eyes when I leave you, lest the sight of it freeze you, too, to stone.'

But the maiden answered nothing, for she could not believe his words. And then, suddenly looking up, she pointed to the sea, and shrieked— 'There he comes, with the sunrise, as they promised. I must die now. How shall I endure it? Oh, go! Is it not dreadful enough to be torn piecemeal, without having you to look on?' And she tried to thrust him away.

But he said, 'I go; yet promise me one thing **ere** I go: that if I slay this beast you will be my wife, and come back with me to my kingdom in fruitful Argos, for I am a king's heir. Promise me, and seal it with a kiss.'

Then she lifted up her face, and kissed him; and Perseus laughed for joy, and flew upward, while Andromeda crouched trembling on the rock, waiting for what might befall.

Part Two

On came the great sea-monster, coasting along like a huge black **galley** *[omission]*, and stopping at times by creek or headland to watch for the laughter of girls **at their bleaching**, or cattle pawing on the sand-hills, or boys bathing on the beach. His great sides were fringed with clustering shells and sea-weeds, and the water gurgled in and out of his wide jaws, as he rolled along, dripping and glistening in the beams of the morning sun.

At last he saw Andromeda, and shot forward to take his prey, while the waves foamed white behind him, and before him the fish fled leaping. Then down from the height of the air fell Perseus like a shooting star; down to the crests of the waves, while Andromeda hid her face as he shouted; and then there was silence for a while.

At last she looked up trembling, and saw Perseus springing toward her; and instead of the monster a long black rock, with the sea rippling quietly round it.

Who then so proud as Perseus, as he leapt back to the rock, and lifted his fair Andromeda in his arms, and flew with her to the cliff-top, as a falcon carries a dove? Who so proud as Perseus, and who so joyful as all the Aethiop people?

For they had stood watching the monster from the cliffs, wailing for the maiden's fate. And already a messenger had gone to Cepheus and Cassiopeia, where they sat **in sackcloth and ashes** on the ground, in the innermost palace chambers, awaiting their daughter's end. And they came, and all the city with them, to see the wonder, with songs and with dances, with cymbals and harps, and received their daughter back again, as one alive from the dead.

Part Three

Then Cepheus said, 'Hero of the Hellenes, stay here with me and be my son-in-law, and I will give you the half of my kingdom.'

'I will be your son-in-law,' said Perseus, 'but of your kingdom I will have none, for I long after the pleasant land of Greece, and my mother who waits for me at home.'

Then Cepheus said, 'You must not take my daughter away at once, for she is to us like one alive from the dead. Stay with us here a year, and after that you shall return with honour.' And Perseus consented; but before he went to the palace he bade the people bring stones and wood, and built three altars, one to Athena, and one to Hermes, and one to Father Zeus, and offered bullocks and rams.

And some said, 'This is a pious man.' Yet the priests said, '[The sea gods will be yet more angry with us, because the monster is slain.]' But they were afraid to speak aloud, for they feared the Gorgon's head.

So they went up to the palace; and when they came in, there stood in the hall **Phineus**, the brother of Cepheus, chafing like a bear robbed of her [cubs], and with him his sons, and his servants, and many an armed man; and he cried to Cepheus— 'You shall not marry your daughter to this stranger, of whom no one knows even the name. Was not Andromeda **betrothed to my son**? And now she is safe again, has he not a right to claim her?'

But Perseus laughed, and answered, 'If your son is in want of a bride, let him save a maiden for himself. As yet he seems but a helpless bride-groom. He left this one to die, and dead she is to him. I saved her alive, and alive she is to me, but to no one else. Ungrateful man! have I not saved your land, and the lives of your sons and daughters, and will you requite me thus? Go, or it will be worse for you.' But all the men-at-arms drew their swords, and rushed on him like wild beasts.

Then he unveiled the Gorgon's head, and said, 'This has delivered my bride from one wild beast: it shall deliver her from many.' And as he spoke Phineus and all his men-at-arms stopped short, and stiffened each man as he stood; and before Perseus had drawn the goatskin over the face again, they were all turned into stone. Then Perseus bade the people bring levers and roll them out; and what was done with them after that I cannot tell.

So they made a great wedding-feast, which lasted seven whole days, and who [was] so happy as Perseus and Andromeda?

Part Four

But on the eighth night Perseus dreamed a dream; and he saw standing beside him Pallas Athena, as he had seen her in Seriphos, seven long years before; and she stood and called him by name, and said— 'Perseus, you have played the man, and see, you have your reward. *[omission]* Now give me here the sword Harpe, and the sandals, and the hat of darkness, that I may give them back to their owners; but the Gorgon's head you shall keep awhile, for you will need it in your land of Greece. Then you shall lay it up in my temple at Seriphos, that I may wear it on my shield forever, a terror to the Titans and the monsters, and the foes of gods and men.' *[omission]*

And Perseus rose to give her the sword, and the cap, and the sandals; but he woke, and his dream vanished away. And yet it was not altogether a dream; for the goatskin with the head was in its place; but the sword, and the cap, and the sandals were gone, and Perseus never saw them more.

Then a great awe fell on Perseus; and he went out in the morning to the people, and told his dream, and bade them build altars to Zeus, the Father of gods and men, and to Athena, who gives wisdom to heroes; and fear no more the earthquakes and the floods, but sow and build in peace.

[omission for content]

The Heroes

Narration and Discussion

Who do you think showed more courage, Perseus or Andromeda?

Do you think Perseus was sorry to give back the magic things?

If you could have just one of the three (the sword, the sandals, or the hat), which would you choose?

For further thought: There are many questions that may be raised about beliefs and superstitions that could lead to a situation such as Andromeda's. There are one or two points that might be brought out: first, that this is (as Kingsley keeps telling us) a fairy tale that includes jealous mermaids and destructive sea monsters. So, yes, obviously there is injustice here, but it's within the realm of imagination, and not necessarily a commentary on particular religious practices. Second, we can ask something like, "Suppose we run across someone in real life who is stuck and seems to need help. What if helping might be dangerous, or might cause them additional trouble? How do you decide what is the right thing to do?"
   (And then realize that's a question we'll be asking all our lives.)

> *"But Rush, he has such a horrible time."*
>
> *"Maybe he doesn't think of it like you do. People never feel pitiful to themselves. They feel sore, or mad, or blue or something; but they don't ever feel pitiful."*
>
> *"How do you know?"*
>
> *"I just know, that's all."*
>
> *Randy accepted this as wisdom.*
>
> (Elizabeth Enright, *Then There Were Five* [AO Free Reading, Year Three])

Lesson #9

Introduction

In this last story about Perseus, we are pretty much prepared for what he is about to do with the Gorgon's head. But what about Acrisius, the wicked grandfather, who (it was prophesied) would also die at the hands of Danae's son?

Sailors and Seababies

Vocabulary

vermilion: red

pitch: a waterproofing material like tar

dowry: money or other property that a bride brings with her when she marries

upon the threshold: in the doorway

on the board: on the table

quoits: Kingsley seems to have the wrong game here, as traditionally (and logically) what Perseus threw in these games was a **discus**. Quoits is a game of accuracy, but a discus is thrown for distance.

five fathoms: 30 feet (about 9.1 m)

the prophecy had declared that he should kill his grandfather: There are other versions of this story. One of them is that Perseus, trying to restore his grandfather to his rightful throne, turns his great-uncle Proetus to stone with the Gorgon's head. However, Acrisius reverts to his wicked behaviour, and Perseus turns the head on his grandfather as well, thus fulfilling the prophecy in a different way. In any case, Athena eventually takes the Gorgon's head and displays it on her shield.

with the Gorgon's head: Some old star atlases depicted the constellation Perseus as holding the head, but this is not common.

beacon: signal light

People

Phoenicians from Tyre: The Phoenicians were famous as sailors and builders of ships.

Teutamides: king of Larissa (Kingsley spells it Teutamenes)

Pelasgians: a name for the inhabitants of a region near the **Aegean Sea**

Places

Crete: a large island near mainland Greece

Aegean (Sea): the part of the **Mediterranean Sea** between Greece and Asia

Larissa: the largest city in **Thessaly**

Reading

Part One

And when a year was ended Perseus hired **Phoenicians from Tyre**, and cut down cedars, and built himself a noble galley; and painted its [bows] with **vermilion**, and pitched its sides with **pitch**; and in it he put Andromeda, and all her **dowry** of jewels, and rich shawls, and spices from the East; and great was the weeping when they rowed away. But the remembrance of his brave deed was left behind; and Andromeda's rock was shown [there] till more than a thousand years were past.

So Perseus and the Phoenicians rowed to the westward, across the sea of **Crete**, till they came to the blue **Aegean** and the pleasant Isles of Hellas, and Seriphos, his ancient home. Then he left his galley on the beach, and went up as of old; and he embraced his mother, and Dictys his good foster-father, and they wept over each other a long while, for it was seven years and more since they had met.

Then Perseus went out, and up to the hall of Polydectes; and underneath the goatskin he bore the Gorgon's head.

Part Two

And when he came into the hall, Polydectes sat at the table-head, and all his nobles and landowners on either side, each according to his rank, feasting on the fish and the goat's flesh, and drinking the blood-red wine. The harpers harped, and the revelers shouted, and the wine-cups rang merrily as they passed from hand to hand, and great was the noise in the hall of Polydectes.

Then Perseus stood **upon the threshold**, and called to the king by name. But none of the guests knew Perseus, for he was changed by his long journey. He had gone out a boy, and he was come home a hero; his eye shone like an eagle's, and his beard was like a lion's beard, and he stood up like a wild bull in his pride.

But Polydectes the wicked knew him, and hardened his heart still more; and scornfully he called— 'Ah, foundling! have you found it more easy to promise than to fulfil?'

'Those whom the gods help fulfil their promises; and those who despise them, reap as they have sown. Behold the Gorgon's head!' Then Perseus drew back the goatskin, and held aloft the Gorgon's head.

Pale grew Polydectes and his guests as they looked upon that dreadful face. They tried to rise up from their seats: but from their seats they never rose, but stiffened, each man where he sat, into a ring of cold grey stones. Then Perseus turned and left them, and went down to his galley in the bay; and he gave the kingdom to good Dictys, and sailed away with his mother and his bride.

And Polydectes and his guests sat still, with the wine-cups before them **on the board**, till the rafters crumbled down above their heads, and the walls behind their backs, and the table crumbled down between them, and the grass sprung up about their feet: but Polydectes and his guests sit on the hillside, a ring of grey stones until this day.

Part Three

But Perseus rowed westward toward Argos, and landed, and went up to the town. And when he came, he found that Acrisius his grandfather had fled. For Proetus his wicked brother had made war against him afresh; and had come across the river from Tiryns, and conquered Argos, and Acrisius had fled to **Larissa**, in the country of the wild Pelasgians.

Then Perseus called the Argives together, and told them who he was, and all the noble deeds which he had done. And all the nobles and the yeomen made him king, for they saw that he had a royal heart; and they fought with him against Argos, and took it, and killed Proetus, and made the Cyclopes serve them, and build them walls round Argos, like the walls which they had built at Tiryns; and there were great rejoicings in the vale of Argos, because they had got a king from Father Zeus.

But Perseus' heart yearned after his grandfather, and he said, 'Surely he is my flesh and blood, and he will love me now that I am come home with honour. I will go and find him, and bring him home, and we will reign together in peace.'

Part Four

So Perseus sailed away with his Phoenicians, [until] he came to the town of Larissa *[omission]*. And when he came there, all the people were in the fields, and there was feasting, and all kinds of games; for **Teutamides** their king wished to honour Acrisius, because he was the king of a mighty land. Perseus did not tell his name, but went up to the games unknown; for he said, 'If I carry away the prize in the games, my grandfather's heart will be softened toward me.'

So he threw off his helmet, and his [armour], and all his clothes, and stood among the youths of Larissa, while all wondered at him, and said, 'Who is this young stranger, who stands like a wild bull in his pride? Surely he is one of the Heroes, the sons of the Immortals, from Olympus.'

And when the games began, they wondered yet more; for Perseus was the best man of all at running, and leaping, and wrestling and throwing the javelin; and he won four crowns, and took them, and then he said to himself, 'There is a fifth crown yet to be won: I will win that, and lay them all upon the knees of my grandfather.'

And as he spoke, he saw where Acrisius sat, by the side of Teutamides the king, with his white beard flowing down upon his knees, and his royal staff in his hand; and Perseus wept when he looked at him, for his heart yearned after his kin; and he said, 'Surely he is a kingly old man, yet he need not be ashamed of his grandson.'

Then he took the **quoits**, and hurled them, **five fathoms** beyond all the rest; and the people shouted, 'Further yet, brave stranger! There has never been such a hurler in this land.'

Then Perseus put out all his strength, and hurled. But a gust of wind came from the sea, and carried the quoit aside, and far beyond all the rest; and it fell on the foot of Acrisius, and he swooned away with the pain. Perseus shrieked, and ran up to him; but when they lifted the old man up he was dead, for his life was slow and feeble.

Then Perseus rent his clothes, and cast dust upon his head, and wept a long while for his grandfather. At last he rose, and called to all the people aloud, and said— 'The gods are true, and what they have ordained must be. I am Perseus, the grandson of this dead man, the far-famed slayer of the Gorgon.'

Then he told them how **the prophecy had declared that he should kill his grandfather**, and all the story of his life. So they made a great mourning for Acrisius, and burnt [his body]; and Perseus went to the temple, and was purified from the guilt of the death, because he had done it unknowingly.

Part Five

Then he went home to Argos, and reigned there well with fair Andromeda; and they had four sons and three daughters, and died in a good old age. And when they died, the ancients say, Athena took them up into the sky, with Cepheus and Cassiopeia. And there on starlight nights you may see them shining still; Cepheus with his kingly crown, and Cassiopeia in her ivory chair, plaiting her star-spangled tresses, and Perseus **with the Gorgon's head**, and fair Andromeda beside him, spreading her long white arms across the heaven *[omission]*. [There is also a constellation for Cetus, the sea monster.]

All night long, they shine, for a beacon to wandering sailors; but all day they feast with the gods, on the still blue peaks of Olympus.

Narration and Discussion

Do you think Dictys was a good choice to be king in Seriphos?

What do you think might have happened if Perseus had *not* struck his grandfather with the discus?

For the curious: Have you ever heard of any of these constellations? The constellation Cassiopeia the Queen (formerly called Cassiopeia's Chair) is one that can easily be picked out when the Big Dipper (Ursa Major) is also in view. The constellation Andromeda can be seen in the autumn, in the northern and sometimes in the southern hemispheres. A good star map (or app) will help you find them. One online resource is the website www.thoughtco.com; use the search bar to search for *constellation andromeda*, or whatever you're looking for.

> *"Didn't you ever heard about the Perseids?"*
> *"No. What are they?"*

Sailors and Seababies

"They're the shooting stars you've been looking at. Every August they come, the sky is full of them. Specially around the tenth. I've counted more'n a hundred some nights..."

"Gee, I learn more from you than I learn in a whole year at school," said Rush admiringly...

(Elizabeth Enright, Then There Were Five*)*

Examination Questions for Perseus

Tell one of these stories:

1. How Perseus acted at Polydectes' feast

2. How Perseus found the Three Grey Sisters

3. How Athena and Hermes came to the help of Perseus

4. How Perseus slew the Gorgon

Sailors and Seababies

Lesson #10 (Jason)

Introduction

> Three thousand years and more they sailed away, into the unknown Eastern seas; and great nations have come and gone since then, and many a storm has swept the earth; and many a mighty armament, to which *Argo* would be but one small boat; English and French, Turkish and Russian, have sailed those waters since; yet the fame of that small *Argo* lives forever, and her name is become a proverb among men. (Kingsley)

As "The Golden Fleece" is also told in Nathaniel Hawthorne's *Tanglewood Tales*, some students will remember hearing it in an earlier year.

The first big problem we hear about is that the restless spirit of Prince Phrixus is roaming around Greece, trying to enlist someone brave enough to go to Colchis and retrieve his golden fleece. So far there are no takers.

The second problem is that of his cousin King Aeson, who is driven out of his kingdom by his wicked brother. Aeson, wanting to protect his young son from the usurper, comes up with a plan to move him somewhere safe. The two of them climb up a mountain, and hear someone singing in a cave. "Trust me on this," says Aeson, and the boy, though confused, obeys him and goes in.

Vocabulary

strait: a narrow passage of water, often connecting two seas

torrent: a rushing stream, and sometimes a waterfall

People

Socrates (SOH-kra-teez): a famous Greek philosopher

ladies who went out last year: the volunteer nurses, led by Florence Nightingale, who served in the Crimean War

Argonauts: those who sailed with Jason in the ship *Argo*

Phrixus and Helle: mythical twins whose parents were a king and a cloud goddess. There is a whole story about how they escaped from their evil stepmother, and how Phrixus ended up in **Colchis** (see below).

Minyans or **Minyae (MIN-yee):** a tribe who lived in the Greek region of **Boeotia**. (Kingsley spells this word **Minuai**.)

Chalciope (Kal-SEE-o-pee)

Aietes (Ay-EE-teez or Eye-EE-teez): I have kept Kingsley's spelling, as it is easier to read than other versions.

Aeson (EE-sahn)

Pelias (PEEL-ee-us)

Places

Thermopylae: the site of a famous battle in 480 B.C.

Thracian Chersonese: a peninsula (strip of land) between Europe and Asia

Hellespont: also called the Strait of Gallipoli and the Dardanelles; a **strait** in northwestern Turkey that forms part of the boundary between Europe and Asia

Colchis (KOHL-kiss): an ancient region at the eastern end of the Black Sea. The city of **Kutaisi** in **Georgia** is believed to be in the place where the Golden Fleece was found.

Circassian coast: the Russian Black Sea Coast

Hellas: Greece

Iolcos (or Iolcus, Iolkos): an ancient city in **Thessaly**, Greece

Anauros (or Anavros): a **torrent** near Iolcos

Pelion: a mountain in southeastern Thessaly

Reading

Prologue

I have told you of a hero who fought with wild beasts and with wild men; but now I have a tale of heroes who sailed away into a distant land, to win themselves renown forever, in the adventure of the Golden Fleece.

Whither they sailed, my children, I cannot clearly tell. It all happened long ago; so long that it has all grown dim, like a dream which you dreamt last year. And why they went I cannot tell: some say that it was to win gold. It may be so; but the noblest deeds which have been done on earth have not been done for gold. It was not for the sake of gold that the Lord came down and died, and the Apostles went out to preach the good news in all lands. The Spartans looked for no reward in money when they fought and died at **Thermopylae**; and **Socrates** the wise asked no pay from his countrymen, but lived poor and barefoot all his days, only caring to make men good. And there are heroes in our days also, who do noble deeds, but not for gold. Our discoverers did not go to make themselves rich when they sailed out one after another into the dreary frozen seas; nor did the **ladies who went out last year** to drudge in the hospitals of the East, making themselves poor, that they might be rich in noble works *[omission]*. No, children, there is a better thing on earth than wealth, a better thing than life itself; and that is, to have done something before you die, for which good men may honour you, and God your Father smile upon your work.

Therefore we will believe—why should we not?—of these same **Argonauts** of old, that they too were noble men, who planned and did a noble deed; and that therefore their fame has lived, and been told in story and in song, mixed up, no doubt, with dreams and fables, and yet true and right at heart. So we will honour these old Argonauts, and listen to their story as it stands; and we will try to be like them, each of us in our place; for each of us has a Golden Fleece to seek, and a wild sea to sail over ere we reach it, and dragons to fight ere it be ours.

Part One: Before Jason

And what was that first Golden Fleece? [This is the legend]: **Phrixus and Helle** were the children of [a] cloud-nymph, and of Athamas the **Minyan** king. And when a famine came upon the land, their cruel step-mother Ino wished to kill them, that her own children might reign, and said that they must be sacrificed on an altar, to turn away the anger of the gods. So the poor children were brought to the altar, and the priest stood ready with his knife—when out of the clouds came the Golden Ram, and took them on his back, and vanished. Then madness came upon that foolish king, Athamas, and ruin upon Ino and her children.

[Omission for length and content.]

But the ram carried the two children far away over land and sea, till he came to the **Thracian Chersonese**, and there Helle fell into the sea. So those narrow **straits** are called the **Hellespont**, after her; and they bear that name until this day.

Then the ram flew on with Phrixus to the north-east across the [Black] Sea *[omission]*. And at last, they say, he stopped at **Colchis**, on the steep **Circassian coast**; and there Phrixus married **Chalciope**, the daughter of **Aietes** the king; and offered the ram in sacrifice; and Aietes nailed the ram's fleece to a beech [tree], in the grove of Ares the war-god.

And after a while Phrixus died, and was buried, but his spirit had no rest; for he was buried far from his native land, and the pleasant hills of **Hellas**. So he came in dreams to the heroes of the **Minyae**, and called sadly by their beds, 'Come and set my spirit free, that I may go home *[omission]* to my kinsfolk, and the pleasant Minyan land.'

And they asked, 'How shall we set your spirit free?'

'You must sail over the sea to Colchis, and bring home the golden fleece; and then my spirit will come back with it, and I shall sleep with my fathers and have rest.'

He came thus, and called to them often; but when they woke they looked at each other, and said, 'Who dare sail to Colchis, or bring home the golden fleece?' And in all the country none was brave enough to try it; for the man and the time were not come.

Part Two

Phrixus had a cousin called **Aeson**, who was king in **Iolcos** by the sea. There he ruled over the rich Minyan heroes, as Athamas his uncle ruled in Boeotia; and, like Athamas, he was an unhappy man. For he had a step-brother named **Pelias**, [who was fearless and lawless]; and at last [Pelias] drove out Aeson, and then his own brother Neleus, and took the kingdom to himself, and ruled over the rich Minyan heroes, in Iolcos by the sea.

And Aeson, when he was driven out, went sadly away out of the town, leading his little son by the hand; and he said to himself, 'I must hide the child in the mountains; or Pelias will surely kill him, because he is the heir.'

So he went up from the sea across the valley, through the vineyards and the olive groves, and across the **torrent** of **Anauros**, toward **Pelion** the ancient mountain, whose brows are white with snow. He went up and up into the mountain, over marsh, and crag, and down, till the boy was tired and footsore, and Aeson had to bear him in his arms, till he came to the mouth of a lonely cave, at the foot of a mighty cliff.

Above the cliff the snow-wreaths hung, dripping and cracking in the sun; but at its foot around the cave's mouth grew all fair flowers and herbs, as if in a garden, ranged in order, each sort by itself. There they grew gaily in the sunshine, and the spray of the torrent from above; while from the cave came the sound of music, and a man's voice singing to the harp.

Then Aeson put down the lad, and whispered—

'Fear not, but go in, and whomsoever you shall find, lay your hands upon his knees, and say, *In the name of Zeus, the father of gods and men, I am your guest from this day forth.*' Then the lad went in without trembling, for he too was a hero's son; but when he was within, he stopped in wonder to listen to that magic song.

Narration and Discussion

What was the biggest difference between the two fathers (Athamas and Aeson) in this passage?

Who or what do you think might be in the cave?

For further thought: Kingsley says "each of us has a Golden Fleece to seek, and a wild sea to sail over ere we reach it, and dragons to fight ere it be ours." What do you think he means?

> ...*the four dwarves sat round the table, and talked about mines and gold and troubles with the goblins, and the depredations of dragons, and lots of other things which he did not understand, and did not want to, for they sounded much too adventurous ...* (J. R. R. Tolkien, **The Hobbit** *[AO Literature, Year Six])*

Lesson #11

Introduction

We now learn about the education of Jason—because this hidden place in the mountains is a (very) unusual school.

Vocabulary

Centaur: part man, part horse

ether: sky

valiant: brave, courageous

lyre: a harp with a U-shaped frame

resound: echo

according to his deserts: in the way that each of them deserved

downs: hills

People

Aeolids: legendary rulers in Greece; the descendants of **Aeolus**

Cheiron (KY-run) (also spelled **Chiron, Kheiron**)

Aeneas: He would grow up to be one of the heroes of the Trojan war.

Peleus: He would grow up to be king of Phthia, and the father of **Achilles**.

Caeneus: either he or his son (depending on the version told) became one of the Argonauts

Asclepius: He would grow up to be a great healer.

Reading

Part One

And there he saw the singer lying upon bear-skins and fragrant boughs: **Cheiron**, the ancient **Centaur**, the wisest of all things beneath the sky. Down to the waist he was a man, but below he was a noble horse; his white hair rolled down over his broad shoulders, and his white beard over his broad brown chest; and his eyes were wise and mild, and his forehead like a mountain-wall. And in his hands he held a harp of gold, and struck it with a golden key; and as he struck, he sang till his eyes glittered, and filled all the cave with light.

And he sang of the birth of Time, and of the heavens and the dancing stars; and of the ocean, and the **ether**, and the fire, and the shaping of the wondrous earth. And he sang of the treasures of the hills, and the hidden jewels of the mine, and the veins of fire and metal, and the virtues of all healing herbs, and of the speech of birds, and of prophecy, and of hidden things to come.

Then he sang of health, and strength, and manhood, and a **valiant** heart; and of music, and hunting, and wrestling, and all the games which heroes love: and of travel, and wars, and sieges, and a noble death in fight; and then he sang of peace and plenty, and of equal justice in the land; and as he sang the boy listened wide-eyed, and forgot his errand in the song.

And at the last old Cheiron was silent, and called the lad with a soft voice. And the lad ran trembling to him, and would have laid his hands upon his knees; but Cheiron smiled, and said, 'Call hither your father Aeson, for I know you, and all that has befallen, and saw you both afar in the valley, even before you left the town.'

Then Aeson came in sadly, and Cheiron asked him, 'Why camest you not yourself to me, Aeson the **Aeolid**?'

And Aeson said— 'I thought, Cheiron will pity the lad if he sees him come alone; and I wished to try whether he was fearless, and dare venture like a hero's son. But now I entreat you by Father Zeus, let the boy be your guest till better times, and train him among the sons of the heroes, that he may avenge his father's house.'

Then Cheiron smiled, and drew the lad to him, and laid his hand upon his golden locks, and said, 'Are you afraid of my horse's hoofs, fair boy, or will you be my pupil from this day?'

'I would gladly have horse's hoofs like you, if I could sing such songs as yours.'

And Cheiron laughed, and said, 'Sit here by me till sundown, when your playfellows will come home, and you shall learn like them to be a king, worthy to rule over gallant men.' Then he turned to Aeson, and said, 'Go back in peace, and bend before the storm like a prudent man. This boy shall not cross the Anauros again, till he has become a glory to you and to the house of **Aeolus**.'

And Aeson wept over his son and went away; but the boy did not weep, so full was his fancy of that strange cave, and the centaur, and his song, and the playfellows whom he was to see.

Part Two

Then Cheiron put the **lyre** into his hands, and taught him how to play it, till the sun sank low behind the cliff, and a shout was heard outside. And then in came the sons of the heroes, **Aeneas**, and Heracles, and **Peleus**, and many another mighty name.

And great Cheiron leapt up joyfully, and his hoofs made the cave **resound**, as they shouted, 'Come out, Father Cheiron; come out and see our game.'

And one cried, 'I have killed two deer'; and another, 'I took a wild cat among the crags'; and Heracles dragged a wild goat after him by its horns, for he was as huge as a mountain crag; and **Caeneus** carried a bear-cub under each arm, and laughed when they scratched and bit, for neither tooth nor steel could wound him. And Cheiron praised them all, each **according to his deserts**.

Only one walked apart and silent, **Asclepius**, the too-wise child, with his [tunic front] full of herbs and flowers, and round his wrist a spotted snake; he came with downcast eyes to Cheiron, and whispered how he had watched the snake cast its old skin, and grow young again before his eyes, and how he had gone down into a village in the vale, and cured a dying man with a herb which he had seen a sick goat eat.

And Cheiron smiled, and said, 'To each Athena and Apollo give some gift, and each is worthy in his place; but to this child they have given an honour beyond all honours, to cure while others kill.'

Then the lads brought in wood, and split it, and lighted a blazing fire; and others skinned the deer and quartered them, and set them to roast before the fire; and while the [meat] was cooking they bathed in the snow-torrent, and washed away the dust and sweat. And then all ate till they could eat no more (for they had tasted nothing since the dawn), and drank of the clear spring water, for wine is not fit for growing lads. And when the remnants were put away, they all lay down upon the skins and leaves about the fire, and each took the lyre in turn, and sang and played with all his heart. And after a while they all went out to a plot of grass at the cave's mouth, and there they boxed, and ran, and wrestled, and laughed till the stones fell from the cliffs.

Then Cheiron took his lyre, and all the lads joined hands; and as be played, they danced to his measure, in and out, and round and round. There they danced hand in hand, till the night fell over land and sea, while the black glen shone with their broad white limbs and the gleam of their golden hair.

And the lad danced with them, delighted, and then slept a wholesome sleep, upon fragrant leaves of bay, and myrtle, and marjoram, and flowers of thyme; and [he] rose at the dawn, and bathed in the torrent, and became a schoolfellow to the Heroes' sons, and forgot Iolcos, and his father, and all his former life. But he grew strong, and brave and cunning, upon the pleasant **downs** of Pelion, in the keen hungry mountain air. And he learnt to wrestle, and to box, and to hunt, and to play upon the harp; and next he learnt to ride, for old Cheiron used to mount him on his back; and he learnt the virtues of all herbs and how to cure all wounds; and Cheiron called him Jason the Healer, and that is his name until this day.

Narration and Discussion

Would you like to go to Cheiron's school? Why or why not? Is it anything like your school (or homeschool)?

For further thought: Do you think Jason really forgot Iolcos and his father?

Creative narration #1: Draw a poster, or act out a commercial for "Cheiron's King and Hero School."

Creative narration #2: Make up a song that the boys might have sung around the fire.

Lesson #12

Introduction

Ten years have gone by, and school is done. We first get a "where are they now" for Jason's friends; but what will Jason himself do next? The immediate problem, as he is reminded here, is that his uncle has stolen his father's throne. Does Cheiron have any advice for a kingdom-restorer? Yes, he does—but it's not what Jason was expecting.

Vocabulary

fledged: able to fly on its own

arbutus: a kind of flowering shrub

pomegranate: a fruit-bearing shrub. (Have you ever eaten pomegranate seeds?)

mantle: cloak

heifer: young cow

awful: awe-inspiring

try if: see if

People

Lapithai (or Lapiths): a legendary people of Thessaly, related to the Centaurs. Cheiron sings a song about them in **Lesson #15**.

Hera: an important Greek goddess

Places

Peloponnese: the southern part of Greece

Troy: an ancient city located in present-day Turkey; the site of the Trojan War

Lake of Boebe (or Boibe): Boebeis Lake in Thessaly, now called **Lake Karla**

Pineios: a river in Thessaly

Tempe: a gorge in northern Thessaly

Magnesia: a region of ancient Greece

Ossa: a mountain in Thessaly

Pagasae (or Pagasai): a town in Thessaly

Haemonia: another name for Thessaly, because Haemon was the father of Thessalus.

Reading

Prologue

And ten years came and went, and Jason was grown to be a mighty man. Some of his fellows were gone, and some were growing up by his side.

Asclepius was gone into **Peloponnese** to work his wondrous cures on men; and some say he used to raise the dead to life.

And Heracles was gone to Thebes to fulfil those famous labours which have become a proverb among men.

And Peleus had married a sea-nymph, and his wedding is famous to this day.

And Aeneas was gone home to **Troy**, and many a noble tale you will read of him, and of all the other gallant heroes, the scholars of Cheiron the just.

Part One

And it happened on a day that Jason stood on the mountain, and looked north and south and east and west; and Cheiron stood by him and watched him, for he knew that the time was come.

And Jason looked and saw the plains of Thessaly, where the **Lapithai** breed their horses; and the **Lake of Boebe**, and the stream which runs northward to **Pineios** and **Tempe**; and he looked north, and saw the mountain wall which guards the **Magnesian** shore; Olympus, the seat of the Immortals, and **Ossa**, and Pelion, where he stood. Then he looked east and saw the bright blue sea, which stretched away forever toward the dawn. Then he looked south, and saw a pleasant land, with white-walled towns and farms, nestling along the shore of a land-locked bay, while the smoke rose blue among the trees; and he knew it for the bay of **Pagasae**, and the rich lowlands of **Haemonia**, and Iolcos by the sea.

Then he sighed, and asked, 'Is it true what the heroes tell me—that I am heir of that fair land?'

'And what good would it be to you, Jason, if you were heir of that fair land?'

'I would take it and keep it.'

'A strong man has taken it and kept it long. Are you stronger than Pelias the Terrible?'

'I can try my strength with his,' said Jason.

But Cheiron sighed, and said— 'You have many a danger to go through before you rule in Iolcos by the sea; many a danger and many a woe; and strange troubles in strange lands, such as man never saw before.'

'The happier I,' said Jason, 'to see what man never saw before.'

And Cheiron sighed again, and said, 'The eaglet must leave the nest when it is **fledged**. Will you go to Iolcos by the sea? Then promise me two things before you go.' Jason promised, and Cheiron answered, 'Speak harshly to no soul whom you may meet, and stand by the word which you shall speak.'

Jason wondered why Cheiron asked this of him; but he knew that the Centaur was a prophet, and saw things long before they came. So he promised, and leapt down the mountain, to take his fortune like a man.

Part Two

He went down through the **arbutus** thickets, and across the downs of thyme, till he came to the vineyard walls, and the **pomegranates** and the olives in the glen; and among the olives roared Anauros, all foaming with a summer flood.

And on the bank of Anauros sat a woman, all wrinkled, grey, and old; her head shook *[omission]*, and her hands shook *[omission]* ; and when she saw Jason, she spoke whining, 'Who will carry me across the flood?'

Jason was bold and hasty, and was just going to leap into the flood; and yet he thought twice before he leapt, so loud roared the torrent down, all brown from the mountain rains, and silver-veined with melting snow; while underneath he could hear the boulders rumbling like the tramp of horsemen or the roll of wheels, as they ground along the narrow channel, and shook the rocks on which he stood.

But the old woman whined all the more, 'I am weak and old, fair youth. For **Hera**'s sake, carry me over the torrent.' And Jason was going to answer her scornfully, when Cheiron's words came to his mind.

So he said, 'For Hera's sake, the Queen of the Immortals on Olympus, I will carry you over the torrent, unless we both are drowned midway.'

Then the old dame leapt upon his back, as nimbly as a goat; and Jason staggered in, wondering; and the first step was up to his knees.

The first step was up to his knees, and the second step was up to his waist; and the stones rolled about his feet, and his feet slipped about the stones; so he went on staggering, and panting, while the old woman cried from off his back— 'Fool, you have wet my **mantle**! Do you make game of poor old souls like me?'

Jason had half a mind to drop her, and let her get through the torrent by herself;

but Cheiron's words were in his mind, and he said only, 'Patience, mother; the best horse may stumble someday.'

At last he staggered to the shore, and set her down upon the bank; and a strong man he needed to have been, or that wild water he never would have crossed. He lay panting awhile upon the bank, and then leapt up to go upon his journey; but he cast one look at the old woman, for he thought, 'She should thank me once at least.'

And as he looked, she grew fairer than all women, and taller than all men on earth; and her garments shone like the summer sea, and her jewels like the stars of heaven; and over her forehead was a veil woven of the golden clouds of sunset; and through the veil she looked down on him, with great soft **heifer's** eyes; with great eyes, mild and **awful**, which filled all the glen with light.

And Jason fell upon his knees, and hid his face between his hands.

And she spoke, 'I am the Queen of Olympus, Hera the wife of Zeus. As thou hast done to me, so will I do to thee. Call on me in the hour of need, and **try if** the Immortals can forget.'

And when Jason looked up, she rose from off the earth, like a pillar of tall white cloud, and floated away across the mountain peaks, toward Olympus the holy hill.

Then a great fear fell on Jason: but after a while he grew light of heart; and he blessed old Cheiron, and said, 'Surely the Centaur is a prophet, and guessed what would come to pass, when he bade me speak harshly to no soul whom I might meet.'

Narration and Discussion

Does Jason now seem "fledged?" How do you know?

Cheiron's first bit of advice has come true. What might happen with the second one?

Creative narration: If you have a group of students, have each one write a postcard or note to Jason, as if they were Jason's recently-graduated friends. Tell something they have been up to lately, remind them of a joke, invite them to visit, etc.

For further thought: Can you think of any other stories in which a similar kindness is later rewarded? (Perhaps *The King of the Golden River*?)

Lesson #13

Introduction

Jason enters Iolcos, prepared to fight his uncle for the throne (in spite of having only one shoe). However, his uncle's way of fighting is not what he expects.

Vocabulary

> **oracle:** prophecy, particularly one given through a priest (or priestess) who claims to be acting as the voice of a god. The word can also refer to the priest, or to the place where the message is given, such as the temple at **Delphi**.
>
> **doleful:** sad
>
> **our uncle's spirit:** technically Phrixus would be a cousin to them rather than an uncle, but it doesn't really matter
>
> **slandered me:** told lies about me
>
> **forthwith:** right away
>
> **swore a great oath:** made a solemn promise or agreement

Reading

Part One

Then Jason went down toward Iolcos; and as he walked he found that he had lost one of his sandals in the flood.

And as he went through the streets, the people came out to look at him, so tall and fair was he; but some of the elders whispered together; and at last one of them stopped Jason, and called to him, 'Fair lad, who are you, and whence come you; and what is your errand in the town?'

'My name, good father, is Jason, and I come from Pelion up above; and my errand is to Pelias your king; tell me then where his palace is.'

But the old man started, and grew pale, and said, 'Do you not know the **oracle**, my son, that you go so boldly through the town with but one sandal on?'

'I am a stranger here, and know of no oracle; but what of my one sandal? I lost the other in Anauros, while I was struggling with the flood.'

Then the old man looked back to his companions; and one sighed, and another smiled; at last he said, 'I will tell you, lest you rush upon your ruin unawares. The oracle in **Delphi** has said that a man wearing one sandal should take the kingdom from Pelias, and keep it for himself. Therefore beware how you go up to his palace, for he is the fiercest and most cunning of all kings.'

Then Jason laughed a great laugh, like a war-horse in his pride. 'Good news, good father, both for you and me. For that very end I came into the town.'

Then he strode on toward the palace of Pelias, while all the people wondered at his bearing. And he stood in the doorway and cried, 'Come out, come out, Pelias the valiant, and fight for your kingdom like a man.'

Pelias came out wondering, and 'Who are you, bold youth?' he cried.

'I am Jason, the son of Aeson, the heir of all this land.'

Then Pelias lifted up his hands and eyes, and wept, or seemed to weep; and blessed the heavens which had brought his nephew to him, never to leave him more. 'For,' said he, 'I have but three daughters, and no son to be my heir. You shall be my heir then, and rule the kingdom after me, and marry whichsoever of my daughters you shall choose; though a sad kingdom you will find it, and whosoever rules it a miserable man. But come in, come in, and feast.'

So he drew Jason in, whether he would or not, and spoke to him so lovingly and feasted him so well, that Jason's anger passed.

Part Two

After supper his three cousins came into the hall, and Jason thought that he should like well enough to have one of them for his wife. But at last he said to Pelias, 'Why do you look so sad, my uncle? And what did you mean just now when you said that this was a **doleful** kingdom, and its ruler a miserable man?'

Then Pelias sighed heavily again and again and again, like a man who had to tell some dreadful story, and was afraid to begin; but at last—

'For seven long years and more have I never known a quiet night; and no more will he who comes after me, till the golden fleece be brought home.' Then he told Jason the story of [his cousin] Phrixus, and of the golden fleece; and told him, too, which was a lie, that Phrixus's spirit tormented him, calling to him day and night. And his daughters came, and told the same tale (for their father had taught them their parts), and wept, and said, 'Oh who will bring home the golden fleece, that **our uncle's spirit** may rest; and that we may have rest also, whom he never lets sleep in peace?'

Jason sat awhile, sad and silent; for he had often heard of that golden fleece; but he looked on it as a thing hopeless and impossible for any mortal man to win it.

But when Pelias saw him silent, he began to talk of other things, and courted Jason more and more, speaking to him as if he was certain to be his heir, and asking his advice about the kingdom; till Jason, who was young and simple, could not help saying to himself, 'Surely he is not the dark man whom people call him. Yet why did he drive my father out?'

And he asked Pelias boldly, 'Men say that you are terrible, and a man of blood; but I find you a kind and hospitable man; and as you are to me, so will I be to you. Yet why did you drive my father out?'

Pelias smiled, and sighed. 'Men have **slandered me** in that, as in all things. Your father was growing old and weary, and he gave the kingdom up to me of his own will. You shall see him tomorrow, and ask him; and he will tell you the same.'

Jason's heart leapt in him when he heard that he was to see his father; and he believed all that Pelias said, forgetting that his father might not dare to tell the truth.

'One thing more there is,' said Pelias, 'on which I need your advice; for, though you are young, I see in you a wisdom beyond your years. There is one neighbour of mine, whom I dread more than all men on earth. I am stronger than he now, and can command him; but I know that if he stay among us, he will work my ruin in the end.

Can you give me a plan, Jason, by which I can rid myself of that man?'

After a while Jason answered, half laughing, 'Were I you, I would send him to fetch that same golden fleece; for if he once set forth after it you would never be troubled with him more.'

And at that a bitter smile came across Pelias' lips, and a flash of wicked joy into his eyes; and Jason saw it, and started; and over his mind came the warning of the old man, and his own one sandal, and the oracle, and he saw that he was taken in a trap.

But Pelias only answered gently, 'My son, he shall be sent **forthwith**.'

'You mean me?' cried Jason, starting up, 'because I came here with one sandal?' And he lifted his fist angrily, while Pelias stood up to him like a wolf at bay; and whether of the two was the stronger and the fiercer it would be hard to tell.

But after a moment Pelias spoke gently, 'Why then so rash, my son? You, and not I, have said what is said; why blame me for what I have not done? Had you bid me love the man of whom I spoke, and make him my son-in-law and heir, I would have obeyed you; and what if I obey you now, and send the man to win himself immortal fame? I have not harmed you, or him. One thing at least I know, that he will go, and that gladly; for he has a hero's heart within him, loving glory, and scorning to break the word which he has given.'

Part Three

Jason saw that he was entrapped; but his second promise to Cheiron came into his mind, and he thought, 'What if the Centaur were a prophet in that also, and meant that I should win the fleece!' Then he cried aloud— 'You have well spoken, cunning uncle of mine! I love glory, and I dare keep to my word. I will go and fetch this golden fleece. Promise me but this in return, and keep your word as I keep mine. Treat my father lovingly while I am gone, for the sake of the all-seeing Zeus; and give me up the kingdom for my own on the day that I bring back the golden fleece.'

Then Pelias looked at him and almost loved him, in the midst of all his hate; and said, 'I promise, and I will perform. It will be no shame to give up my kingdom to the man who wins that fleece.' Then they **swore a great oath** between them; and afterwards both went in, and lay down to sleep.

But Jason could not sleep for thinking of his mighty oath, and how he was to fulfil it, all alone, and without wealth or friends. So he tossed a long time upon his bed, and thought of this plan and of that; and sometimes Phrixus seemed to call him, in a thin voice, faint and low, as if it came from far across the sea, 'Let me come home to my fathers and have rest.' And sometimes he seemed to see the eyes of Hera, and to hear her words again— 'Call on me in the hour of need, and see if the Immortals can forget.'

[The next day Jason offered a sacrifice]; and as he stood by the altar Hera sent a thought into his mind; and he went back to Pelias, and said— 'If you are indeed in earnest, give me two heralds, that they may go round to all the princes of the Minyae, who were pupils of the Centaur with me, that we may fit out a ship together, and take what shall befall.'

At that Pelias praised his wisdom, and hastened to send the heralds out; for he said in his heart, 'Let all the princes go with him, and, like him, never return; for so I shall be lord of all the Minyae, and the greatest king in Hellas.'

Narration and Discussion

Why did Pelias seem so happy at first to see Jason?

Why did Jason finally agree to take Pelias's challenge?

For further thought: Why does Pelias believe that the task is an impossible one?

Lesson #14

Introduction

Jason gathers fifty of his old schoolmates (including some we haven't yet heard of), and they plan their expedition to Colchis.

Vocabulary

coats of mail: armour

greaves: leg protectors

lances: spears

pitch, vermilion: we have seen these words before in the story of Perseus

pine-trunk rollers: One way to move a heavy object, such as a ship, is to put a series of logs in its path, and as they roll forward the object will move with them. The logs at the back are then used again at the front. (As children, we were told that this is how the ancient Egyptians moved giant stones to build the pyramids, and we replicated it with small objects and a handful of coloured pencils. Try it for yourself!)

cordage: ships' ropes

People

Hylas (HIGH-las)

Tiphys (TYE-fis)

Castor and Polydeuces: or Castor and Pollux

The Heroes

Thetis (THEH-tis): Peleus tells us more about her in the next lesson.

Orpheus (OR-fee-us): the most musical of the Argonauts. I have omitted the story of his lost love Eurydice, and his search for her through the underworld; AO students will read it later in *Age of Fable*.

Places

Thrace: (also mentioned in "Perseus") **Thrace** was a region (and later a Roman province) in southeastern Europe, between the **Balkan Mountains**, the **Aegean Sea**, and the **Black Sea**. Parts of it are in present-day Bulgaria, Greece, and Turkey.

Rhodope: The Rhodopes are a mountain range in southeastern Europe.

Haliacmon: the longest river flowing entirely in Greece

Dodona the town of Zeus: a sacred place, similar to **Delphi**

Reading

Part One

So the heralds went out, and cried to all the heroes of the Minyae, 'Who dare come to the adventure of the golden fleece?'

And Hera stirred the hearts of all the princes, and they came from all their valleys to the yellow sands of Pagasae. And first came Heracles the mighty, with his lion's skin and club, and behind him Hylas his young squire, who bore his arrows and his bow; and **Tiphys**, the skillful steersman; and Butes, the fairest of all men; and **Castor and Polydeuces** the twins, the sons of the magic swan; and Caeneus, the strongest of mortals, whom the Centaurs tried in vain to kill, and overwhelmed him with trunks of pine-trees, but even so he would not die; and thither came Zetes and Calais, the winged sons of the north wind; and Peleus *[omission]*, whose bride was silver-footed **Thetis**, the goddess of the sea.

And thither came Telamon and Oileus *[omission]*; and Mopsus, the wise soothsayer, who knew the speech of birds; and Idmon, to whom Phoebus gave a tongue to prophesy of things to come; and Ancaeus, who could read the stars, and knew all the circles of the heavens; and Argus, the famed shipbuilder, and many a hero more, in helmets of brass and gold with tall dyed horse-hair crests, and embroidered shirts of linen beneath their **coats of mail**, and **greaves** of polished tin to guard their knees in fight; with each man his shield upon his shoulder, of many a fold of tough bull's hide, and his sword of tempered bronze in his silver-studded belt; and in his right hand a pair of **lances** [made of heavy white ash-wood].

So they came down to Iolcos, and all the city came out to meet them, and were never tired with looking at their height, and their beauty, and their gallant bearing, and the glitter of their inlaid arms. And some said, 'Never was such a gathering of the heroes since the Hellenes conquered the land.' But the women sighed over them, and whispered, 'Alas! they are all going to their death!'

Part Two

Then they felled the pines on Pelion, and shaped them with the axe, and Argus taught them to build a galley, the first long ship which ever sailed the seas. They pierced her for fifty oars—an oar for each hero of the crew—and pitched her with coal-black **pitch**, and painted her bows with **vermilion**; and they named her *Argo* after Argus, and worked at her all day long. And at night Pelias feasted them like a king, and they slept in his palace-porch.

But Jason went away to the northward, and into the land of **Thrace**, till he found **Orpheus**, the prince of minstrels, where he dwelt in his cave under **Rhodope** *[omission]*. And he asked him, 'Will you leave your mountains, Orpheus, my fellow-scholar in old times, and cross [the river] Strymon once more with me, to sail with the heroes of the Minyae, and bring home the golden fleece, and charm for us all men and all monsters with your magic harp and song?'

Then Orpheus sighed, 'Have I not had enough of toil and of weary wandering, far and wide since I lived in Cheiron's cave, above Iolcos by the sea? *[omission]*. And now I must go out again, to the ends of all the earth, far away into the misty darkness, to the last wave of the Eastern Sea. But what is doomed must be, and a friend's demand obeyed; for prayers are the daughters of Zeus, and who honours them honours him.'

Then Orpheus rose up, sighing, and took his harp, and went over Strymon.

He led Jason to the south-west, up the banks of **Haliacmon** and over the spurs of Pindus, to **Dodona the town of Zeus**. [There Orpheus bade Jason cut down a bough of the holy oak tree, and make a sacrifice to Hera and to Zeus.] And they took the bough and came to Iolcos, and nailed it to the beak-head of the ship.

Part Three

And at last the ship was finished, and they tried to launch her down the beach; but she was too heavy for them to move her, and her keel sank deep into the sand. Then all the heroes looked at each other blushing; but Jason spoke, and said, 'Let us ask the magic bough; perhaps it can help us in our need.'

Then a voice came from the bough, and Jason heard the words it said, and bade Orpheus play upon the harp, while the heroes waited round, holding the **pine-trunk rollers**, to help her toward the sea.

Then Orpheus took his harp, and began his magic song—

> How sweet it is to ride upon the surges, and to leap from wave to wave, while the wind sings cheerful in the **cordage**, and the oars flash fast among the foam!
>
> How sweet it is to roam across the ocean, and see new towns and

wondrous lands, and to come home laden with treasure, and to win undying fame!

And the good ship *Argo* heard him, and longed to be away and out at sea; till she stirred in every timber, and heaved from stem to stern, and leapt up from the sand upon the rollers, and plunged onward like a gallant horse; and the heroes fed her path with pine-trunks, till she rushed into the whispering sea.

Then they stored her well with food and water, and pulled the ladder up on board, and settled themselves each man to his oar, and kept time to Orpheus's harp; and away across the bay they rowed southward, while the people lined the cliffs; and the women wept, while the men shouted, at the starting of that gallant crew.

Narration and Discussion

Why is Orpheus such an asset to the crew of the *Argo*? Do you think his special gifts may be important later on? (But will he ever stop sighing?)

Creative narration: You are a news reporter on the scene of the big boat launch at Iolcos. Tell about what you are seeing, and perhaps talk to someone who is going on the journey, or watching from the shore.

Lesson #15

Introduction

The heroes start off on their journey, with a stop to visit Cheiron (and Achilles, the son of Peleus, who is now being schooled by the Centaur).

Vocabulary

crowned with olive: wearing a leafy crown such as were worn in athletic games

awful: solemn

corn: grain, such as wheat or barley

venison: deer meat

hawsers: ropes that moor the ship

People

Achilles (Ah-KEE-leez): The son of Peleus and Thetis, who (as his father says) would become famous in his own right

Cyzicus (SIH-zi-cus)

Places

Aphetae (or Aphetai): a port across the bay from Iolcos

Reading

Prologue

What happened next, my children, whether it be true or not, stands written in ancient songs, which you shall read for yourselves someday. And grand old songs they are, written in grand old rolling verse; and they call them the Songs of Orpheus, or the Orphics, to this day.

They tell how the heroes came to **Aphetae**, across the bay, and waited for the south-west wind, and chose themselves a captain from their crew; and how all called for Heracles, because he was the strongest and most huge; but Heracles refused, and called for Jason, because he was the wisest of them all. So Jason was chosen captain; and Orpheus heaped a pile of wood, and slew a bull, and offered it to Hera, and called all the heroes to stand round, each man's head **crowned with olive**, and to strike their swords into the bull. Then he filled a golden goblet with the bull's blood, and with wheaten flour, and honey, and wine, and the bitter salt-sea water, and bade the heroes taste. So each tasted the goblet, and passed it round, and vowed an **awful** vow: and they vowed before the sun, and the night, and the blue-haired sea who shakes the land, to stand by Jason faithfully in the adventure of the golden fleece; and whosoever shrank back, or disobeyed, or turned traitor to his vow, then justice should minister against him *[omission]*.

Then Jason lighted the pile, and burnt the carcass of the bull; and they went to their ship and sailed eastward, like men who have a work to do; and the place from which they went was called Aphetae, the sailing-place, from that day forth. Three thousand years and more they sailed away, into the unknown Eastern seas; and great nations have come and gone since then, and many a storm has swept the earth; and many a mighty armament, to which *Argo* would be but one small boat; English and French, Turkish and Russian, have sailed those waters since; yet the fame of that small *Argo* lives forever, and her name is become a proverb among men.

Part One

So they sailed past the Isle of Sciathos, with the Cape of Sepius on their left, and turned to the northward toward Pelion, up the long Magnesian shore. On their right hand was the open sea, and on their left old Pelion rose, while the clouds crawled round his dark pine-forests, and his caps of summer snow. And their hearts yearned for the dear old mountain, as they thought of pleasant days gone by, and of the sports of their

The Heroes

boyhood, and their hunting, and their schooling in the cave beneath the cliff.

And at last Peleus spoke, 'Let us land here, friends, and climb the dear old hill once more. We are going on a fearful journey; who knows if we shall see Pelion again? Let us go up to Cheiron our master, and ask his blessing ere we start. And I have a boy, too, with him, whom he trains as he trained me once—the son whom Thetis brought me, the silver-footed lady of the sea, whom I caught in the cave, and tamed her, though she changed her shape seven times. For she changed, as I held her, into water, and to vapour, and to burning flame, and to a rock, and to a black-maned lion, and to a tall and stately tree. But I held her and held her ever, till she took her own shape again, and led her to my father's house, and won her for my bride *[omission]*. And now let me see my son; for it is not often I shall see him upon earth: famous he will be, but short-lived, and die in the flower of youth.'

So Tiphys the helmsman steered them to the shore under the crags of Pelion; and they went up through the dark pine-forests towards the Centaur's cave.

And they came into the misty hall, beneath the snow-crowned crag; and saw the great Centaur lying, with his huge limbs spread upon the rock; and beside him stood **Achilles**, the child whom no steel could wound, and played upon his harp right sweetly, while Cheiron watched and smiled.

Then Cheiron leapt up and welcomed them, and kissed them every one, and set a feast before them of swine's flesh, and **venison**, and good wine; and young Achilles served them, and carried the golden goblet round. And after supper all the Heroes clapped their hands, and called on Orpheus to sing; but he refused, and said, 'How can I, who am the younger, sing before our ancient host?' So they called on Cheiron to sing, and Achilles brought him his harp; and he began a wondrous song; a famous story of old time, of the fight between the Centaurs and the Lapithai, which you may still see carved in stone. He sang how his brothers came to ruin by their folly, when they were mad with wine; and how they and the heroes fought, with fists, and teeth, and the goblets from which they drank; and how they tore up the pine-trees in their fury, and hurled great crags of stone, while the mountains thundered with the battle, and the land was wasted far and wide; till the Lapithai drove them from their home in the rich Thessalian plains to the lonely glens of Pindus, leaving Cheiron all alone. And the Heroes praised his song right heartily; for some of them had helped in that great fight.

Then Orpheus took the lyre, and sang of Chaos, and the making of the wondrous World, and how all things sprang from Love, who could not live alone in the Abyss. And as he sang, his voice rose from the cave, above the crags, and through the tree-tops, and the glens of oak and pine. And the trees bowed their heads when they heard it, and the grey rocks cracked and rang, and the forest beasts crept near to listen, and the birds forsook their nests and hovered round. And old Cheiron clapped his hands together, and beat his hoofs upon the ground, for wonder at that magic song.

Then Peleus kissed his boy, and wept over him, and they went down to the ship; and Cheiron came down with them, weeping, and kissed them one by one, and blest them, and promised to them great renown. And the Heroes wept when they left him, till their great hearts could weep no more; for he was kind and just and pious, and wiser than all beasts and men. Then he went up to a cliff, and prayed for them, that they might come home safe and well; while the heroes rowed away, and watched him standing on his cliff above the sea, with his great hands raised toward heaven, and his white locks waving in the wind; and they strained their eyes to watch him to the last, for they felt that they should look on him no more.

Part Two: A Very Sad Story

So they rowed on over the long swell of the sea, past Olympus, the seat of the Immortals, and past the wooded bays of Athos, and Samothrace the sacred isle; and they came past Lemnos to the Hellespont, and through the narrow strait of Abydos, and so on into the Propontis, which we call Marmora now. And there they met with [a ruler named] **Cyzicus** *[omission]*, who, the songs say, was the son of Aeneas *[omission]*. Now Cyzicus, the songs say, welcomed the Heroes, for his father had been one of Cheiron's scholars; so he welcomed them, and feasted them, and stored their ship with **corn** and wine, and cloaks and rugs *[omission]*, and shirts, of which no doubt they stood in need.

But at night, while they lay sleeping, [there] came down on them terrible [beasts with six arms], and they fought with young firs and pines. But Heracles killed them all before morn with his deadly poisoned arrows; but among them, in the darkness, he slew Cyzicus the kindly prince.

Then they got to their ship and to their oars, and Tiphys bade them cast off the **hawsers** and go to sea. But as he spoke a whirlwind came, and spun the *Argo* round, and twisted the hawsers together, so that no man could loose them. Then Tiphys dropped the rudder from his hand, and cried, 'This comes from the gods above.' But Jason went forward, and asked counsel of the magic bough.

Then the magic bough spoke, and answered, 'This is because you have slain Cyzicus your friend. You must appease his soul, or you will never leave this shore.' Jason went back sadly, and told the Heroes what he had heard. And they leapt on shore, and searched till dawn; and at dawn they found the body, all rolled in dust and blood, among the corpses of those monstrous beasts.

And they wept over their kind host, and laid him on a fair bed, and heaped a huge mound over him, and offered black sheep at his tomb, and Orpheus sang a magic song to him, that his spirit might have rest. And then they held games at the tomb, after the custom of those times, and Jason gave prizes to each winner. To Ancaeus he gave a golden cup, for he wrestled best of all; and to Heracles a silver one, for he was the strongest of all; and to Castor, who rode best, a golden crest; and Polydeuces the boxer had a rich carpet, and to Orpheus for his song a sandal with golden wings. But Jason himself was the best of all the archers, and the Minyae crowned him with an olive crown; and so, the songs say, the soul of good Cyzicus was appeased and the heroes went on their way in peace.

But when Cyzicus's wife heard that he was dead, she died likewise of grief; and her tears became a fountain of clear water, which flows the whole year round.

Narration and Discussion

Would you say this journey has gotten off to a good start?

Does it seem stranger to make a sacrifice of sheep at a funeral, or to have wrestling and archery games? Why do you think they did these things?

For further thought: Orpheus sang a song about the creation of all things. Have you ever heard of another story with such a song?

> *The Lion was pacing to and fro about that empty land and singing his new song. It was…a gentle, rippling music. And as he walked and sang the valley grew green with grass. (C. S. Lewis,* The Magician's Nephew *[AO Free Reading, Year Four]*

Lesson #16

Introduction

Jason and the Argonauts continue their journey to Colchis. Finally (though decreased by a few), they arrive at Colchis, and decide to declare straight out what they have come for. King Aietes is not in a mood to be co-operative, but certain members of his family feel differently.

Note: There are several omissions in this reading, for the sake of length and moving the story along.

Vocabulary

by stealth: secretly

carried him down under the lake to be their playfellow…: One might say that Hylas became a water-baby.

heron: waterbird

withies: willow branches

appease the nymphs: do something to satisfy them, or atone for a wrong done

scepter (British, sceptre): an ornamented staff carried by royalty

kept ward: kept watch

base: cowardly

sow them with serpents' teeth: Those who have read *Tanglewood Tales* may remember the story of Cadmus sowing dragon's teeth, and how a race of warriors sprang from the ground. Although Jason is challenged here to do something similar, it is not the same story.

nine ells high: 33.75 feet (about 11 m)

People

Harpies: legendary winged creatures who swoop down and steal food. Their story is shortened here, as AO students will read more about them in *Age of Fable*.

Ancaeus: King of the Island of Samos, who became helmsman after Tiphys

King Aietes (Ay-EE-teez or Eye-EE-teez): Introduced in **Lesson #10**.

Medea (Meh-DEE-ah or Meh-DAY-ah): daughter of King Aietes. See introductory note **Tell me about Medea**.

Chalciope: see **Lesson #10**

Argus, Phrixus's son: Not the shipbuilder, but another by the same name.

Brimo: an angry goddess

Circe (SUR-see)

Idas: a prince of Messene

Places

Rhyndacus: the ancient name for a river in Anatolia (part of present-day Turkey)

Mount Arganthonius: a mountain range in ancient **Bithynia** (a kingdom in the northwest part of Asia Minor, now part of Turkey)

Caucasus: the mountains between the Black Sea and the Caspian Sea

Phasis: now called the Rioni; the main river of western Georgia

Reading

Part One

Then they rowed away, the songs say, along the Mysian shore, and past the mouth of the **Rhyndacus**, till they found a pleasant bay, sheltered by the long ridges of **Mount**

The Heroes

Arganthonius, and by high walls of basalt rock. And there they ran the ship ashore upon the yellow sand, and furled the sail, and took the mast down, and lashed it in its crutch. And next they let down the ladder, and went ashore to sport and rest.

And there Heracles went away into the woods, bow in hand, to hunt wild deer; and Hylas the fair boy slipped away after him, and followed him **by stealth**, until he [Hylas] lost himself among the glens, and sat down weary to rest himself by the side of a lake; and there the water nymphs came up to look at him, and loved him, and **carried him down under the lake to be their playfellow**, forever happy and young. And Heracles sought for him in vain, shouting his name till all the mountains rang; but Hylas never heard him, far down under the sparkling lake. So while Heracles wandered searching for him, a fair breeze sprang up, and Heracles was nowhere to be found; and the *Argo* sailed away, and Heracles was left behind.

[Omissions for length: Polydeuces boxes with a giant. Zetes and Calais fight with the Harpies.]

Sidebar: The Harpies

Some readers may be disappointed after that last note. How can you tell the story of Jason without the Harpies? For those who insist, we include the following. Those who don't care about it can move on, because this is already quite a long reading.

And the Minyae went on up the Bosphorus, till they came to the city of Phineus, the fierce Bithynian king; for Zetes and Calais bade Jason land there, because they had a work to do.

And they went up from the shore toward the city, through forests white with snow; and Phineus came out to meet them with a lean and woeful face, and said, 'Welcome, gallant heroes, to the land of bitter blasts, the land of cold and misery; yet I will feast you as best I can.' And he led them in, and set meat before them; but before they could put their hands to their mouths, down came two fearful monsters, the like of whom man never saw; for they had the faces and the hair of fair maidens, but the wings and claws of hawks; and they snatched the meat from off the table, and flew shrieking out above the roofs.

Then Phineus beat his breast and cried, 'These are the Harpies, whose names are the Whirlwind and the Swift, the daughters of Wonder and of the Amber-nymph, and they rob us night and day *[omission]*. They haunt me, and my people, and the Bosphorus, with fearful storms; and sweep away our food from off our tables, so that we starve in spite of all our wealth.'

Then up rose Zetes and Calais, the winged sons of the North-wind, and said, 'Do you not know us, Phineus, and these wings which grow upon our backs?' And Phineus hid his face in terror; but he answered not a word.

[omission for content: Zetes and Calais list the terrible sins of Phineus, and force him to change his ways.]

But Zetes and Calais rose up sadly and said, 'Farewell now, heroes all; farewell, our dear companions, with whom we played on Pelion in old times; for a fate is laid upon us, and our day is come at last, in which we must hunt the whirlwinds over land and sea forever; and if we catch them they die, and if not, we die ourselves.'

At that all the heroes wept; but the two young men sprang up, and aloft into the air after the Harpies. [And the Heroes did not see them again.]

[omission for length]

Part Two

The Argonauts went eastward, and out into the open sea, which we now call the Black Sea, but it was called the Euxine then. No Hellene had ever crossed it, and all feared that dreadful sea, and its rocks, and shoals, and fogs, and bitter freezing storms; and they told strange stories of it, some false and some half-true, how it stretched northward to the ends of the earth, and the sluggish Putrid Sea, and the everlasting night, and the regions of the dead. So the heroes trembled, for all their courage, as they came into that wild Black Sea, and saw it stretching out before them, without a shore, as far as eye could see.

And first Orpheus spoke, and warned them, 'We shall come now to the wandering blue rocks; my mother [Calliope, the immortal muse,] warned me of them.' And soon they saw the blue rocks shining like spires and castles of grey glass, while an ice-cold wind blew from them and chilled all the heroes' hearts. And as they neared they could see them heaving, as they rolled upon the long sea-waves, crashing and grinding together, till the roar went up to heaven. The sea sprang up in spouts between them, and swept round them in white sheets of foam; but their heads swung nodding high in air, while the wind whistled shrill among the crags.

The heroes' hearts sank within them, and they lay upon their oars in fear; but Orpheus called to Tiphys the helmsman, 'Between them we must pass; so look ahead for an opening, and be brave, for Hera is with us.' But Tiphys the cunning helmsman stood silent, clenching his teeth, till he saw a **heron** come flying mast-high toward the rocks, and hover awhile before them, as if looking for a passage through. Then he cried, 'Hera has sent us a pilot; let us follow the cunning bird.'

Then the heron flapped to and fro a moment, till he saw a hidden gap, and into it he rushed like an arrow, while the heroes watched what would befall.

And the blue rocks clashed together as the bird fled swiftly through; but they struck but a feather from his tail, and then rebounded apart at the shock. Then Tiphys cheered the heroes, and they shouted; and the oars bent like **withies** beneath their strokes as they rushed between those toppling ice-crags and the cold blue lips of death. And ere the rocks could meet again they had passed them, and were safe out in the open sea.

*[Omission for length: the loss of two more of the crew, including Tiphys the helmsman, who was replaced by **Ancaeus**.]*

Part Three

And they rowed three days to the eastward, while **Caucasus** rose higher hour by hour, till they saw the dark stream of **Phasis** rushing headlong to the sea, and, shining above the tree-tops, the golden roofs of **King Aietes**, the child of the Sun.

Then out spoke Ancaeus the helmsman, 'We are come to our goal at last, for there are the roofs of Aietes, and the woods where all poisons grow; but who can tell us where among them is hid the golden fleece? Many a toil must we bear ere we find it, and bring it home to Greece.'

But Jason cheered the heroes, for his heart was high and bold; and he said, 'I will go alone up to Aietes, though he be the child of the Sun, and win him with soft words. Better so than to go altogether, and to come to blows at once.' But the Minyae would not stay behind, so they rowed boldly up the stream.

And a dream came to Aietes, and filled his heart with fear. He thought he saw a shining star, which fell into his daughter's lap; and that **Medea** his daughter took it gladly, and carried it to the riverside, and cast it in, and there the whirling river bore it down, and out into the Euxine Sea.

Then he leapt up in fear, and bade his servants bring his chariot, that he might go down to the riverside and **appease the nymphs**, and the heroes whose spirits haunt the bank. So he went down in his golden chariot, and his daughters by his side, Medea the fair witch-maiden, and **Chalciope**, who had been Phrixus's wife, and behind him a crowd of servants and soldiers, for he was a rich and mighty prince.

And as he drove down by the reedy river he saw *Argo* sliding up beneath the bank, and many a hero in her, like Immortals for beauty and for strength, as their weapons glittered round them in the level morning sunlight, through the white mist of the stream. But Jason was the noblest of all; for Hera, who loved him, gave him beauty and tallness and terrible manhood.

And when they came near together and looked into each other's eyes the heroes were awed before Aietes as he shone in his chariot, like his father the glorious Sun; for his robes were of rich gold tissue, and the rays of his diadem flashed fire; and in his hand he bore a jeweled **scepter**, which glittered like the stars; and sternly he looked at them under his brows, and sternly he spoke and loud—

'Who are you, and what want you here *[omission]*? Do you take no account of my rule, nor of my people the Colchians who serve me, who never tired yet in the battle, and know well how to face an invader?'

And the heroes sat silent awhile before the face of that ancient king.

But Hera the awful goddess put courage into Jason's heart, and he rose and shouted loudly in answer, 'We are no pirates nor lawless men. We come not to plunder and to ravage, or carry away slaves from your land; but my uncle, the son of Poseidon, Pelias the Minyan king, he it is who has set me on a quest to bring home the golden fleece.

And these too, my bold comrades, they are no nameless men; for some are the sons of Immortals, and some of heroes far renowned. And we too never tire in battle, and know well how to give blows and to take: yet we wish to be guests at your table: it will be better so for both.'

Then Aietes' race rushed up like a whirlwind, and his eyes flashed fire as he heard; but he crushed his anger down in his breast, and spoke mildly a cunning speech—

'If you will fight for the fleece with my Colchians, then many a man must die. But do you indeed expect to win from me the fleece in fight? So few you are that if you be worsted I can load your ship with your corpses. But if you will be ruled by me, you will find it better far to choose the best man among you, and let him fulfil the labours which I demand. Then I will give him the golden fleece for a prize and a glory to you all.' So saying, he turned his horses and drove back in silence to the town.

And the Minyae sat silent with sorrow, and longed for Heracles and his strength; for there was no facing the thousands of the Colchians and the fearful chance of war.

But Chalciope, Phrixus's widow, went weeping to the town; for she remembered her Minyan husband, and all the pleasures of her youth, while she watched the fair faces of his kinsmen, and their long locks of golden hair. And she whispered to Medea her sister, 'Why should all these brave men die? why does not my father give them up the fleece, that my husband's spirit may have rest?'

And Medea's heart pitied the heroes, and Jason most of all; and she answered, 'Our father is stern and terrible, and who can win the golden fleece?' But Chalciope said, 'These men are not like our men; there is nothing which they cannot dare nor do.'

And Medea thought of Jason and his brave countenance, and said, 'If there was one among them who knew no fear, I could show him how to win the fleece.'

Part Four

So in the dusk of evening they went down to the river-side, Chalciope and Medea *[omission]*, and **Argus, Phrixus's son**. And Argus the boy crept forward, among the beds of reeds, till he came where the heroes were sleeping, on the thwarts of the ship, beneath the bank, while Jason **kept ward** on shore, and leant upon his lance full of thought. And the boy came to Jason, and said— 'I am the son of Phrixus, your cousin; and Chalciope my mother waits for you, to talk about the golden fleece.'

Then Jason went boldly with the boy, and found the two princesses standing; and when Chalciope saw him she wept, and took his hands, and cried— 'O cousin of my beloved, go home before you die!'

'It would be **base** to go home now, fair princess, and to have sailed all these seas in vain.' Then both the princesses besought him; but Jason said, 'It is too late.'

'But you know not,' said Medea, 'what he must do who would win the fleece. He must tame the two brazen-footed bulls, who breathe devouring flame; and with them he must plough ere nightfall four acres in the field of Ares; and he must **sow them with serpents' teeth**, of which each tooth springs up into an armed man. Then he must fight with all those warriors; and little will it profit him to conquer them, for the fleece is guarded by a serpent, more huge than any mountain pine; and over his body you must step if you would reach the golden fleece.'

Then Jason laughed bitterly. 'Unjustly is that fleece kept here, and by an unjust and lawless king; and unjustly shall I die in my youth, for I will attempt it ere another sun be set.'

Then Medea trembled, and said, 'No mortal man can reach that fleece unless I guide him through. For round it, beyond the river, is a wall full **nine ells high**, with lofty towers and buttresses, and mighty gates of threefold brass; and over the gates the wall is arched, with golden battlements above. And over the gateway sits **Brimo**, the wild witch-huntress of the woods, brandishing a pine-torch in her hands, while her mad hounds howl around. No man dare meet her or look on her, but only I her priestess, and she watches far and wide lest any stranger should come near.'

'No wall so high but it may be climbed at last, and no wood so thick but it may be crawled through; no serpent so wary but he may be charmed, or witch-queen so fierce but spells may soothe her; and I may yet win the golden fleece, if a wise maiden help bold men.'

And he looked at Medea cunningly, and held her with his glittering eye, till she blushed and trembled, and said— 'Who can face the fire of the bulls' breath, and fight ten thousand armed men?'

'He whom you help,' said Jason, flattering her, 'for your fame is spread over all the earth. Are you not the queen of all enchantresses, wiser even than your sister **Circe**, in her fairy island in the West?'

'Would that I were with my sister Circe in her fairy island in the West, far away from sore temptation and thoughts which tear the heart! But if it must be so—for why should you die?—I have an ointment here; I made it from the magic ice-flower which sprang from Prometheus's wound, above the clouds on Caucasus, in the dreary fields of snow. Anoint yourself with that, and you shall have in you seven men's strength; and anoint your shield with it, and neither fire nor sword can harm you. But what you begin you must end before sunset, for its virtue lasts only one day. And anoint your helmet with it before you sow the serpents' teeth; and when the sons of earth spring up, cast your helmet among their ranks, and the deadly crop of the War-god's field will mow itself, and perish.'

Then Jason fell on his knees before her, and thanked her and kissed her hands; and she gave him the vase of ointment, and fled trembling through the reeds. And Jason told his comrades what had happened, and showed them the box of ointment; and all rejoiced but **Idas**, and he grew mad with envy.

Narration and Discussion

Why does King Aietes not want to give up the golden fleece?

Why do you think Medea is so interested in helping Jason? (Some versions of the story say that Aphrodite, the goddess of love, made Medea fall in love with Jason, and that this false start was one reason for the difficulties they had later on.)

For further thought: Jason says, "No wall so high but it may be climbed at last, and no wood so thick but it may be crawled through." Do you agree? Have you ever had to do something that seemed impossible? (What changed the impossible to possible?)

Lesson #17

Introduction

Jason carries out the "labours" King Aietes demands. But when Aietes goes back on his word (are you at all surprised?), the Argonauts are forced to use Plan B.

Vocabulary

goaded: drove

till Prometheus heard them from his crag: As Prometheus is supposed to be up in the high mountains, this must have been very loud indeed.

vowed to her that she should be their queen: From this time on, Medea seems to be not only Jason's "love interest," but also his wife (Queen Arete refers to her as such in **Lesson #20**).

The lot is cast: There is no turning back

ravening: ferociously hungry

kine: cattle

paean: a song of praise or triumph

People

Aethalides (Ee-THAL-i-deez or Ee-thal-LEE-deez): the herald of the Argonauts; known for his gift of never forgetting anything

Apsyrtus (or Absyrtus): young brother of Medea

Reading

Part One

And at sunrise Jason went and bathed, and anointed himself from head to foot, and his shield, and his helmet, and his weapons, and bade his comrades try the spell. So they tried to bend his lance, but it stood like an iron bar; and Idas (in spite) hewed at it with his sword, but the blade flew to splinters in his face. Then they hurled their lances at his shield, but the spear-points turned like lead; and Caeneus tried to throw him, but he never stirred a foot; and Polydeuces struck him with his fist a blow which would have killed an ox, but Jason only smiled, and the heroes danced about him with delight; and he leapt, and ran, and shouted in the joy of that enormous strength, till the sun rose, and it was time to go and to claim Aietes' promise.

So he sent up Telamon and **Aethalides** to tell Aietes that he was ready for the fight; and they went up among the marble walls, and beneath the roofs of gold, and stood in Aietes' hall, while he grew pale with rage.

'Fulfil your promise to us, child of the blazing Sun. Give us the serpents' teeth, and let loose the fiery bulls; for we have found a champion among us who can win the golden fleece.'

And Aietes bit his lips, for he fancied that they had fled away by night; but he could not go back from his promise; so he gave them the serpents' teeth. Then he called for his chariot and his horses, and sent heralds through all the town; and all the people went out with him to the dreadful War-god's field.

And there Aietes sat upon his throne, with his warriors on each hand, thousands and tens of thousands, clothed from head to foot in steel chain-mail. And the people and the women crowded to every window and bank and wall; while the Minyae stood together, a mere handful in the midst of that great host.

And Chalciope was there and [the boy] Argus, trembling, and Medea, wrapped closely in her veil; but Aietes did not know that she was muttering cunning spells between her lips.

Then Jason cried, 'Fulfil your promise, and let your fiery bulls come forth.'

Then Aietes bade open the gates, and the magic bulls leapt out. Their brazen hoofs rang upon the ground, and their nostrils sent out sheets of flame, as they rushed with lowered heads upon Jason; but he never flinched a step. The flame of their breath swept round him, but it singed not a hair of his head; and the bulls stopped short and trembled when Medea began her spell.

Then Jason sprang upon the nearest and seized him by the horn; and up and down they wrestled, till the bull fell groveling on his knees; for the heart of the brute died within him, and his mighty limbs were loosed *[omission]*. So both the bulls were tamed and yoked; and Jason bound them to the plough, and **goaded** them onward with his lance till he had ploughed the sacred field.

And all the Minyae shouted; but Aietes bit his lips with rage, for the half of Jason's work was over, and the sun was yet high in heaven.

Part Two

Then he took the serpents' teeth and sowed them, and waited what would befall *[omission]*. And every furrow heaved and bubbled, and out of every clod arose a man.

Out of the earth they rose by thousands, each clad from head to foot in steel, and drew their swords and rushed on Jason, where he stood in the midst alone.

Then the Minyae grew pale with fear for him; but Aietes laughed a bitter laugh. 'See! if I had not warriors enough already round me, I could call them out of the bosom of the earth.'

But Jason snatched off his helmet, and hurled it into the thickest of the throng. And blind madness came upon them, suspicion, hate, and fear; and one cried to his fellow, 'Thou didst strike me!' and another, 'Thou art Jason; thou shalt die!' So fury seized those earth-born phantoms, and each turned his hand against the rest; and they fought and were never weary, till they all lay dead upon the ground *[omission]*.

Then the Minyae rose and shouted, **till Prometheus heard them from his crag**. And Jason cried, 'Lead me to the fleece this moment, before the sun goes down.'

But Aietes thought, 'He has conquered the bulls, and sown and reaped the deadly crop. Who is this who is proof against all magic? He may kill the serpent yet.' So he delayed, and sat taking counsel with his princes till the sun went down and all was dark. Then he bade a herald cry, 'Every man to his home for to-night. Tomorrow we will meet these heroes, and speak about the golden fleece.'

Then he turned and looked at Medea. 'This is your doing, false witch-maid! You have helped these yellow-haired strangers, and brought shame upon your father and yourself!'

Medea shrank and trembled, and her face grew pale with fear; and Aietes knew that she was guilty, and whispered, 'If they win the fleece, you die!'

But the Minyae marched toward their ship, growling like lions cheated of their prey; for they saw that Aietes meant to mock them, and to cheat them out of all their toil. Oileus said, 'Let us go to the grove together, and take the fleece by force.' And Idas the rash cried, 'Let us draw lots who shall go in first; for, while the dragon is devouring one, the rest can slay him and carry off the fleece in peace.'

But Jason held them back, though he praised them; for he hoped for Medea's help.

Part Three

And after a while Medea came trembling, and wept a long while before she spoke. And at last— 'My end is come, and I must die; for my father has found out that I have helped you. You he would kill if he dared; but he will not harm you, because you have been his guests. Go then, go, and remember poor Medea when you are far away across the sea.'

But all the heroes cried— 'If you die, we die with you; for without you we cannot win the fleece, and home we will not go without it, but fall here fighting to the last man.'

'You need not die,' said Jason. 'Flee home with us across the sea. Show us first how to win the fleece; for you can do it. Why else are you the priestess of the grove? Show us but how to win the fleece, and come with us, and you shall be my queen, and rule over the rich princes of the Minyae, in Iolcos by the sea.'

And all the heroes pressed round, and **vowed to her that she should be their queen**.

Medea wept, and shuddered, and hid her face in her hands; for her heart yearned after her sisters and her playfellows, and the home where she was brought up as a child. But at last she looked up at Jason, and spoke between her sobs— 'Must I leave my home and my people, to wander with strangers across the sea? **The lot is cast**, and I must endure it. I will show you how to win the golden fleece. Bring up your ship to the wood-side, and moor her there against the bank; and let Jason come up at midnight, and one brave comrade with him, and meet me beneath the wall.'

Then all the heroes cried together, 'I will go!' 'and I!' 'and I!' And Idas the rash grew mad with envy; for he longed to be foremost in all things.

But Medea calmed them, and said, 'Orpheus shall go with Jason, and bring his magic harp; for I hear of him that he is the king of all minstrels, and can charm all things on earth.'

And Orpheus laughed for joy, and clapped his hands, because the choice had fallen on him; for in those days poets and singers were as bold warriors as the best.

Part Four

So at midnight they went up the bank, and found Medea; and beside came **Apsyrtus** her young brother, leading a yearling lamb. Then Medea brought them to a thicket beside the War-god's gate; and there she bade Jason dig a ditch, and kill the lamb, and leave it there, and strew on it magic herbs and honey from the honeycomb.

Then sprang up through the earth, with the red fire flashing before her, Brimo the wild witch-huntress, while her mad hounds howled around. She had one head like a horse's, and another like a **ravening** hound's, and another like a hissing snake's, and a sword in either hand. And she leapt into the ditch with her hounds, and they ate and drank their fill, while Jason and Orpheus trembled, and Medea hid her eyes. And at last the witch-queen vanished, and fled with her hounds into the woods; and the bars of the gates fell down, and the brazen doors flew wide, and Medea and the heroes ran forward and hurried through the poison wood, among the dark stems of the mighty beeches, guided by the gleam of the golden fleece, until they saw it hanging on one vast tree in the midst.

And Jason would have sprung to seize it; but Medea held him back, and pointed, shuddering, to the tree-foot, where the mighty serpent lay, coiled in and out among the roots, with a body like a mountain pine. His coils stretched many a fathom, spangled with bronze and gold; and half of him they could see, but no more, for the rest lay in the darkness far beyond.

And when he saw them coming he lifted up his head, and watched them with his small bright eyes, and flashed his forked tongue, and roared like the fire among the woodlands, till the forest tossed and groaned. For his cries shook the trees from leaf to root, and swept over the long reaches of the river, and over Aietes' hall, and woke the sleepers in the city, till mothers clasped their children in their fear.

But Medea called gently to him, and he stretched out his long spotted neck, and licked her hand, and looked up in her face, as if to ask for food. Then she made a sign to Orpheus, and he began his magic song. And as he sung, the forest grew calm again, and the leaves on every tree hung still; and the serpent's head sank down, and his brazen coils grew limp, and his glittering eyes closed lazily, till he breathed as gently as a child, while Orpheus called to pleasant Slumber, who gives peace to men, and beasts, and waves.

Then Jason leapt forward warily, and stepped across that mighty snake, and tore the fleece from off the tree-trunk; and the four rushed down the garden, to the bank where the *Argo* lay. There was a silence for a moment, while Jason held the golden fleece on high. Then he cried, 'Go now, good *Argo*, swift and steady, if ever you would see Pelion more.'

And she went, as the heroes drove her, grim and silent all, with muffled oars, till the pine-wood bent like willow in their hands, and stout *Argo* groaned beneath their strokes. On and on, beneath the dewy darkness, they fled swiftly down the swirling stream; underneath black walls, and temples, and the castles of the princes of the East; past sluice-mouths, and fragrant gardens, and groves of all strange fruits; past marshes where fat **kine** lay sleeping, and long beds of whispering reeds; till they heard the merry music of the surge upon the bar, as it tumbled in the moonlight all alone.

Into the surge they rushed, and *Argo* leapt the breakers like a horse; for she knew the time was come to show her mettle, and win honour for the heroes and herself. Into the surge they rushed *[omission]*, till the heroes stopped all panting, each man upon his oar, as she slid into the still broad sea.

Then Orpheus took his harp and sang a **paean**, till the heroes' hearts rose high again; and they rowed on stoutly and steadfastly, away into the darkness of the West.

Narration and Discussion

Tell these events from a non-speaking character's point of view (e.g. Brimo, Apsyrtus, the dragon).

For further thought: How did "suspicion, hate, and fear" kill the dragons-teeth soldiers? Is there a useful thought there for our own lives?

Lesson #18

Introduction

The Argonauts find that it is harder work than they thought to get the Golden Fleece back to Iolcos.

The Heroes

Vocabulary

struck on a shoal: hit a sandbank or rocky area

shoals of fish: large numbers of fish swimming together. (It's interesting that Kingsley uses two different meanings of the word in one passage.)

whelp: puppy

our ship is foul with guilt: In Kingsley's version of the story, the Argonauts are still trying to get themselves to the place where they can be purified.

People

Lynceus (LIN-sooss or LIN-see-us): known for his excellent vision

Enceladus the giant: one of the ancient beings who (according to the myths) participated in a war against the Olympian gods, and who was buried under Mount Etna in Sicily. What do you think Kingsley is describing here?

Charybdis (Ka-RIB-diss): one of a pair of sea monsters who lived in either side of a narrow channel

Scylla [SEE-lah]: the other of the pair

Amphitrite (Am-fi-TRI-tee): the wife of Poseidon the sea god

Places

Ierne: Ireland

Aeaea (Ay-EE-ah): the island home of Circe, thought to be somewhere west of Italy

Sardinia: the second-largest island in the Mediterranean, located west of Italy

Anthemusa (or Anthemoessa): an island, possibly in the Gulf of Naples

Lilybaeum: the western tip of the island of **Sicily**; on the site of present-day Marsala

Reading

Part One

So they fled away in haste to the westward; but Aietes manned his fleet and followed them. And **Lynceus** the quick-eyed saw him coming, while he was still many a mile away, and cried, 'I see a hundred ships, like a flock of white swans, far in the east.' And at that they rowed hard, like heroes; but the ships came nearer every hour.

Sailors and Seababies

Then Medea *[omission]* laid a cruel and a cunning plot; for she killed Absyrtus her young brother, and cast him into the sea; and said, 'Ere my father can take up his corpse and bury it, he must wait long, and be left far behind.' And all the heroes shuddered, and looked one at the other for shame; yet they did not punish that dark witch-woman, because she had won for them the golden fleece.

And when Aietes came to the place, he saw the floating corpse; and he stopped a long while, and bewailed his son, and took him up, and went home. But he sent on his sailors toward the westward, and bound them by a mighty curse [if they returned without Medea].

So the Argonauts escaped for that time: but Father Zeus saw that foul crime; and out of the heavens he sent a storm, and swept the ship far from her course. Day after day the storm drove her, amid foam and blinding mist, till they knew no longer where they were, for the sun was blotted from the skies. And at last the ship **struck on a shoal**, amid low isles of mud and sand, and the waves rolled over her and through her, and the Heroes lost all hope of life.

Then Jason cried to Hera, 'Fair queen, who hast befriended us till now, why hast thou left us in our misery, to die here among unknown seas? It is hard to lose the honour which we have won with such toil and danger, and hard never to see Hellas again, and the pleasant bay of Pagasae.'

Then out spoke the magic bough which stood upon the Argo's beak, 'Because Father Zeus is angry, all this has fallen on you; for a cruel crime has been done on board, and the sacred ship is foul with blood.'

At that some of the heroes *[omission]* seized Medea, to hurl her into the sea, and atone for the young boy's death; but the magic bough spoke again, 'Let her live till her crimes are full. Vengeance waits for her, slow and sure; but she must live, for you need her still. She must show you the way to her sister Circe, who lives among the islands of the West. To her you must sail, a weary way, and she shall cleanse you from your guilt.'

Then all the heroes wept aloud *[omission]*; for they knew that a dark journey lay before them, and years of bitter toil. And some upbraided the dark witch-woman, and some said, 'Nay, we are her debtors still; without her we should never have won the fleece.' But most of them bit their lips in silence, for they feared the witch's spells.

And now the sea grew calmer, and the sun shone out once more, and the heroes thrust the ship off the sand-bank, and rowed forward on their weary course under the guiding of the dark witch-maiden, into the wastes of the unknown sea.

[Omission for length: The Argonauts sail "for many a weary day," till even the magic bough complains that it has had enough.]

But ere they could pass **Ierne**, the land of mists and storms, the wild wind came down, dark and roaring, and caught the sail, and strained the ropes. And away they drove twelve nights, on the wide wild western sea, through the foam, and over the rollers, while they saw neither sun nor stars. And they cried again, 'We shall perish, for we know not where we are. We are lost in the dreary damp darkness, and cannot tell north from south.'

But Lynceus the long-sighted called gaily from the bows, 'Take heart again, brave sailors; for I see a pine-clad isle, and the halls of the kind Earth-mother, with a crown of clouds around them.'

But Orpheus said, 'Turn from them, for no living man can land there: there is no harbour on the coast, but steep-walled cliffs all round.'

Part Two

So Ancaeus turned the ship away; and for three days more they sailed on, till they came to **Aeaea**, Circe's home, and the fairy island of the West. And there Jason bid them land, and seek about for any sign of living man. And as they went inland Circe met them, coming down toward the ship; and they trembled when they saw her, for her hair, and face, and robes shone like flame.

And she came and looked at Medea; and Medea hid her face beneath her veil. And Circe cried, 'Ah, wretched girl, have you forgotten all your sins, that you come hither to my island, where the flowers bloom all the year round? Where is your aged father, and the brother whom you killed? Little do I expect you to return in safety with these strangers whom you love."

[Omission for length and content: In Kingsley's story, Circe refuses to perform the cleansing ceremony, but sends them on to a place where they can, apparently, do it themselves; so their next adventures are part of the journey there. However, other versions say that Circe did everything necessary, which changes the rest of their journey into their return home.]

They sailed on [past] **Sardinia** *[omission]*, till they came to a flowery island, upon a still bright summer's eve. And as they neared it, slowly and wearily, they heard sweet songs upon the shore. But when Medea heard it, she started, and cried, 'Beware, all heroes, for these are the rocks of the Sirens. You must pass close by them, for there is no other channel; but those who listen to that song are lost.'

Then Orpheus spoke, the king of all minstrels, 'Let them match their song against mine. I have charmed stones, and trees, and dragons, how much more the hearts of men!' So he caught up his lyre, and stood upon the [deck], and began his magic song.

And now they could see the Sirens on **Anthemusa**, the flowery isle; three fair maidens sitting on the beach, beneath a red rock in the setting sun, among beds of crimson poppies and golden asphodel. Slowly they sung and sleepily, with silver voices, mild and clear, which stole over the golden waters, and into the hearts of all the Heroes, in spite of Orpheus's song.

And all things stayed around and listened; the gulls sat in white lines along the rocks; on the beach great seals lay basking, and kept time with lazy heads; while silver **shoals of fish** came up to hearken, and whispered as they broke the shining calm. The Wind overhead hushed his whistling, as he shepherded his clouds toward the west; and the clouds stood in mid blue, and listened dreaming, like a flock of golden sheep.

And as the heroes listened, the oars fell from their hands, and their heads drooped on their breasts, and they closed their heavy eyes; and they dreamed of bright still gardens, and of slumbers under murmuring pines, till all their toil seemed foolishness, and they thought of their renown no more.

Part Three

Then one lifted his head suddenly, and cried, 'What use in wandering forever? Let us stay here and rest awhile.' And another, 'Let us row to the shore, and hear the words they sing.' And another, 'I care not for the words, but for the music. They shall sing me to sleep, that I may rest.' *[omission]* Then Medea clapped her hands together, and cried, 'Sing louder, Orpheus, sing a bolder strain; wake up these hapless sluggards, or none of them will see the land of Hellas more.'

Then Orpheus lifted his harp, and crashed his cunning hand across the strings; and his music and his voice rose like a trumpet through the still evening air; into the air it rushed like thunder, till the rocks rang and the sea; and into their souls it rushed like wine, till all hearts beat fast within their breasts.

And he sang the song of Perseus, how the gods led him over land and sea, and how he slew the loathly Gorgon, and won himself a peerless bride; and how he sits now with the gods upon Olympus, a shining star in the sky, immortal with his immortal bride, and honoured by all men below.

So Orpheus sang, and the Sirens, answering each other across the golden sea, till Orpheus's voice drowned the Sirens', and the heroes caught their oars again.

And they cried, 'We will be men like Perseus, and we will dare and suffer to the last. Sing us his song again, brave Orpheus, that we may forget the Sirens and their spell.'

[Omission for length and content: Butes, "the fairest of all mortal men," was so entranced by the music that he "forgot all heaven and earth" and was taken by the Sirens.]

And as Orpheus sang, they dashed their oars into the sea, and kept time to his music, as they fled fast away; and the Sirens' voices died behind them, in the hissing of the foam along their wake.

But when the Sirens saw that they were conquered, they shrieked for envy and rage, and leapt from the beach into the sea, and were changed into rocks until this day.

Part Four

Then they came to the straits by **Lilybaeum**, and saw **Sicily**, the three-cornered island, under which **Enceladus the giant** lies groaning day and night, and when he turns the earth quakes, and his breath bursts out in roaring flames from the highest cone of Aetna, above the chestnut woods.

And there **Charybdis** caught them in its fearful coils of wave, and rolled mast-high about them, and spun them round and round; and they could go neither back nor forward, while the whirlpool sucked them in. And while they struggled they saw near them, on the other side [of] the strait, a rock stand in the water, with its peak wrapped round in clouds—a rock which no man could climb, though he had twenty hands and feet, for the stone was smooth and slippery, as if polished by man's hand; and halfway up a misty cave looked out toward the west.

And when Orpheus saw it he groaned, and struck his hands together. 'Little will it help us,' he cried, 'to escape the jaws of the whirlpool; for in that cave lives **Scylla**, the sea-hag with a young **whelp's** voice; my mother warned me of her ere we sailed away from Hellas; she has six heads, and six long necks, and hides in that dark cleft. And from her cave she fishes for all things which pass by—for sharks, and seals, and dolphins, and all the herds of **Amphitrite**. And never ship's crew boasted that they came safe by her rock, for she bends her long necks down to them, and every mouth takes up a man. And who will help us now? For Hera and Zeus hate us, and **our ship is foul with guilt**; so we must die, whatever befalls.'

Then out of the depths came Thetis, Peleus's silver-footed bride, for love of her gallant husband, and all her nymphs around her; and they played like snow-white dolphins, diving on from wave to wave, before the ship, and in her wake, and beside her, as dolphins play. And they caught the ship, and guided her, and passed her on from hand to hand, and tossed her through the billows, as maidens toss the ball. And when Scylla stooped to seize her, they struck back her ravening heads, and foul Scylla whined, as a whelp whines, at the touch of their gentle hands. But she shrank into her cave affrighted—for all bad things shrink from good—and *Argo* leapt safe past her, while a fair breeze rose behind. Then Thetis and her nymphs sank down to their coral caves beneath the sea, and their gardens of green and purple, where live flowers bloom all the year round; while the Heroes went on rejoicing, yet dreading what might come next.

Narration and Discussion

What might have happened if Medea had *not* killed her brother? Did that justify such a terrible act? (Zeus appeared to think not.)

For further thought: "Those who listen to that song are lost." Are there songs (or words, or ideas) against which people should plug their ears? What are some ways to shut them out?

Lesson #19

Introduction

The *Argos* lands near a city ruled by the very wealthy King Alcinous and Queen Arete. What might be a relaxing holiday for the sailors, however, turns into a dangerous situation, as emissaries from Medea's father are already there waiting for them.

Vocabulary

jest: joke

steel mail-shirts: armour

quays: docks, piers

happy: fortunate, blessed

People

Alcinous (Al-KEE-nohs): King of the **Phaeacian**s; the husband of **Arete**. He also appears in *The Odyssey*.

Hephaestus [Heh-FEH-stus or Heh-FEE-stus]: the Greek god of artisans, blacksmiths, and volcanoes.

Places

a long high island: possibly the island of Corfu

Liburnia: part of modern-day Croatia

Reading

Part One

After that they rowed on steadily for many a weary day, till they saw **a long high island**, and beyond it a mountain land. And they searched till they found a harbour, and there rowed boldly in.

[Omission for length: The Argonauts are puzzled by the appearance of an unfamiliar city, especially when they pull the ship in for a closer look and are shouted at rudely by sailors on the pier.]

But they limped ashore, all stiff and weary, with long ragged beards and sunburnt cheeks, and garments torn and weather-stained, and weapons rusted with the spray, while the sailors laughed at them (for they were rough-tongued, though their hearts were frank and kind). And one said, 'These fellows are but raw sailors; they look as if they had been sea-sick all the day.' And another, 'Their legs have grown crooked with much rowing, till they waddle in their walk like ducks.'

At that Idas the rash would have struck them; but Jason held him back, till one of the merchant kings spoke to them, a tall and stately man.

'Do not be angry, strangers; the sailor boys must have their **jest**. But we will treat you justly and kindly, for strangers and poor men come from God; and you seem no common sailors by your strength, and height, and weapons. Come up with me to the palace of **Alcinous**, the rich sea-going king, and we will feast you well and heartily; and after that you shall tell us your name.'

But Medea hung back, and trembled, and whispered in Jason's ear, 'We are betrayed, and are going to our ruin, for I see my countrymen among the crowd; dark-eyed Colchi in **steel mail-shirts**, such as they wear in my father's land.'

'It is too late to turn,' said Jason. And he spoke to the merchant king, 'What country is this, good sir; and what is this new-built town?'

'This is the land of the **Phaeacians**, beloved by all the Immortals; for they come hither and feast like friends with us, and sit by our side in the hall. Hither we came from **Liburnia** to escape the unrighteous Cyclopes; for they robbed us, peaceful merchants, of our hard-earned wares and wealth. So Nausithous, the son of Poseidon, brought us hither, and died in peace; and now his son Alcinous rules us, and **Arete** the wisest of queens.'

So they went up across the square, and wondered still more as they went; for along the **quays** lay in order great cables, and yards, and masts, before the fair temple of Poseidon, the blue-haired king of the seas. And round the square worked the ship-wrights, as many in number as ants, twining ropes, and hewing timber, and smoothing long yards and oars. And the Minyae went on in silence through clean white marble streets, till they came to the hall of Alcinous, and they wondered then still more.

For the lofty palace shone aloft in the sun, with walls of plated brass, from the threshold to the innermost chamber, and the doors were of silver and gold. And on each side of the doorway sat living dogs of gold, who never grew old or died, so well **Hephaestus** had made them in his forges in smoking Lemnos, and gave them to Alcinous to guard his gates by night. And within, against the walls, stood thrones on either side, down the whole length of the hall, strewn with rich glossy shawls; and on them the merchant kings of those crafty sea-roving Phaeacians sat eating and drinking in pride, and feasting there all the year round.

[Omission for length: description of the palace and its orchards and gardens]

Part Two

So they went in, and saw Alcinous sitting, like Poseidon, on his throne, with his golden scepter by him, in garments stiff with gold, and in his hand a sculptured goblet, as he pledged the merchant kings; and beside him stood Arete, his wise and lovely queen, and leaned against a pillar as she spun her golden threads. Then Alcinous rose, and welcomed them, and bade them sit and eat; and the servants brought them tables, and bread, and meat, and wine.

But Medea went on trembling toward Arete the fair queen, and fell at her knees, and clasped them, and cried, weeping, as she knelt— 'I am your guest, fair queen, and I entreat you by Zeus, from whom prayers come. Do not send me back to my father to die some dreadful death; but let me go my way, and bear my burden. Have I not had enough of punishment and shame?'

'Who are you, strange maiden? and what is the meaning of your prayer?'

'I am Medea, daughter of Aietes, and I saw my countrymen here today; and I know that they are come to find me, and take me home to die some dreadful death.'

Then Arete frowned, and said, 'Lead this girl in, my maidens; and let the kings decide, not I.'

And Alcinous leapt up from his throne, and cried, 'Speak, strangers, who are you? And who is this maiden?'

'We are the Heroes of the Minyae,' said Jason; 'and this maiden has spoken truth. We are the men who took the golden fleece, the men whose fame has run round every shore. We came hither out of the ocean, after sorrows such as man never saw before. We went out many, and come back few, for many a noble comrade have we lost. So let us go, as you should let your guests go, in peace; that the world may say, "Alcinous is a just king."'

But Alcinous frowned, and stood deep in thought; and at last he spoke— 'Had not the deed been done which is done, I should have said this day to myself, "It is an honour to Alcinous, and to his children after him, that the far-famed Argonauts are his guests." But these Colchi are my guests, as you are; and for this month they have waited here with all their fleet, for they have hunted all the seas of Hellas, and could not find you, and dared neither go farther, nor go home.'

'Let them choose out their champions, and we will fight them, man for man.'

'No guests of ours shall fight upon our island, and if you go outside they will outnumber you. I will do justice between you, for I know and do what is right.' Then he turned to his kings, and said, 'This may stand over till tomorrow. To-night we will feast our guests, and hear the story of all their wanderings, and how they came hither out of the ocean.'

Part Three

So Alcinous bade the servants take the Heroes in, and bathe them, and give them clothes. And they were glad when they saw the warm water, for it was long since they had bathed. And they washed off the sea-salt from their limbs, and anointed themselves from head to foot with oil, and combed out their golden hair. Then they came back again into the hall, while the merchant kings rose up to do them honour. And each man said to his neighbour, 'No wonder that these men won fame. How they stand now like Giants, or Titans, or Immortals come down from Olympus, though many a winter has worn them, and many a fearful storm. What must they have been when they sailed from Iolcos, in the bloom of their youth, long ago?'

Then they went out to the garden; and the merchant princes said, 'Heroes, run races with us. Let us see whose feet are nimblest.'

'We cannot race against you, for our limbs are stiff from sea; and we have lost our two swift comrades, the sons of the north wind. But do not think us cowards: if you wish to try our strength, we will shoot, and box, and wrestle, against any men on earth.'

And Alcinous smiled, and answered, 'I believe you, gallant guests; with your long limbs and broad shoulders, we could never match you here. For we care nothing here for boxing, or for shooting with the bow; but for feasts, and songs, and harping, and dancing, and running races, to stretch our limbs on shore.'

So they danced there and ran races, the jolly merchant kings, till the night fell, and all went in. And then they ate and drank, and comforted their weary souls, till Alcinous called a herald, and bade him go and fetch the harper.

Part Four

The herald went out, and fetched the harper, and led him in by the hand; and Alcinous cut him a piece of meat, from the fattest of the haunch, and sent it to him, and said, 'Sing to us, noble harper, and rejoice the Heroes' hearts.' So the harper played and sang, while the dancers danced strange figures; and after that the tumblers showed their tricks, till the Heroes laughed again.

Then, 'Tell me, Heroes,' asked Alcinous, 'you who have sailed the ocean round, and seen the manners of all nations, have you seen such dancers as ours here, or heard such music and such singing? We hold ours to be the best on earth.'

'Such dancing we have never seen,' said Orpheus; 'and your singer is a **happy** man, for Phoebus himself must have taught him, or else he is the son of a Muse, as I am also, and have sung once or twice, though not so well as he.'

'Sing to us, then, noble stranger,' said Alcinous; 'and we will give you precious gifts.'

So Orpheus took his magic harp, and sang to them a stirring song of their voyage from Iolcos, and their dangers, and how they won the golden fleece; and of Medea's love, and how she helped them, and went with them over land and sea; and of all their fearful dangers, from monsters, and rocks, and storms, till the heart of Arete was softened, and all the women wept.

And the merchant kings rose up, each man from off his golden throne, and clapped their hands, and shouted, 'Hail to the noble Argonauts, who sailed the unknown sea!'

Then he went on, and told their journey over the sluggish northern main, and through the shoreless outer ocean, to the fairy island of the west; and of the Sirens, and Scylla, and Charybdis, and all the wonders they had seen, till midnight passed and the day dawned; but the kings never thought of sleep. Each man sat still and listened, with his chin upon his hand. And at last, when Orpheus had ended, they all went thoughtful out, and the Heroes lay down to sleep, beneath the sounding porch outside, where Arete had strewn them rugs and carpets, in the sweet still summer night.

Narration and Discussion

Alcinous promised, "I will do justice between you, for I know and do what is right."

If you were Alcinous, what would you do about the dispute between Medea, the Argonauts, and the men from Colchis?

Why couldn't Jason just "have it out" with these enemies?

Creative narration: The song of Orpheus, describing the Heroes' adventures, kept the audience spellbound long into the night. As we are now drawing close to the end of Jason's story, find a creative way (alone or with friends) to illustrate the parts you remember or like best.

Lesson #20

Introduction

According to Kingsley, the Heroes have still not been cleansed from their guilt over the murder; but other tellers, as has been explained, prefer to end that part of the story on Circe's island. In any case, there are still a few adventures left for them all before they arrive home.

Vocabulary

suppliant: one who requests help or mercy

bootless: useless

dragon-car: flying chariot. It's interesting that Jason appears to know this about Medea, since (we assume) she hasn't had any reason to use it during their travels. Keep your eyes open, though—it may come up later on.

ichor: immortal blood

People

Minos the just king: We will hear more about Minos in the story of Theseus.

Talos (or Talus): as explained in the text, a giant bronze "automaton" (or robot), made to protect Princess Europa from kidnappers, pirates, and invaders. (Those who have read *Tanglewood Tales* will have heard of "Talus" there, in the story of Theseus; but he really belongs in this story instead.)

Places

peak of Ida: Mount Ida, the highest mountain on the island of **Crete**.

Reading

Part One

Arete pleaded hard with her husband for Medea, for her heart was softened. And she said, 'The gods will punish her, not we. After all, she is our guest and my **suppliant**, and prayers are the daughters of Zeus. And who, too, dare part man and wife, after all they have endured together?'

And Alcinous smiled. 'The minstrel's song has charmed you: but I must remember what is right, for songs cannot alter justice; and I must be faithful to my name. Alcinous I am called, "the man of sturdy sense"; and Alcinous I will be.' But for all that Arete besought him, until she won him round.

So next morning he sent a herald, and called the kings into the square, and said, 'This is a puzzling matter: remember but one thing. These Minyae live close by us, and we may meet them often on the seas; but Aietes lives afar off, and we have only heard his name. Which, then, of the two is it safer to offend—the men near us, or the men far off?'

The princes laughed, and praised his wisdom; and Alcinous called the Heroes to the square, and the Colchi also; and they came and stood opposite each other, but Medea stayed in the palace. Then Alcinous spoke, 'Heroes of the Colchi, what is your errand about this lady?'

'To carry her home with us, that she may die a shameful death; but if we return without her, we must die the death she should have died.'

'What say you to this, Jason the Aeolid?' said Alcinous, turning to the Minyae.

'I say,' said the cunning Jason, 'that they are come here on a **bootless** errand. Do you think that you can make her follow you, Heroes of the Colchi—her, who knows all spells and charms? She will cast away your ships on quicksands, or call down on you Brimo the wild huntress; or the chains will fall from off her wrists, and she will escape in her **dragon-car**; or if not thus, some other way, for she has a thousand plans and wiles. And why return home at all, and face the long seas again *[omission]*? There is many a fair land round these coasts, which waits for gallant men like you. Better to settle there, and build a city, and let Aietes and Colchis help themselves.'

Then a murmur rose among the Colchi, and some cried 'He has spoken well'; and some, 'We have had enough of roving, we will sail the seas no more!'

And the chief said at last, 'Be it so, then; a plague she has been to us, and a plague to the house of her father, and a plague she will be to you. Take her, since you are no wiser; and we will sail away toward the north.'

Then Alcinous gave them food, and water, and garments, and rich presents of all sorts; and he gave the same to the Minyae, and sent them all away in peace. So *[omission]* the Colchi went northward into the Adriatic, and settled, and built towns along the shore.

Part Two

And the Heroes rowed *[omission]* for many a weary day, till their water was spent, and their food eaten; and they were worn out with hunger and thirst. But at last they saw a long steep island, and a blue peak high among the clouds; and they knew it for the **peak of Ida**, and the famous land of **Crete**. And they said, 'We will land in Crete, and see **Minos the just king**, and all his glory and his wealth; at least he will treat us hospitably, and let us fill our water-casks upon the shore.'

But when they came nearer to the island they saw a wondrous sight upon the cliffs. For on a cape to the westward stood a giant, taller than any mountain pine, who glittered aloft against the sky like a tower of burnished brass. He turned and looked on all sides round him, till he saw the *Argo* and her crew; and when he saw them he came toward them, more swiftly than the swiftest horse, leaping across the glens at a bound, and striding at one step from down to down. And when he came abreast of them he brandished his arms up and down, as a ship hoists and lowers her yards, and shouted with his brazen throat like a trumpet from off the hills, 'You are pirates, you are robbers! If you dare land here, you die.'

Then the Heroes cried, 'We are no pirates. We are all good men and true, and all we ask is food and water'; but the giant cried the more— 'You are robbers, you are pirates all; I know you; and if you land, you shall die the death.'

Then he waved his arms again as a signal, and they saw the people flying inland, driving their flocks before them, while a great flame arose among the hills. Then the giant ran up a valley and vanished, and the Heroes lay on their oars in fear.

But Medea stood watching all from under her steep black brows, with a cunning smile upon her lips, and a cunning plot within her heart. At last she spoke, 'I know this giant. I heard of him in the East. Hephaestus the Fire King made him in his forge in Aetna beneath the earth, and called him Talos, and gave him to Minos for a servant, to guard the coast of Crete. Thrice a day he walks round the island, and never stops to sleep; and if strangers land he leaps into his furnace, which flames there among the hills; and when he is red-hot he rushes on them, and burns them in his brazen hands.'

Then all the Heroes cried, 'What shall we do, wise Medea? We must have water, or we die of thirst. Flesh and blood we can face fairly; but who can face this red-hot brass?'

'I can face red-hot brass, if the tale I hear be true. For they say that he has but one vein in all his body, filled with liquid fire; and that this vein is closed with a nail: but I know not where that nail is placed. But if I can get it once into these hands, you shall water your ship here in peace.' Then she bade them put her on shore, and row off again, and wait what would befall.

And the Heroes obeyed her unwillingly, for they were ashamed to leave her so alone; but Jason said, 'She is dearer to me than to any of you, yet I will trust her freely on shore; she has more plots than we can dream of in the windings of that fair and cunning head.'

Part Three

So they left [Medea] on the shore; and she stood there in her beauty all alone, till the giant strode back red-hot from head to heel, while the grass hissed and smoked beneath his tread.

And when he saw the maiden alone, he stopped; and she looked boldly up into his face without moving, and began her magic song:—

> Life is short, though life is sweet; and even men of brass and fire must die.
>
> The brass must rust, the fire must cool, for time gnaws all things in their turn.
>
> Life is short, though life is sweet: but sweeter to live forever;
>
> sweeter to live ever youthful like the gods, who have **ichor** in their veins—
>
> ichor which gives life, and youth, and joy, and a bounding heart.

Then Talos said, 'Who are you, strange maiden, and where is this ichor of youth?'

Then Medea held up a flask of crystal, and said, 'Here is the ichor of youth. I am Medea the enchantress; my sister Circe gave me this, and said, "Go and reward Talos, the faithful servant, for his fame is gone out into all lands." So come, and I will pour this into your veins, that you may live forever young.'

And he listened to her false words, that simple Talos, and came near; and Medea said, 'Dip yourself in the sea first, and cool yourself, lest you burn my tender hands; then show me where the nail in your vein is, that I may pour the ichor in.'

Then that simple Talos dipped himself in the sea, till it hissed, and roared, and smoked; and came and knelt before Medea, and showed her the secret nail. And she drew the nail out gently, but she poured no ichor in; and instead the liquid fire spouted forth, like a stream of red-hot iron.

And Talos tried to leap up, crying, 'You have betrayed me, false witch-maiden!'

But she lifted up her hands before him, and sang, till he sank beneath her spell. And as he sank, his brazen limbs clanked heavily, and the earth groaned beneath his weight; and the liquid fire ran from his heel, like a stream of lava, to the sea; and Medea laughed, and called to the Heroes, 'Come ashore, and water your ship in peace.'

So they came, and found the giant lying dead; and they fell down, and kissed Medea's feet; and watered their ship, and took sheep and oxen, and so left that inhospitable shore.

Narration and Discussion

What do you think of Jason's advice to the men from Colchis?

One of the men warns Jason in return that "a plague she will be to you." Is Medea more of a help or a problem?

Creative narration: It seems that even bronze robots worry about getting old. Create a commercial or magazine advertisement for Medea's "anti-aging remedy." Alternatively, create a commercial or advertisement that might interest the Heroes.

Lesson #21

Introduction

After many years, the Heroes arrive back in Iolcos; but it has been a very long time! Does the return of the Fleece even matter now?

Vocabulary

wronged her: He left her for another wife.

too terrible to speak of here: Kingsley has no more to say of Medea for now, but we will meet her again in the story of Theseus. As for Jason, the Greek dramatist Euripides suggested a somewhat appropriate ending in his play *Medea*: he said that Jason was asleep under the stern of the rotting *Argo*, and it fell on him.

you must read them for yourselves: Those who go on to AO Year Four (or Groups Form II) will do this, using the book *Age of Fable*.

Places

Cape Maleas: one of the most southerly points of Greece, known for violent storms. In Homer's epic poem *The Odyssey*, the hero **Odysseus** is trying to get around Cape Maleas but is blown off course, which causes his voyage home to take years longer than it should have.

Laconia: a region of Greece in the southeastern part of the Peloponnese

Euboean Strait: an arm of the Aegean between the island of Euboea and the mainland

Reading

Part One

At last, after many more adventures, they came to **Cape Maleas**, at the south-west point of the Peloponnese. And there they offered sacrifices, and Orpheus purged them from their guilt.

Then they rode away again to the northward, past the **Laconian** shore, and came all worn and tired *[omission]* up the long **Euboean Strait**, until they saw once more

Pelion, and Aphetai, and Iolcos by the sea.

And they ran the ship ashore; but they had no strength left to haul her up the beach; and they crawled out on the pebbles, and sat down, and wept till they could weep no more. For the houses and the trees were all altered; and all the faces which they saw were strange; and their joy was swallowed up in sorrow, while they thought of their youth, and all their labour, and the gallant comrades they had lost. And the people crowded round, and asked them 'Who are you, that you sit weeping here?'

'We are the sons of your princes, who sailed out many a year ago. We went to fetch the golden fleece, and we have brought it, and grief therewith. Give us news of our fathers and our mothers, if any of them be left alive on earth.'

Then there was shouting, and laughing, and weeping; and all the kings came to the shore, and they led away the Heroes to their homes, and bewailed the valiant dead.

Part Two

Then Jason went up with Medea to the palace of his uncle Pelias. And when he came in Pelias sat by the hearth, crippled and blind with age; while opposite him sat Aeson, Jason's father, crippled and blind likewise; and the two old men's heads shook together as they tried to warm themselves before the fire.

And Jason fell down at his father's knees, and wept, and called him by his name. And the old man stretched his hands out, and felt him, and said, 'Do not mock me, young hero. My son Jason is dead long ago at sea.'

'I am your own son Jason, whom you trusted to the Centaur upon Pelion; and I have brought home the golden fleece, and a princess of the Sun's race for my bride. So now give me up the kingdom, Pelias my uncle, and fulfil your promise as I have fulfilled mine.'

Then his father clung to him like a child, and wept, and would not let him go; and cried, 'Now I shall not go down lonely to my grave. Promise me never to leave me till I die.'

Part Three

And now I wish that I could end my story pleasantly; but it is no fault of mine that I cannot. The old songs end it sadly, and I believe that they are right and wise; for though the Heroes were purified at Malea, yet **sacrifices cannot make bad hearts good**, and Jason had taken a wicked wife, and he had to bear his burden to the last.

[Omission for content: some of Medea's enchantments, which still seem a bit shocking for a children's book.]

But Jason could not love her, after all her cruel deeds. So he was ungrateful to her, and **wronged her**; and she revenged herself on him. And a terrible revenge she took— **too terrible to speak of here**. But you will hear of it yourselves when you grow up *[omission]*; and whether it be true or not, it stands for ever as a warning to us not to seek for help from evil persons, or to gain good ends by evil means. For if we use an adder even against our enemies, it will turn again and sting us.

Part Four

But of all the other Heroes there is many a brave tale left, which I have no space to tell you, so **you must read them for yourselves**;—of the hunting of the boar in Calydon, which Meleager killed; and of Heracles' twelve famous labours; and of the seven who fought at Thebes, [and others as well].

And what became of Cheiron, the good immortal beast? That, too, is a sad story; for the Heroes never saw him more. He was wounded by a poisoned arrow, at Pholoe among the hills, when Heracles opened the fatal wine-jar, which Cheiron had warned him not to touch. And the Centaurs smelt the wine, and flocked to it, and fought for it with Heracles; but he killed them all with his poisoned arrows, and Cheiron was left alone.

Then Cheiron took up one of the arrows, and dropped it by chance upon his foot; and the poison ran like fire along his veins, and he lay down and longed to die; and cried, 'Through wine I perish, the bane of all my race. Why should I live forever in this agony? Who will take my immortality, that I may die?'

Then Prometheus answered, the good Titan, whom Heracles had set free from Caucasus, 'I will take your immortality and live forever, that I may help poor mortal men.' So Cheiron gave him his immortality, and died, and had rest from pain. And Heracles and Prometheus wept over him, and went to bury him on Pelion; but Zeus took him up among the stars, to live forever, grand and mild, low down in the far southern sky.

And in time the Heroes died *[omission]*, and left behind them valiant sons, but not so great as they had been.

Yet their fame, too, lives till this day, for they fought at the ten years' siege of Troy: and their story is *[omission]* in two of the noblest songs on earth—the *Iliad*, which tells us of the siege of Troy, and Achilles' quarrel with the kings; and the *Odyssey*, which tells the wanderings of **Odysseus**, through many lands for many years *[omission]*. We will read that sweet story, children, by the fire some winter night. And now I will end my tale, and begin another and a more cheerful one, of a hero who became a worthy king, and won his people's love.

Narration and Discussion

At the beginning of the quest, there were two reasons given for getting the fleece: first, to appease the spirit of Phrixus, and, second, to prove that Jason was worthy to take back his father's throne. We don't hear any more about the first motive, but we can assume that the second one comes true (though some versions say that Jason's son became the next king). Were you at all disappointed by the not-too-exciting reunion between Jason, his uncle, and his father? (Were you surprised that they were sitting together?)

Creative narration (following up on the first question): You are putting on a play, or writing a book like Kingsley's. What happens in the final scenes?

How did Cheiron live on forever, but in a better way than he expected? Do you live in a place where you might be able to see the constellation Centaurus? (Have you ever heard of the triple star system Alpha Centauri?)

For further thought: Consider this early paragraph from the story:

> Therefore we will believe—why should we not?—of these same Argonauts of old, that they too were noble men, who planned and did a noble deed; and that therefore their fame has lived, and been told in story and in song, mixed up, no doubt, with dreams and fables, and yet true and right at heart. So we will honour these old Argonauts, and listen to their story as it stands; and we will try to be like them, each of us in our place; for each of us has a Golden Fleece to seek, and a wild sea to sail over ere we reach it, and dragons to fight ere it be ours.

Why do you think "their fame has lived, and been told in story and in song?"

Examination Questions for Jason and the Argonauts

Tell one of these stories:

1. About Scylla and Charybdis

2. How Jason won the Golden Fleece

3. How the Heroes returned

As an alternative, draw a picture and tell about your favourite of the Heroes, and something he did.

The Heroes

Lesson #22 (Theseus)

Introduction

Like Perseus and Jason, Theseus was spoken of as a "divine hero" by the ancient Greeks. He is the subject of one of Plutarch's *Lives*, but he was a legend and a subject of plays and poetry long before that. Theseus is considered to be the founder and first king of Athens, bringing twelve smaller towns together to form a larger city. Although his time as a king comes into this story only briefly, it is helpful to know that Theseus was remembered for his connection to Athens, as there are clues to this scattered throughout. (See the note **A Clue of Thread** in **Lesson #29**.)

Was Theseus a real person, and if so, when did he live? The answer to the first is, we don't know. But if he did, he may have been alive during the Late Bronze Age, shortly before the Trojan War. One clue we do have is the François Vase, believed to have been made in about 570 B.C.; and there are similar images of Theseus, mostly shown killing the Minotaur, from the decades following that. (For those who might like to compare this to other history, the prophet Ezekiel died in 570 B.C. It is also the birthdate of Pythagoras.)

But in another sense, Theseus is very much a "real person," and Kingsley helps us get to know him in the third part of *The Heroes*. In this first reading, we hear how Theseus grew up and discovered the special secret that his mother had been keeping since his birth.

Vocabulary

her husband: King Aegeus of Athens (but we don't need to know this yet, as Theseus doesn't know it either)

plane tree: *Platanus,* one of the best-known trees in Greece (besides the olive tree); also popular in England and elsewhere in Europe

arbutus, lentisk, purple heather-bushes: shrubs of various kinds

all was of no avail: it was hopeless

coursing: chasing

thicket: group of bushes or trees

hilt: handle

Hide them in your bosom: Hide them in your clothes. (Editor's note: Perhaps he was wearing a cloak?)

girdle: surround

cicada (or cicala): an insect which produces a high-pitched droning sound

pledge: a promise or guarantee of help, to be used when needed

sack: destroy

thralldom: slavery

People

Theseus (THEE-see-us, with the TH sound soft as in "thick")

Aethra (EETH-ra): the mother of Theseus. (Kingsley spells it Aithra) Aethra has her own history, but as this is the story of Theseus, we will not go into it here.

Pittheus (Pi-THAY-us): the king of **Troezen (TREE-zin)**, which he had named for his late brother

Aegeus (EE-jee-us or Ee-JEE-us)

Places

The most important places to know, in the beginning, are the **Saronic Gulf** (or Gulf of Aegina), which is part of the **Aegean Sea** and easy to find on any map of Greece. Being able to locate the **Saronic Gulf** will help with future studies; it's a useful landmark.

Look for the city of **Athens**, on its north coast; and (if you're using a historical rather than a current map), the town of **Troezen**, across the gulf in the **Peloponnese**, or southern part of Greece. (The two halves of Greece are divided by the **Isthmus of Corinth**.) **Methana** is another ancient town near **Troezen**.

You should also look for the islands of Salamis (which looks like it was chopped out of Athens), and **Aegina**, which is mentioned here. **Attica** is the region including and surrounding Athens; Kingsley sometimes uses the word **Attic** to mean things in or of that area.

Sounion: Cape Sounion, a promontory at the southern tip of the **Attica** peninsula

Hymettus, Pentelicus: mountains

Pallas's hill: the Acropolis, or "sacred rock," in Athens

Reading

Part One

Once upon a time there was a princess in **Troezen: Aethra**, the daughter of **Pittheus** the king. She had one fair son, named **Theseus**, the bravest lad in all the land; and Aethra never smiled but when she looked at him, for **her husband** had forgotten her, and lived far away. And she used to go up to the mountain above Troezen, to the temple of Poseidon, and sit there all day looking out across the bay, over **Methana**, to the purple peaks of **Aegina** and the **Attic** shore beyond.

And when Theseus was full fifteen years old she took him up with her to the temple, and into the thickets of the grove which grew in the temple-yard. And she led him to a tall **plane tree**, beneath whose shade grew **arbutus**, and **lentisk,** and **purple heather-bushes**. And there she sighed, and said, 'Theseus, my son, go into that thicket and you will find at the plane tree foot a great flat stone; lift it, and bring me what lies underneath.'

Then Theseus pushed his way in through the thick bushes, and saw that they had not been moved for many a year. And searching among their roots he found a great flat stone, all overgrown with ivy, and acanthus, and moss. He tried to lift it, but he could not. And he tried till the sweat ran down his brow from heat, and the tears from his eyes for shame; but **all was of no avail**. And at last he came back to his mother, and said, 'I have found the stone, but I cannot lift it; nor do I think that any man could in all Troezen.'

Then she sighed, and said, 'The gods wait long; but they are just at last. Let it be for another year. The day may come when you will be a stronger man than lives in all Troezen.' Then she took him by the hand, and went into the temple and prayed, and came down again with Theseus to her home.

And when a full year was past she led Theseus up again to the temple, and bade him lift the stone; but he could not.

Then she sighed, and said the same words again, and went down, and came again the next year; but Theseus could not lift the stone then, nor the year after; and he longed to ask his mother the meaning of that stone, and what might lie underneath it; but her face was so sad that he had not the heart to ask.

So he said to himself, 'The day shall surely come when I will lift that stone, though no man in Troezen can.' And in order to grow strong he spent all his days in wrestling, and boxing, and hurling, and taming horses, and hunting the boar and the bull, and **coursing** goats and deer among the rocks; till upon all the mountains there was no hunter so swift as Theseus; and he killed Phaia, the Crommyonian Sow, which wasted all the land; till all the people said, 'Surely the gods are with the lad.'

Part Two

And when his eighteenth year was past, Aethra led him up again to the temple, and said, 'Theseus, lift the stone this day, or never know who you are.' And Theseus went into the **thicket**, and stood over the stone, and tugged at it; and it moved. Then his spirit swelled within him, and he said, 'If I break my heart in my body, it shall [come] up.' And he tugged at it once more, and lifted it, and rolled it over with a shout.

And when he looked beneath it, on the ground lay a sword of bronze, with a **hilt** of glittering gold, and by it a pair of golden sandals; and he caught them up, and burst through the bushes like a wild boar, and leapt to his mother, holding them high above his head.

But when she saw them she wept long in silence, hiding her fair face in her shawl; and Theseus stood by her wondering, and wept also, he knew not why. And when she was tired of weeping, she lifted up her head, and laid her finger on her lips, and said, '**Hide them in your bosom**, Theseus my son, and come with me where we can look down upon the sea.'

Then they went outside the sacred wall, and looked down over the bright blue sea; and Aethra said— 'Do you see this land at our feet?'

And he said, 'Yes; this is Troezen, where I was born and bred.'

And she said, 'It is but a little land, barren and rocky, and looks towards the bleak north-east. Do you see that land beyond?'

'Yes; that is **Attica**, where the **Athenian** people dwell.'

'That is a fair land and large, Theseus my son; and it looks toward the sunny south; a land of olive-oil and honey, the joy of gods and men. For the gods have **girdled** it with mountains, whose veins are of pure silver, and their bones of marble white as snow; and there the hills are sweet with thyme and basil, and the meadows with violet and asphodel, and the nightingales sing all day in the thickets, by the side of ever-flowing streams. There are twelve towns well peopled, the homes of an ancient race *[omission]*, who wear gold **cicadas** among the tresses of their golden hair; for like the cicadas they sprang from the earth, and like the cicadas they sing all day, rejoicing in the genial sun. What would you do, son Theseus, if you were king of such a land?'

Then Theseus stood astonished, as he looked across the broad bright sea, and saw the fair Attic shore, from **Sounion** to **Hymettus** and **Pentelicus**, and all the mountain peaks which girdle Athens round. But Athens itself he could not see, for purple Aegina stood before it, midway across the sea.

Then his heart grew great within him, and he said, 'If I were king of such a land I would rule it wisely and well in wisdom and in might, that when I died all men might weep over my tomb, and cry, "Alas for the shepherd of his people!"'

And Aethra smiled, and said, 'Take, then, the sword and the sandals, and go to **Aegeus**, king of Athens, who lives on **Pallas's hill**; and say to him, "The stone is lifted, but whose is the **pledge** beneath it?" Then show him the sword and the sandals, and take what the gods shall send.'

But Theseus wept, 'Shall I leave you, O my mother?'

But she answered, 'Weep not for me. That which is fated must be; and grief is easy to those who do nought but grieve. Full of sorrow was my youth, and full of sorrow my womanhood *[omission for length]*. Yet shall I be avenged, when the golden-haired Heroes sail against Troy, and **sack** the palaces of Ilium; then my son shall set me free from **thralldom**, and I shall hear the tale of Theseus's fame. Yet beyond that I see new sorrows; but I can bear them as I have borne the past.'

Then she kissed Theseus, and wept over him; and went into the temple, and Theseus saw her no more.

Narration and Discussion

Why didn't Theseus's mother lift the rock for him, or ask someone else to do it?

Have you ever had to wait until you were big or strong enough to do something? Tell about it.

> *[Almanzo] was thinking so hard that words came out of his mouth before he knew it.*
>
> *"Thirty bales to a load, at two dollars a bale," he said. "That's sixty dollars a lo—"*
>
> *He stopped, scared. He knew better than to speak at table, when he wasn't spoken to.*
>
> *"Mercy on us, listen to the boy!" Mother said.*
>
> *"Well, well, son!" said Father. "I see you've been studying to some purpose." He drank the tea out of his saucer, set it down, and looked again at Almanzo. "Learning is best put into practice. What say you ride to town with me tomorrow, and sell that load of hay?"*
>
> (Laura Ingalls Wilder, Farmer Boy *[AO Free Reading, Year Two]*)

For even further thought (for older students and adults): Theseus's mother asked him, "What would you do, son Theseus, if you were king of such a land?" If someone showed you a great land and asked you this, what would you answer? Charlotte Mason says that we each have such a kingdom inside ourselves. "And of all the fair lands which God has made, there is no country more fair than the Kingdom of Mansoul." (*Ourselves*, p. 1)

Lesson #23

Introduction

Theseus, hesitant to approach the king too soon, decides to "win honour and renown" to "prove [himself] worthy of his love."

Vocabulary

glen: narrow valley

down: hill

brake: marshy area

clefts: splits, openings

kites and crows: scavenger birds

coots: waterbirds

People

Eurystheus (Yoo-RISS-tee-us): the king who required Heracles to perform his Twelve Labours

Periphetes: also called **Corynetes**, "the club-bearer"

Places

Isthmus (ISS-mus): the strip of land where the city of **Corinth** is located

Spider mountains: The Arachneo (also called Mount Arachnaeus, or Sapyselaton)

Reading

Part One

So Theseus stood there alone, with his mind full of many hopes. And first he thought of going down to the harbour and hiring a swift ship, and sailing across the bay to Athens; but even that seemed too slow for him, and he longed for wings to fly across the sea, and find his father.

But after a while his heart began to fail him; and he sighed, and said within himself— 'What if my father have other sons about him whom he loves? What if he will not receive me? And what have I done that he should receive me? He has forgotten me ever since I was born: why should he welcome me now?'

Then he thought a long while sadly; and at the last he cried aloud, 'Yes! I will make him love me; for I will prove myself worthy of his love. I will win honour and renown, and do such deeds that Aegeus shall be proud of me, though he had fifty other sons! Did not Heracles win himself honour, though he was oppressed, and the slave of **Eurystheus**? Did he not kill all robbers and evil beasts, and drain great lakes and marshes, breaking the hills through with his club? Therefore it was that all men honoured him, because he rid them of their miseries, and made life pleasant to them and their children after them. Where can I go, to do as Heracles has done? Where can I find strange adventures, robbers, and monsters *[omission]*, the enemies of men? I will go by land, and into the mountains, and round by the way of the **Isthmus**. Perhaps there I may hear of brave adventures, and do something which shall win my father's love.'

Part Two

So he went by land, and away into the mountains, with his father's sword upon his thigh, till he came to the **Spider mountains**, which hang over Epidaurus and the sea, where the **glens** run downward from one peak in the midst, as the rays spread in the spider's web. And he went up into the gloomy glens, between the furrowed marble walls, till the lowland grew blue beneath his feet and the clouds drove damp about his head. But he went up and up for ever, through the spider's web of glens, till he could see the narrow gulfs spread below him, north and south, and east and west; black cracks half-choked with mists, and above all a dreary **down**.

But over that down he must go, for there was no road right or left; so he toiled on through bog and **brake**, till he came to a pile of stones.

And on the stones a man was sitting, wrapped in a bearskin cloak. The head of the bear served him for a cap, and its teeth grinned white around his brows; and the feet were tied about his throat, and their claws shone white upon his chest. And when he saw Theseus he rose, and laughed till the glens rattled.

'And who art thou, fair fly, who hast walked into the spider's web?' But Theseus walked on steadily, and made no answer; but he thought, 'Is this some robber? and has an adventure come already to me?' But the strange man laughed louder than ever, and said— 'Bold fly, know you not that these glens are the web from which no fly ever finds his way out again, and this down the spider's house, and I the spider who sucks the flies? Come hither, and let me feast upon you; for it is of no use to run away, so cunning a web has my father Hephaestus spread for me when he made these **clefts** in the mountains, through which no man finds his way home.'

But Theseus came on steadily, and asked— 'And what is your name among men, bold spider? and where are your spider's fangs?'

Then the strange man laughed again— 'My name is **Periphetes**, the son of Hephaestus and Anticleia the mountain nymph. But men call me **Corynetes** the club-bearer; and here is my spider's fang.' And he lifted from off the stones at his side a mighty club of bronze. 'This my father gave me, and forged it himself in the roots of the mountain; and with it I pound all proud flies till they give out their fatness and their sweetness. So give me up that [shining] sword of yours, and your mantle, and your golden sandals, lest I pound you, and by ill-luck you die.'

But Theseus wrapped his mantle round his left arm quickly, in hard folds, from his shoulder to his hand, and drew his sword, and rushed upon the club-bearer, and the club-bearer rushed on him.

Thrice he struck at Theseus, and made him bend under the blows like a sapling; but Theseus guarded his head with his left arm, and the mantle which was wrapped around it. And thrice Theseus sprang upright after the blow, like a sapling when the storm is past; and he stabbed at the club-bearer with his sword, but the loose folds of the bearskin saved him.

Then Theseus grew mad, and closed with him, and caught him by the throat, and they fell and rolled over together; but when Theseus rose up from the ground the club-bearer lay still at his feet.

Part Three

Then Theseus took [the] club and [the] bearskin, and left [Periphetes] to the **kites and crows**, and went upon his journey down the glens on the farther slope, till he came to a broad green valley, and saw flocks and herds sleeping beneath the trees.

And by the side of a pleasant fountain, under the shade of rocks and trees, were nymphs and shepherds dancing; but no one piped to them while they danced. And when they saw Theseus they shrieked; and the shepherds ran off, and drove away their flocks, while the nymphs dived into the fountain like **coots**, and vanished.

Theseus wondered and laughed: 'What strange fancies have folks here who run away from strangers, and have no music when they dance!' But he was tired, and dusty, and thirsty; so he thought no more of them, but drank and bathed in the clear pool, and then lay down in the shade under a plane tree, while the water sang him to sleep, as it tinkled down from stone to stone.

And when he woke he heard a whispering, and saw the nymphs peeping at him across the fountain from the dark mouth of a cave, where they sat on green cushions of moss. And one said, 'Surely he is not Periphetes'; and another, 'He looks like no robber, but a fair and gentle youth.'

Then Theseus smiled, and called them, 'Fair nymphs, I am not Periphetes. He sleeps among the kites and crows; but I have brought away his bearskin and his club.'

Then they leapt across the pool, and came to him, and called the shepherds back. And he told them how he had slain the club-bearer: and the shepherds kissed his feet and sang, 'Now we shall feed our flocks in peace, and not be afraid to have music when we dance; for the cruel club-bearer has met his match, and he will listen for our pipes no more.'

Then they brought him kid's flesh and wine, and the nymphs brought him honey from the rocks, and he ate, and drank, and slept again, while the nymphs and shepherds danced and sang. And when he woke, they begged him to stay; but he would not. 'I have a great work to do,' he said; 'I must be away toward the Isthmus, that I may go to Athens.'

[Omission for length: The shepherds warn Theseus that the journey to Athens may be a dangerous one. He should beware especially of a man who bends pine trees; a robber who makes people wash his feet and then kicks them over a cliff to be eaten by a tortoise; and a king who challenges all comers to wrestle with him, and then kills the losers.]

Then Theseus frowned, and said, 'This seems indeed an ill-ruled land, and adventures enough in it to be tried. But if I am the heir of it, I will rule it and right it, and here is my royal scepter.'

And he shook his club of bronze, while the nymphs and shepherds clung round him, and entreated him not to go. But on he went nevertheless, till he could see both the seas and the citadel of Corinth towering high above all the land.

Narration and Discussion

Tell about one of Theseus's adventures during this time.

How does he know that he is finally ready to go to Athens?

For further thought: Theseus badly wants to earn the respect of his father, King Aegeus. But he also notices that the land seems "ill-ruled." Does that give us any clues about what might happen when the two men meet?

Lesson #24

Introduction

In this reading, Theseus does indeed take on two of the people he was warned about.

Vocabulary

smote: struck

People

Sinis (SIH-nis): the bender of pine trees

Sciron (SKY-ron): the robber who throws people off a cliff. Also spelled **Skeiron**.

Pausanias: a Greek traveler, geographer, and writer of the 2nd century A.D.

Places

Megara (MEG-ah-ra): a town in the west part of **Attica**

Cliffs of Sciron (SKY-ron)

Reading

Part One

[Theseus passed] swiftly along the Isthmus, for his heart burned to meet that cruel **Sinis**; and in a pinewood at last he met him, where the Isthmus was narrowest and the road ran between high rocks. There he sat upon a stone by the wayside, with a young fir-tree for a club across his knees, and a cord laid ready by his side; and over his head, upon the fir-tops, hung the bones of murdered men.

Then Theseus shouted to him, 'Holla, thou valiant pine-bender, hast thou two fir-trees left for me?'

And Sinis leapt to his feet, and answered, pointing to the bones above his head, 'My larder has grown empty lately, so I have two fir-trees ready for thee.' And he rushed on Theseus, lifting his club, and Theseus rushed upon him.

Then they hammered together till the greenwoods rang; but the metal was tougher than the pine, and Sinis's club broke right across, as the bronze came down upon it. Then Theseus heaved up another mighty stroke, and **smote** Sinis down upon his face; and knelt upon his back, and bound him with his own cord, and said, 'As thou hast done to others, so shall it be done to thee.' Then he bent down two young fir-trees, and bound Sinis between them for all his struggling and his prayers; and let them go, and ended Sinis, and went on, leaving him to the hawks and crows.

Part Two

Then he went over the hills toward **Megara**, keeping close along the Saronic Gulf, till he came to the **cliffs of Sciron**, and the narrow path between the mountain and the sea. And there he saw **Sciron** sitting by a fountain, at the edge of the cliff. On his knees was a mighty club; and he had barred the path with stones, so that everyone must stop who came up.

Then Theseus shouted to him, and said, 'Holla, thou tortoise-feeder, do thy feet need washing today?'

And Sciron leapt to his feet, and answered— 'My tortoise is empty and hungry, and my feet need washing today.' And he stood before his barrier, and lifted up his club in both hands.

Then Theseus rushed upon him; and sore was the battle upon the cliff, for when Sciron felt the weight of the bronze club, he dropped his own, and closed with Theseus, and tried to hurl him by main force over the cliff.

But Theseus was a wary wrestler, and dropped his own club, and caught him by the throat and by the knee, and forced him back against the wall of stones, and crushed him up against them, till his breath was almost gone. And Sciron cried panting, 'Loose me, and I will let thee pass.'

But Theseus answered, 'I must not pass till I have made the rough way smooth;' and he forced him back against the wall till it fell, and Sciron rolled head over heels.

Then Theseus lifted him up all bruised, and said, 'Come hither and wash my feet.' And he drew his sword, and sat down by the well, and said, 'Wash my feet, or I cut you piecemeal.'

And Sciron washed his feet trembling; and when it was done, Theseus rose, and cried, 'As thou hast done to others, so shall it be done to thee. Go feed thy tortoise thyself'; and he kicked him over the cliff into the sea.

The Heroes

And whether the tortoise ate him, I know not; for some say that earth and sea both disdained to take his body, so foul it was with sin. So the sea cast it out upon the shore, and the shore cast it back into the sea, and at last the waves hurled it high into the air in anger; and it hung there long without a grave, till it was changed into a desolate rock, which stands there in the surge until this day.

This at least is true, which **Pausanias** tells, that in the royal porch at Athens he saw the figure of Theseus modelled in clay, and by him Sciron the robber falling headlong into the sea.

Narration and Discussion

How did Theseus's years of bodybuilding benefit him later on? Can you imagine something that you are working at now being useful when you are older?

Creative narration: These readings lend themselves especially to drama and artwork.

Lesson #25

Introduction

Theseus meets Cercyon, the wrestling and murdering king; but he also encounters someone more interesting, and perhaps even more dangerous.

Vocabulary

> **the sacred strait of the sea-fight:** The Battle of Salamis was fought in 480 B.C.
>
> **kine:** cattle
>
> **by stealth:** without letting the other one see they were doing it
>
> **mastiff:** dog
>
> **venison:** deer meat
>
> **churlish:** rude

People

> **Cercyon (KER-ky-on):** the wrestling king with quite an awful family history
>
> **Furies:** Greek goddesses of vengeance. Bulfinch's *Age of Fable* says, "The Erinnyes, or Furies, were three goddesses who punished by their secret stings the crimes of those who escaped or defied public justice."

Earth-mother: the goddess **Demeter**. Every now and again, Kingsley likes to slip an extra myth into the main story.

sons of Phytalus: the descendants of an ancient king named Phytalus, who (the legend says) was kind to **Demeter** and was therefore revered in **Eleusis**.

Places

Cithaeron (Several different possible pronunciations; KIH-ther-on is one)

Thriasian plain

Eleusis (Ih-LEW-siss)

Aphidnai

Cephisus (Seh-FIH-sus or Keh-FIH-sus)

Parnes (PAR-nays)

Reading

Prologue

Then he went a long day's journey, past Megara, into the Attic land, and high before him rose the snow-peaks of **Cithaeron**, all cold above the black pine-woods, where haunt the **Furies** *[omission]*, far aloft upon the dreary mountains, where the storms howl all day long. And on his right hand was the sea always, and Salamis, with its island cliffs, and **the sacred strait of the sea-fight**, where afterwards the Persians fled before the Greeks.

So he went all day until the evening, till he saw the **Thriasian plain**, and the sacred city of **Eleusis**, where the **Earth-mother's** temple stands. For there she met Triptolemus, when all the land lay waste, **Demeter** the kind Earth-mother, and in her hands a sheaf of corn. And she taught him to plough the fallows, and to yoke the lazy **kine**; and she taught him to sow the seed-fields, and to reap the golden grain; and sent him forth to teach all nations, and give corn to labouring men. So at Eleusis all men honour her, whosoever tills the land; [and also] Triptolemus her beloved, who gave corn to labouring men.

Part One

And he went along the plain into Eleusis, and stood in the marketplace, and cried—'Where is **Cercyon**, the king of the city? I must wrestle a fall with him today.'

Then all the people crowded round him, and cried, 'Fair youth, why will you die? Hasten out of the city, before the cruel king hears that a stranger is here.' But Theseus went up through the town, while the people wept and prayed, and through the gates of the palace-yard, and through the piles of bones and skulls, till he came to the door of Cercyon's hall, the terror of all mortal men. And there he saw Cercyon sitting at the table in the hall alone; and before him was a whole sheep roasted, and beside him a whole jar of wine.

And Theseus stood and called him, 'Holla, thou valiant wrestler, wilt thou wrestle a fall today?'

And Cercyon looked up and laughed, and answered, 'I will wrestle a fall today; but come in, for I am lonely and thou weary, and eat and drink before thou die.'

Then Theseus went up boldly, and sat down before Cercyon at the board; and he ate his fill of the sheep's flesh, and drank his fill of the wine; and Theseus ate enough for three men, but Cercyon ate enough for seven. But neither spoke a word to the other, though they looked across the table **by stealth**; and each said in his heart, 'He has broad shoulders; but I trust mine are as broad as his.'

At last, when the sheep was eaten and the jar of wine drained dry, King Cercyon rose, and cried, 'Let us wrestle a fall before we sleep.' So they tossed off all their garments, and went forth in the palace-yard; and Cercyon bade [the servants] strew fresh sand in an open space between the bones. And there the [two] stood, face to face, while their eyes glared like [those of] wild bulls; and all the people crowded at the gates to see what would befall.

And there they stood and wrestled, till the stars shone out above their heads; up and down and round, till the sand was stamped hard beneath their feet. And their eyes flashed like stars in the darkness, and their breath went up like smoke in the night air; but neither took nor gave a footstep, and the people watched silent at the gates.

But at last Cercyon grew angry, and caught Theseus round the neck, and shook him as a **mastiff** shakes a rat; but he could not shake him off his feet. But Theseus was quick and wary, and clasped Cercyon round the waist, and slipped *[omission]* underneath him, while he caught him by the wrist; and then he hove a mighty heave, a heave which would have stirred an oak, and lifted Cercyon, and pitched him right over his shoulder on the ground.

Then he leapt on him, and called, 'Yield, or I kill thee!' but Cercyon said no word; for his heart was burst within him with the fall, and the meat, and the wine.

Part Two

Then Theseus opened the gates, and called in all the people; and they cried, 'You have slain our evil king; be you now our king, and rule us well.'

'I will be your king in Eleusis, and I will rule you right and well; for this cause I have slain all evil-doers—Sinis, and Sciron, and this man last of all.'

Then an aged man stepped forth, and said, 'Young hero, hast thou slain Sinis? Beware then of Aegeus, king of Athens *[omission]*, for he is near of kin to Sinis.'

'Then I have slain my own kinsman,' said Theseus, 'though well he deserved to die. Who will purge me from his death, for rightfully I slew him, unrighteous and accursed as he was?'

And the old man answered— 'That will the Heroes do, the **sons of Phytalus**, who dwell beneath the elm-tree in **Aphidnai,** by the bank of silver **Cephisus**; for they know the mysteries of the gods. Thither you shall go and be purified, and after you shall be our king.'

So he took an oath of the people of Eleusis, that they would serve him as their king, and went away next morning across the Thriasian plain, and over the hills toward Aphidnai, that he might find the sons of Phytalus.

Part Three

And as he was skirting the Vale of Cephisus, along the foot of lofty **Parnes**, a very tall and strong man came down to meet him, dressed in rich garments. On his arms were golden bracelets, and round his neck a collar of jewels; and he came forward, bowing courteously, and held out both his hands, and spoke—

'Welcome, fair youth, to these mountains; happy am I to have met you! For what greater pleasure to a good man, than to entertain strangers? But I see that you are weary. Come up to my castle, and rest yourself awhile.'

'I give you thanks,' said Theseus: 'but I am in haste to go up the valley, and to reach Aphidnai in the Vale of Cephisus.'

'Alas! you have wandered far from the right way, and you cannot reach Aphidnai to-night, for there are many miles of mountain between you and it, and steep passes, and cliffs dangerous after nightfall. It is well for you that I met you, for my whole joy is to find strangers, and to feast them at my castle, and hear tales from them of foreign lands. Come up with me, and eat the best of **venison**, and drink the rich red wine, and sleep upon my famous bed, of which all travelers say that they never saw the like. For whatsoever the stature of my guest, however tall or short, that bed fits him to a hair, and he sleeps on it as he never slept before.'

And he laid hold on Theseus's hands, and would not let him go.

Theseus wished to go forwards: but he was ashamed to seem **churlish** to so hospitable a man; and he was curious to see that wondrous bed; and besides, he was hungry and weary. Yet he shrank from the man, he knew not why; for, though his voice was gentle and fawning, it was dry and husky like a toad's; and though his eyes were gentle, they were dull and cold like stones.

But he consented, and went with the man up a glen which led from the road toward the peaks of Parnes, under the dark shadow of the cliffs.

Narration and Discussion

"Here I am, I have killed all your enemies," Theseus says. How is the old man's response not exactly what Theseus expects? How does Theseus react?

Do you think Theseus should accept the hospitality of this well-dressed stranger? Are there any hints that it might not be a good idea?

For further thought: Sinis was undoubtedly evil, but Theseus had still committed a crime by killing a relative. While that isn't a choice most of us we would have to make, we do sometimes have to decide between relationships and doing what is right. For instance, is it wrong to tell an adult if a friend is doing something wrong?

For even further thought: Consider stories from the Bible about people who needed to be cleansed from sin. How do their stories differ from this one?

Lesson #26

Introduction

Theseus discovers the identity of his new "friend."

Vocabulary

doleful: gloomy, sad

Hades: the Greek god of the dead and "king of the underworld"; Hades also means the Underworld itself

maw: mouth

requite: pay back

lops: cuts

hew: chop

countenance: face

spoil (verb): rob, plunder

spoil (noun): treasure

prowess: skill

People

Procrustes (Pro-KROO-steez or PRO-kroo-stays)

Places

Thebes (Theebs)

Acharnai (Ah-CHAR-nayss) or **Acharnes:** now a suburb of Athens

Reading

Part One

And as they went up, the glen grew narrower, and the cliffs higher and darker, and beneath them a torrent roared, half seen between bare limestone crags. And around there was neither tree nor bush, while from the white peaks of Parnes the snow-blasts swept down the glen, cutting and chilling till a horror fell on Theseus as he looked round at that **doleful** place. And he asked at last, 'Your castle stands, it seems, in a dreary region.'

'Yes; but once within it, hospitality makes all things cheerful. But who are these?' and he looked back, and Theseus also; and far below, along the road which they had left, came a string of laden [donkeys], and merchants walking by them, watching their ware.

'Ah, poor souls!' said the stranger. 'Well for them that I looked back and saw them! And well for me too, for I shall have the more guests at my feast. Wait awhile till I go down and call them, and we will eat and drink together the livelong night. Happy am I, to whom Heaven sends so many guests at once!'

And he ran back down the hill, waving his hand and shouting, to the merchants, while Theseus went slowly up the steep pass. But as he went up he met an aged man, who had been gathering driftwood in the torrent-bed. He had laid down his [bundle of sticks] in the road, and was trying to lift it again to his shoulder. And when he saw Theseus, he called to him, and said— 'O fair youth, help me up with my burden, for my limbs are stiff and weak with years.'

Then Theseus lifted the burden on his back. And the old man blessed him, and then looked earnestly upon him, and said— 'Who are you, fair youth, and wherefore travel you this doleful road?'

'Who I am my parents know; but I travel this doleful road because I have been invited by a hospitable man, who promises to feast me, and to make me sleep upon I know not what wondrous bed.'

Then the old man clapped his hands together and cried— 'O house of **Hades**, man-devouring! will thy **maw** never be full? Know, fair youth, that you are going to torment and to death, for he who met you (I will **requite** your kindness by another) is a robber and a murderer of men. Whatsoever stranger he meets he entices him hither to death; and as for this bed of which he speaks, truly it fits all comers, yet none ever rose alive off it save me.'

'Why?' asked Theseus, astonished.

'Because, if a man be too tall for it, he **lops** his limbs till they be short enough, and if he be too short, he stretches his limbs till they be long enough: but me only he spared, seven weary years agone; for I alone of all fitted his bed exactly, so he spared me, and made me his slave. And once I was a wealthy merchant, and dwelt in brazen-gated **Thebes**; but now I **hew** wood and draw water for him, the torment of all mortal men.'

Then Theseus said nothing; but he ground his teeth together.

'Escape, then,' said the old man, 'for he will have no pity on thy youth. But yesterday he brought up hither a young man and a maiden, and fitted them upon his bed; and the young man's hands and feet he cut off, but the maiden's limbs he stretched until she died, and so both perished miserably—but I am tired of weeping over the slain. And therefore he is called **Procrustes** the stretcher, though his father called him Damastes. Flee from him: yet whither will you flee? The cliffs are steep, and who can climb them? and there is no other road.'

But Theseus laid his hand upon the old man's mouth, and said, 'There is no need to flee;' and he turned to go down the pass. 'Do not tell him that I have warned you, or he will kill me by some evil death'; and the old man screamed after him down the glen; but Theseus strode on in his wrath.

Part Two

And he said to himself, 'This is an ill-ruled land; when shall I have done ridding it of monsters?' And as he spoke, Procrustes came up the hill, and all the merchants with him, smiling and talking gaily. And when he saw Theseus, he cried, 'Ah, fair young guest, have I kept you too long waiting?'

But Theseus answered, 'The man who stretches his guests upon a bed and hews off their hands and feet, what shall be done to him, when right is done throughout the land?' Then Procrustes' **countenance** changed, and his cheeks grew as green as a lizard, and he felt for his sword in haste; but Theseus leapt on him, and cried— 'Is this true, my host, or is it false?' and he clasped Procrustes round waist and elbow, so that he could not draw his sword.

'Is this true, my host, or is it false?' But Procrustes answered never a word.

Then Theseus flung him from him, and lifted up his dreadful club; and before Procrustes could strike him he had struck, and felled him to the ground. And once again he struck him; and his evil soul fled forth, and went down to Hades squeaking like a bat into the darkness of a cave.

Then Theseus stripped him of his gold ornaments, and went up to his house, and found there great wealth and treasure, which he had stolen from the passers-by. And he called the people of the country, whom Procrustes had **spoiled** a long time, and parted the **spoil** among them, and went down the mountains, and away.

And he went down the glens of Parnes, through mist, and cloud, and rain, down the slopes of oak, and lentisk, and arbutus, and fragrant bay, till he came to the Vale of Cephisus, and the pleasant town of Aphidnai, and the home of the Phytalid Heroes, where they dwelt beneath a mighty elm.

And there they built an altar, and bade him bathe in Cephisus, and offer a yearling ram, and purified him from the blood of Sinis, and sent him away in peace.

And he went down the valley by **Acharnai**, and by the silver-swirling stream, while all the people blessed him, for the fame of his **prowess** had spread wide, till he saw the plain of Athens, and the hill where Athena dwells.

Narration and Discussion

Does Theseus now feel ready to confront his father? How do you know?

The image of Procrustes forcing people into his one-size-fits-all bed has come down through the ages, and it is still used today. As an example, a 1904 article in Charlotte Mason's *Parents' Review* magazine says "girls are not so much subject as boys to the Procrustean system of schools…" Another phrase we use today is "trying to fit a square peg into a round hole." Have you ever been in a situation where you felt squeezed like that? What did you do?

Lesson #27

Introduction

We meet King Aegeus and his wife Medea—THAT Medea.

Vocabulary

> **leeches who suck his blood:** A leech is an annelid worm, often found in water, that attaches itself to animals or people. However, the "leeches" Theseus means are lazy, greedy people who have attached themselves to the king.
>
> **tumblers:** acrobats
>
> **discover:** reveal

People

> **His cousins; sons of Pallas; Pallantides:** Why are the cousins feasting in the hall while King Aegeus hides in a private chamber? What Kingsley does not explain very well is that there have been family power struggles in Athens, and Aegeus now appears to be a weak and fearful man, unsure if he is "master in his own hall." Even his wife **Medea**, with her many powers, does not seem able to restore the balance of things.
>
> **Medea:** see the introductory notes to *The Heroes*

Reading

Part One

So Theseus went up through Athens, and all the people ran out to see him; for his fame had gone before him and everyone knew of his mighty deeds. And all cried, 'Here comes the hero who slew Sinis, and Phaia the wild sow of Crommyon, and conquered Cercyon in wrestling, and slew Procrustes the pitiless.' But Theseus went on sadly and steadfastly, for his heart yearned after his father; and he said, 'How shall I deliver him from these **leeches who suck his blood**?'

So he went up the holy stairs, and into the Acropolis, where Aegeus's palace stood; and he went straight into Aegeus's hall, and stood upon the threshold, and looked round. And there he saw **his cousins** sitting about the table at the wine: many a son of Pallas, but no Aegeus among them. There they sat and feasted, and laughed, and passed the wine-cup round; while harpers harped, and slave-girls sang, and the **tumblers** showed their tricks. Loud laughed the **sons of Pallas**, and fast went the wine-cup round; but Theseus frowned, and said under his breath, 'No wonder that the land is full of robbers, while such as these bear rule.'

Then the **Pallantides** saw him, and called to him, half-drunk with wine, 'Holla, tall stranger at the door, what is your will today?'

'I come hither to ask for hospitality.'

'Then take it, and welcome. You look like a hero and a bold warrior; and we like such to drink with us.'

'I ask no hospitality of you; I ask it of Aegeus the king, the master of this house.'

At that some growled, and some laughed, and shouted, 'Heyday! we are all masters here.'

'Then I am master as much as the rest of you,' said Theseus, and he strode past the table up the hall, and looked around for Aegeus; but he was nowhere to be seen.

The Pallantids looked at him, and then at each other, and each whispered to the man next him, 'This is a forward fellow; he ought to be thrust out at the door.' But each man's neighbour whispered in return, 'His shoulders are broad; will you rise and put him out?' So they all sat still where they were.

Part Two

Then Theseus called to the servants, and said, 'Go tell King Aegeus, your master, that Theseus of Troezen is here, and asks to be his guest awhile.'

A servant ran and told Aegeus, where he sat in his chamber within, by Medea the dark witch-woman *[omission]*. And when Aegeus heard of Troezen he turned pale and red again, and rose from his seat trembling, while Medea watched him like a snake.

'What is Troezen to you?' she asked.

But he said hastily, 'Do you not know who this Theseus is? The hero who has cleared the country from all monsters; but that he came from Troezen, I never heard before. I must go out and welcome him.'

So Aegeus came out into the hall; and when Theseus saw him, his heart leapt into his mouth, and he longed to fall on his neck and welcome him; but he controlled himself, and said, 'My father may not wish for me, after all. I will try him before I **discover** myself'; and he bowed low before Aegeus, and said, 'I have delivered the king's realm from many monsters; therefore I am come to ask a reward of the king.'

And old Aegeus looked on him, and loved him, as what fond heart would not have done? But he only sighed, and said— 'It is little that I can give you, noble lad, and nothing that is worthy of you; for surely you are no mortal man, or at least no mortal's son.'

'All I ask,' said Theseus, 'is to eat and drink at your table.'

'That I can give you,' said Aegeus, 'if at least I am master in my own hall.'

Then he bade them put a seat for Theseus, and set before him the best of the feast; and Theseus sat and ate so much, that all the company wondered at him; but always he kept his club by his side.

Narration and Discussion

Why does Theseus decide to be cautious before revealing his identity?

Why don't any of the cousins "rise and put him out?"

Creative narration: Retell the events told here in dramatic or artistic format.

Lesson #28

Introduction

A lot happens here, and very quickly! The palace is suddenly a much quieter place, and Theseus and his father are able to spend some time together. But it appears that Aegeus has bigger troubles than even Theseus can understand or solve.

Vocabulary

cur: dog, especially a mongrel (so not a compliment)

more beautiful than the day: An interesting phrase, especially for those who have read *Five Children and It* by Edith Nesbit (AO Free Reading, Year Two). The phrase may actually come from Shakespeare's play *Love's Labour's Lost*, where a woman is said to be "As fair as day."

flask: container for liquids; bottle

Nepenthe: a drug said to banish grief and trouble from the mind

spring equinox: the first day of spring

tribute: something which must be paid, like a tax

lamentation: sound of wailing and grief

Panathenaic games: A sporting and religious event held every four years in Athens

People

Minos (American, **MEE-nohs**; British, **MY-nohs**)

Androgeos (AN-dra-jee-us)

Reading

Part One

But Medea *[omission]* had been watching him all the while. She saw how Aegeus turned red and pale when the lad said that he came from Troezen. She saw, too, how his heart was opened toward Theseus; and how Theseus bore himself before all the sons of Pallas, like a lion among a pack of **curs**. And she said to herself, 'This youth will be master here; perhaps he is nearer to Aegeus already than mere fancy. At least the Pallantides will have no chance by the side of such as he.'

Then she went back into her chamber modestly, while Theseus ate and drank; and all the servants whispered, 'This, then, is the man who killed the monsters! How noble are his looks, and how huge his size! Ah, would that he were our master's son!'

But presently Medea came forth, decked in all her jewels, and her rich Eastern robes, and looking **more beautiful than the day**, so that all the guests could look at nothing else. And in her right hand she held a golden cup, and in her left a **flask** of gold; and she came up to Theseus, and spoke in a sweet, soft, winning voice—

'Hail to the hero, the conqueror, the unconquered, the destroyer of all evil things! Drink, Hero, of my charmed cup, which gives rest after every toil, which heals all wounds, and pours new life into the veins. Drink of my cup, for in it sparkles the wine of the East, and **Nepenthe**, the comfort of the Immortals.'

And as she spoke, she poured the flask into the cup; and the fragrance of the wine spread through the hall, like the scent of thyme and roses.

And Theseus looked up in her fair face and into her deep dark eyes. And as he looked, he shrank and shuddered; for they were dry like the eyes of a snake. And he rose, and said, 'The wine is rich and fragrant, and the wine-bearer as fair as the Immortals; but let her pledge me first herself in the cup, that the wine may be the sweeter from her lips.'

Then Medea turned pale, and stammered, 'Forgive me, fair hero; but I am ill, and dare drink no wine.'

And Theseus looked again into her eyes, and cried, 'Thou shalt pledge me in that cup, or die.' And he lifted up his brazen club, while all the guests looked on aghast.

Medea shrieked a fearful shriek, and dashed the cup to the ground, and fled; and where the wine flowed over the marble pavement, the stone bubbled, and crumbled, and hissed *[omission]*.

But Medea called her dragon chariot, and sprang into it and fled aloft, away over land and sea, and no man saw her more.

Part Two

And Aegeus cried, 'What hast thou done?' But Theseus pointed to the stone, 'I have rid the land of an enchantment; now I will rid it of one more.'

He came close to Aegeus, and drew from his bosom the sword and the sandals, and said the words which his mother bade him. And Aegeus stepped back a pace, and looked at the lad till his eyes grew dim; and then he cast himself on his neck and wept, and Theseus wept on his neck, till they had no strength left to weep more.

Then Aegeus turned to all the people, and cried, 'Behold my son *[omission]*, a better man than his father was before him.'

Who, then, were mad but the Pallantids, though they had been mad enough before? And one shouted, 'Shall we make room for an upstart, a pretender, who comes from we know not where?' And another, 'If he be one, we are more than one; and the stronger can hold his own.' And one shouted one thing, and one another; for they were hot and wild with wine: but all caught swords and lances off the wall, where the weapons hung around, and sprang forward to Theseus, and Theseus sprang forward to them.

And he cried, 'Go in peace, if you will, my cousins; but if not, your blood be on your own heads.'

[Omission for length: Some of the Pallantids did try to fight Theseus, but he drove them out. The people of Athens "rejoiced all the night long, because their king had found a noble son, and an heir to his royal house."]

Part Three

So Theseus stayed with his father all the winter: and when the **spring equinox** drew near, all the Athenians grew sad and silent, and Theseus saw it, and asked the reason; but no one would answer him a word.

Then he went to his father, and asked him: but Aegeus turned away his face and wept. 'Do not ask, my son, beforehand, about evils which must happen: it is enough to have to face them when they come.'

And when the spring equinox came, a herald came to Athens, and stood in the market, and cried, 'O people and King of Athens, where is your yearly **tribute**?' Then a great **lamentation** arose throughout the city.

But Theseus stood up to the herald, and cried— 'And who are you, dog-faced, who dare demand tribute here? If I did not reverence your herald's staff, I would brain you with this club.'

And the herald answered proudly, for he was a grave and ancient man— 'Fair youth, I am not dog-faced or shameless; but I do my master's bidding, **Minos, the King of hundred-citied Crete**, the wisest of all kings on earth. And you must be surely a stranger here, or you would know why I come, and that I come by right.'

'I am a stranger here. Tell me, then, why you come.'

'To fetch the tribute which King Aegeus promised to Minos, and confirmed his promise with an oath. For Minos conquered all this land, and Megara which lies to the east, when he came hither with a great fleet of ships, enraged about the murder of his son. For his son **Androgeos** came hither to the **Panathenaic games**, and overcame all the Greeks in the sports, so that the people honoured him as a hero. But when Aegeus saw his valour, he envied him, and feared lest he should join the sons of Pallas, and take away the scepter from him. So he plotted against his life, and slew him basely, no man knows how or where *[omission]*. But Aegeus says that the young men killed him from envy, because he had conquered them in the games. So Minos came hither and avenged him, and would not depart till this land had promised him tribute—seven youths and seven maidens every year, who go with me in a black-sailed ship, till they come to hundred-citied Crete.'

And Theseus ground his teeth together, and said, 'Wert thou not a herald I would kill thee for saying such things of my father; but I will go to him, and know the truth.' So he went to his father, and asked him; but he turned away his head and wept, and said, 'Blood was shed in the land unjustly, and by blood it is avenged. Break not my heart by questions; it is enough to endure in silence.'

Narration and Discussion

Did the reunion with Aegeus turn out as Theseus had hoped?

Why doesn't Aegeus want Theseus to help with the King Minos problem?

Creative narration: Imagine someone arriving back at the palace who has been away for a few days. Explain what has changed recently.

Lesson #29

Introduction

Here we have one of the most famous stories about Theseus: how he went to Crete, entered the labyrinth, and fought the Minotaur.

Vocabulary

those youths and maidens die: There are versions of the story that say the ship came for the young people only every few years, and that only one pair were sent into the Labyrinth each year.

labyrinth: a confusing structure with many passages and dead ends; a maze

Minotaur (American, MEE-nah-tor; British, MYE-nah-tor): "the monster who feeds upon the flesh of men"

A boon: [Grant me] a favour

clue of thread: See note below

hid the sword in his bosom: As in an earlier lesson, Theseus (somehow) concealed it under his clothes.

doleful gulf: deep, dark pit

chasm: space, opening

People

Daedalus (DAY-da-lus): (Kingsley spells it Daidalos)

Ariadne (American, Air-ee-AD-nee; British, Ah-ree-AD-nee)

Places

Knossos (NOHSS-us, sometimes KNOHSS-us): The oldest known settlement on Crete.

peaks of Ida: Mount Ida is the highest mountain on the island of Crete.

Naxos: an island in the Aegean Sea

A Clue of Thread

A "clew" or "clewe" originally meant something round, such as a ball of yarn. But how did the word change to mean a fact or bit of information leading to the solution of a puzzle? It all goes back to the story of Theseus, Ariadne, and the labyrinth.

The fourteenth-century poet Geoffrey Chaucer was the first writer to tell the story in English (Middle English, but still English), in a poem called "The Legend of Good Women." He wrote about Theseus, "By a clewe of twyn as he hath gon / The same weye he may returne a-non / ffolwynge alwey the thred as he hath come." People began to use "a clew of thread" to mean something which points the way to an end.

Eventually the thread part was dropped, and the word "clew" or "clue" began to stand on its own, especially (in the nineteenth century) with the development of detective stories.

However, writers such as Bulfinch and Kingsley kept the phrase alive, even if it puzzled their readers, by using it in their retellings of this story. (Hawthorne, in *Tanglewood Tales*, stepped around it altogether.)

> ***Kingsley:*** *"I will give you a sword, and with that perhaps you may slay the beast; and a clue of thread…"*
>
> ***Bulfinch:*** *She furnished him with a sword, with which to encounter the Minotaur, and with a clew of thread by which he might find his way out of the labyrinth.*
>
> ***Hawthorne:*** *"That is the Minotaur's noise," whispered Ariadne, closely grasping the hand of Theseus… "Stay! take the end of this silken string; I will hold the other end; and then, if you win the victory, it will lead you again to this spot. Farewell, brave Theseus."*

And, just for interest, here is another instance you might come across of someone following a thread into a dangerous place.

> *"If ever you find yourself in any danger—such, for example, as you were in this same evening—you must…follow the thread wherever it leads you…But, remember, it may seem to you a very roundabout way indeed, and you must not doubt the thread. Of one thing you may be sure, that while you hold it, I hold it too."*
> *(George MacDonald,* The Princess and the Goblin *[AO Free Reading, Year Three])*

Reading

Part One

Then Theseus groaned inwardly, and said, 'I will go myself with these youths and maidens, and kill Minos upon his royal throne.'

And Aegeus shrieked, and cried, 'You shall not go, my son, the light of my old age, to whom alone I look to rule this people after I am dead and gone. You shall not go, to die horribly, as **those youths and maidens die**; for Minos thrusts them into a **labyrinth**, which **Daedalus** made for him among the rocks *[omission]*. From that labyrinth no one can escape, entangled in its winding ways, before they meet the **Minotaur**, the monster who feeds upon the flesh of men. There he devours them horribly, and they never see this land again.'

Then Theseus *[omission]* stood awhile like a tall stone pillar on the cliffs above some hero's grave; and at last he spoke— 'Therefore all the more I will go with them, and slay the accursed beast. Have I not slain all evil-doers and monsters, that I might free this land? Where are Periphetes, and Sinis, and Cercyon, and Phaia the wild sow? Where are the fifty sons of Pallas? And this Minotaur shall go the road which they have gone, and Minos himself, if he dare stay me.'

'But how will you slay him, my son? For you must leave your club and your armour behind, and be cast to the monster, defenseless and naked like the rest.'

And Theseus said, 'Are there no stones in that labyrinth; and have I not fists and teeth? Did I need my club to kill Cercyon, the terror of all mortal men?'

Then Aegeus clung to his knees; but he would not hear; and at last he let him go, weeping bitterly, and said only this one word— 'Promise me but this, if you return in peace, though that may hardly be: take down the black sail of the ship (for I shall watch for it all day upon the cliffs), and hoist instead a white sail, that I may know afar off that you are safe.'

And Theseus promised, and went out, and to the market-place where the herald stood, while they drew lots for the youths and maidens, who were to sail in that doleful crew. And the people stood wailing and weeping, as the lot fell on this one and on that; but Theseus strode into the midst, and cried— 'Here is a youth who needs no lot. I myself will be one of the seven.'

And the herald asked in wonder, 'Fair youth, know you whither you are going?'

And Theseus said, 'I know. Let us go down to the black-sailed ship.'

So they went down to the black-sailed ship, seven maidens, and seven youths, and Theseus before them all, and the people following them lamenting.

[omission for length]

Part Two

And at last they came to Crete, and to **Knossos**, beneath the **peaks of Ida**, and to the palace of Minos the great king, to whom Zeus himself taught laws. So he was the wisest of all mortal kings, and conquered all the Aegean isles; and his ships were as many as the seagulls, and his palace like a marble hill. And he sat among the pillars of the hall, upon his throne of beaten gold, and around him stood the speaking statues which **Daedalus** had made by his skill.

[Omission for length: stories about Daedalus]

But Theseus stood before Minos, and they looked each other in the face.

And Minos [ordered them taken] to prison, and cast to the monster one by one, that the death of Androgeos might be avenged. Then Theseus cried— '**A boon**, O Minos! Let me be thrown first to the beast. For I came hither for that very purpose, of my own will, and not by lot.'

'Who art thou, then, brave youth?'

'I am the son of him whom of all men thou hatest most, Aegeus the king of Athens, and I am come here to end this matter.'

And Minos pondered awhile, looking steadfastly at him, and he thought, 'The lad means to atone by his own death for his father's sin;' and he answered at last mildly— 'Go back in peace, my son. It is a pity that one so brave should die.'

But Theseus said, 'I have sworn that I will not go back till I have seen the monster face to face.'

And at that Minos frowned, and said, 'Then thou shalt see him; take the madman away.' And they led Theseus away into the prison, with the other youths and maids.

But **Ariadne**, Minos' daughter, saw him, as she came out of her white stone hall; and she loved him for his courage and his majesty, and said, 'Shame that such a youth should die!' And by night she went down to the prison, and told him all her heart; and said— 'Flee down to your ship at once, for I have bribed the guards before the door. Flee, you and all your friends, and go back to Greece *[omission]*; and take me, take me with you! for I dare not stay after you are gone; for my father will kill me miserably, if he knows what I have done.'

And Theseus stood silent awhile; for he was astonished and confounded by her beauty: but at last he said, 'I cannot go home in peace, till I have seen and slain this Minotaur, and avenged the deaths of the youths and maidens, and put an end to the terrors of my land.'

'And will you kill the Minotaur? How, then?'

'I know not, nor do I care: but he must be strong if he be too strong for me.'

Then she said *[omission]*, 'But when you have killed him, how will you find your way out of the labyrinth?'

'I know not, neither do I care: but it must be a strange road, if I do not find it out before I have eaten up the monster's carcass.'

Then she loved him all the more, and said— 'Fair youth, you are too bold; but I can help you, weak as I am. I will give you a sword, and with that perhaps you may slay the beast; and a **clue of thread**, and by that, Perhaps, you may find your way out again. Only promise me that if you escape safe you will take me home with you to Greece; for my father will surely kill me, if he knows what I have done.'

Then Theseus laughed, and said, 'Am I not safe enough now?' And he **hid the sword in his bosom**, and rolled up the **clue** in his hand; and then he swore [his love] to Ariadne, and fell down before her, and kissed her hands and her feet; and she wept over him a long while, and then went away; and Theseus lay down and slept sweetly.

Part Three

When the evening came, the guards came in and led him away to the labyrinth. And he went down into that **doleful gulf**, through winding paths among the rocks, under caverns, and arches, and galleries, and over heaps of fallen stone.

And he turned on the left hand, and on the right hand, and went up and down, till his head was dizzy; but all the while he held his clue. For when he went in he had fastened it to a stone, and left it to unroll out of his hand as he went on; and it lasted him till he met the Minotaur, in a narrow **chasm** between black cliffs.

And when he saw him he stopped awhile, for he had never seen so strange a beast. His body was a man's: but his head was the head of a bull; and his teeth were the teeth of a lion, and with them he tore his prey. And when he saw Theseus he roared, and put his head down, and rushed right at him.

But Theseus stepped aside nimbly, and as he passed by, cut him in the knee; and ere he could turn in the narrow path, he followed him, and stabbed him again and again from behind, till the monster fled bellowing wildly; for he never before had felt a wound. And Theseus followed him at full speed, holding the clue of thread in his left hand.

Then on, through cavern after cavern, under dark ribs of sounding stone, and up rough glens and torrent-beds, among the sunless roots of Ida, and to the edge of the eternal snow, went they, the hunter and the hunted, while the hills bellowed to the monster's bellow. And at last Theseus came up with him, where he lay panting on a slab among the snow, and caught him by the horns, and forced his head back, and drove the keen sword through his throat.

Part Four

Then he turned, and went back limping and weary, feeling his way down by the clue of thread, till he came to the mouth of that doleful place and saw waiting for him, whom but Ariadne!

And he whispered 'It is done!' and showed her the sword; and she laid her finger on her lips, and led him to the prison, and opened the doors, and set all the prisoners free, while the guards lay sleeping heavily; for she had silenced them with wine.

Then they fled to their ship together, and leapt on board, and hoisted up the sail; and the night lay dark around them, so that they passed through Minos's ships, and escaped all safe to **Naxos**; and there Ariadne became Theseus's wife.

Narration and Discussion

How does Theseus show that he has truly become a Hero?

Do you think King Minos will react with even more anger when he finds out that the Minotaur is dead? (Has Theseus created more of a problem than ever?)

Creative narration: There are many ways to act, write about, or illustrate this story. Choose one that you or your group enjoy.

For the curious: Kingsley does not explain much about the labyrinth, other than its "winding paths" that made Theseus go "up and down, till his head was dizzy." Find out what you can about the labyrinth on Crete, or about other labyrinths.

The Heroes

Lesson #30

Introduction

We are hoping for a happy ending for Theseus, but get instead a mixed bag of mighty deeds and broken promises. Even heroes sometimes "go their own ways."

Vocabulary

a painting of old Titian's: *Bacchus and Ariadne*, painted 1522-1523

took Hippolyta (Hi-POH-li-ta) their queen to be his wife: This is a tangled bit of Theseus's story, as various sources bring Hippolyta into (and out of) his life at quite different times. (He also had another wife, named Phaedra.) One place where we see Theseus and Hippolyta engaged to be married is in Shakespeare's play *A Midsummer Night's Dream*.

People

Dionysus: or Bacchus; the god of wine, among other things

One was a youth, dressed only in a fawn-skin, with vine-leaves wreathed in his curly hair... You felt, as Edmund said when he saw him a few days later, "There's a chap who might do anything—absolutely anything." (C. S. Lewis, Prince Caspian [AO Free Reading, Year Four])

Pirithous (Pie-RIH-thoo-us)

Persephone (PER-se-fah-nee; **Per-SEPH-ah-nee** is also common**)**

Lycomedes (LIKE-oh-me-deez)

Places

Skyros (SKY-ross is one possibility; **SKEER-ohss** is another.)

Reading

Part One: Two Sad Developments

But that fair Ariadne never came to Athens with her husband. Some say that Theseus left her sleeping on Naxos among the Cyclades; and that **Dionysus** *[omission]* found her, and took her up into the sky, as you shall see some day in **a painting of old Titian's**—one of the most glorious pictures upon earth. And some say that Dionysus drove away Theseus, and took Ariadne from him by force: but however that may be, in his haste or in his grief, Theseus forgot to put up the white sail.

Now Aegeus his father sat and watched on Sounion day after day, and strained his old eyes across the sea to see the ship afar. And when he saw the black sail, and not the white one, he gave up Theseus for dead, and in his grief he fell into the sea, and died; so it is called the Aegean to this day.

Part Two: A Good Reign

And now Theseus was king of Athens, and he guarded it and ruled it well.

For he killed the Bull of Marathon, which had killed Androgeos, Minos's son; and he drove back the famous Amazons, the warlike women of the East, when they came from Asia and conquered all Hellas, and broke into Athens itself. But Theseus stopped them there, and conquered them, and **took Hippolyta their queen to be his wife**.

Then he went out to fight against the Lapithai, and **Pirithous** their famous king: but when the two Heroes came face to face they *[omission]* embraced, and became noble friends; so that the friendship of Theseus and Pirithous is a proverb even now.

And he gathered (so the Athenians say) all the boroughs of the land together, and knit them into one strong people, while before they were all parted and weak.

And many another wise thing he did, so that his people honoured him after he was dead, for many a hundred years, as the father of their freedom and their laws. And six hundred years after his death, in the famous fight at Marathon, men said that they saw the ghost of Theseus, with his mighty brazen club, fighting in *[omission]* battle against the invading Persians, for the country which he loved.

Part Three: But a Bad Ending

And twenty years after Marathon his bones (they say) were found in **Skyros**, an isle beyond the sea; and they were bigger than the bones of mortal man. So the Athenians brought them home in triumph; and all the people came out to welcome them; and they built over them a noble temple, and adorned it with sculptures and paintings in which we are told all the noble deeds of Theseus, and the Centaurs, and the Lapithai, and the Amazons; and the ruins of it are standing still.

But why did they find his bones in Skyros? Why did he not die in peace at Athens, and sleep by his father's side?

Because after his triumph he grew proud, and broke the laws of God and man. And one thing worst of all he did, which brought him to his grave with sorrow. For he went down (they say beneath the earth) with that bold Pirithous his friend to help him to carry off **Persephone**, the queen of the world below. But Pirithous was killed miserably, in the dark fire-kingdoms underground; and Theseus was chained to a rock in everlasting pain. And there he sat for years, till Heracles the mighty came down to bring up the three-headed dog who sits at Pluto's gate. So Heracles loosed him from his chain, and brought him up to the light once more.

But when he came back his people had forgotten him, *[omission]* and another king ruled [Athens], who drove out Theseus shamefully, and he fled across the sea to Skyros. And there he lived in sadness, in the house of **Lycomedes** the king, till Lycomedes killed him by treachery, and there was an end of all his labours.

Epilogue

So it is still, my children, and so it will be to the end. In those old Greeks, and in us also, all strength and virtue come from God. But if men grow proud and self-willed, and misuse God's fair gifts, He lets them go their own ways, and fall pitifully, that the glory may be His alone. God help us all, and give us wisdom, and courage to do noble deeds! But God keep pride from us when we have done them, lest we fall, and come to shame!

Narration and Discussion

In the first reading about Theseus (**Lesson #22**), Theseus said, 'If I were king of such a land I would rule it wisely and well in wisdom and in might, that when I died all men might weep over my tomb, and cry, "Alas for the shepherd of his people!"' Did he achieve his goal?

For further thoughts: What are some ways that Theseus used "God's fair gifts" well? How did he misuse them?

Creative narration: As noted earlier, the oldest "Theseus" artifact we know of is a vase, believed to have been made in 570 B.C., and discovered in 1844 in an ancient tomb. (The vase is now in a museum, the Museo Archeologico in Florence, Italy.) Create your own "Theseus vase" or other artifact, showing a favourite scene from his life. (This could be just a drawing, or an actual object.)

Examination Questions for Theseus

Tell one of these stories:

1. About the boyhood of Theseus

2. About Theseus and the Club Bearer

3. About Theseus and Medea

4. About Theseus and Ariadne

5. About the slaying of the Minotaur

Book II: The Water-Babies

Introduction: Swimming With *The Water-Babies*

What is *The Water-Babies?*

The Water-Babies is a moralistic, yet fun, fairy tale from the mind of the English minister-professor-naturalist-poet Charles Kingsley (1819–1875). He apparently wrote it after his wife complained that their three older children (Rose, Maurice, and Mary) already had a book, *The Heroes*, dedicated to them, but that their youngest, Grenville, needed a book too. Kingsley, reportedly, went into his study and plotted out this "fairy tale for a land-baby."

Its style and themes are planted solidly in the mid-Victorian world, but reflect Kingsley's sense of humour and sometimes slightly unorthodox Christian beliefs. AmblesideOnline students reading *The Water-Babies* in Year Three (or Form I) will also be reading Kingsley's version of several Greek myths, *The Heroes* (*The Water-Babies* contains references to Epimetheus, Prometheus, and Pandora). Those who continue with AO's Year Four (Form II) will also find the style of *Madam How and Lady Why* very familiar, as Kingsley continues the conversation with the young boy whom he addresses as "my little man" in *The Water-Babies*. (The last Kingsley book used in the AO Curriculum is *Westward Ho!* in Year Eight.)

How our family discovered this book

A lot of people have heard of *The Water-Babies* and may be aware of a few images and scenes from it; however, few have actually read it. British writer J.G. Ballard echoed a common reaction to *The Water-Babies* when he called it "a masterpiece in its bizarre way, but one of the most unpleasant works of fiction I have ever read..." (in an essay included in *The Pleasure of Reading*).

My own early exposure to it was (mainly) being loaned a cousin's copy, thinking it looked way too long, not understanding it at all, and giving it back again fairly quickly. I read an illustrated (and probably slightly abridged) edition with my oldest daughter when she was about nine, but it was one of her less-enjoyed AO books (although I do remember her giving a good narration of Mr. Grimes stuck in a chimney).

A few years later, we acquired a set of *My Book House* volumes, one of which contained a very short version of *The Water-Babies*. I read it to my book-loving first-grader, but told her that there really was more to the story than that; so she asked to be read The Real Thing. I hesitated, remember my older daughter's ambivalence about the story; but we started off, skipping things here and there but otherwise enjoying the story. My six-year-old didn't seem to worry as much about the questions of death/existence/metaphysics as an older child might; she accepted the book on a simpler, fairy tale level.

So some of the "why read this?" will depend on your child's age. For a young child, it's simply Tom's marvelous adventures underwater, and his struggle not to be greedy and to become better than he has been. When the book says that the fairies came and took Ellie away after her accident, a young child may take that fairly literally; and although it may not be theologically proper, in Kingsley's fairy-tale it is exactly what he means, just as in a Narnia story there can be centaurs and dryads, and Deep Magic that doesn't necessarily correspond to the way things operate in our world.

However, the story is suggested for AO Year Three students who will be about eight to ten years old, and somewhat beyond my first-grader's experience. For those using AO for Groups, it's possible that six- or seven-year-old students in Form I will also be listening in. Year Three students might find the story either somewhat disturbing (too much emphasis on death); or boring (too much talk). So if they are both too old and too young for *The Water-Babies*, why read it to them?

Year Threes are at about the right age to enjoy *Alice in Wonderland*, although Kingsley didn't have Lewis Carroll's gift for verbal nonsense and general lunacy. His more restrained but rambling style; his tendency to moralize; and the problematic device of having human entrance into his "other world" come through death, prevents the story from being as appealing as *Alice*. Still, there are strong characters that make up for the weaknesses in the plot: Tom himself, especially in his periods of mischief; the ugly-but-just Mrs. Bedonebyasyoudid (who people usually remember, incorrectly, by her sister's name); and some of the animal characters. There are memorable scenes, such as Tom and Grimes' final reunion at the chimney. The writing is often gently humorous, sometimes even echoing Dickens' style:

> As for chimney-sweeping, and being hungry, and being beaten, he took all that for the way of the world, like the rain and snow and thunder, and stood manfully with his back to it till it was over, as his old donkey did to a hailstorm; and then shook his ears and was as jolly as ever; and thought of the fine times coming, when he would be a man, and a master sweep, and sit in the public-house with a quart of beer and a long pipe, and play cards for silver money, and wear velveteens and ankle-jacks, and keep a white bulldog with one grey ear, and carry her puppies in his pocket, just like a man.

And strangely enough, Kingsley himself didn't take his own moral fable too seriously. The last chapter starts: "Here begins the never-to-be-too-much-studied account of the nine-hundred-and-ninety-ninth part of the wonderful things which Tom saw on his journey to the Other-end-of-Nowhere." The "moral," tacked on at the end of the book, is summed up by "Don't Hurt Efts," and a reminder to "stick to hard work and cold water." This suggests that, while Kingsley may have been less amusing (on picnics or in writing) than Lewis Carroll, and therefore less successful in his attempt at fantasy, he didn't see his story as only something "improving." I don't think he aimed at being remembered as the author of "one of the most unpleasant works of fiction" for children. His funny bits, often at the expense of academics and other pompous types (such as the poor professor who was thrown into a state of mental anguish until he admitted that he did believe in water-babies) really are good, too, although they sometimes get off-track.

So we hope that young Grenville appreciated his book.

Why is this not a lesson-book?

Unlike *The Heroes*, *The Water-Babies* is not set as a literature book in the AO curriculum. It can be read at any pace you like, and all the extra material, including narration suggestions and exam questions, is entirely optional. Maybe all you will do is read it together, and that's fine.

If parents/teachers wish to use the book in place of another literature book, or perhaps for a Year 3.5 option, the lessons are there to be used. If you incorporate the book into weekly school study, please consider having your student(s) narrate in some form (probably orally, but possibly using some creative format such as drama or visual art). You might choose to use something from the story as copywork; or to learn one of Kingsley's poems (or one of the verses that begin the chapters). If students are keen to know more about the creatures mentioned, or what chimney sweeps do, go ahead and let them explore that (helping as needed). If they want to talk more about some of the big ideas in the book, that's good too.

But let's not turn Kingsley's story into something for which he might send Mrs. Bedonebyasyoudid after us with her birch rod.

What is it about? (Spoilers included)

The main character, Tom, starts out as a mistreated apprentice chimney-sweep. During a job at a country estate, he accidentally goes down a chimney into a little girl's bedroom, which causes uproar in the house and causes him to be chased off as a thief. After a mad dash across the moors and down a cliff, he ends up in a river where he is turned into a "water-baby" and begins a new life (although his human body is discovered floating in the river and he is assumed to be dead).

Tom-the-water-baby lives in the river for some time, but eventually becomes lonely for others like himself and finds his way out to sea. At first he cannot find any water-babies there either, but after showing kindness to a trapped lobster, his eyes and ears are opened and he suddenly sees them swimming and hears them singing. The water-babies take him to their home under the sea, where they are visited on Fridays by ugly Mrs. Bedonebyasyoudid, and on Sundays by her beautiful sister Mrs. Doasyouwouldbedoneby.

Although Tom misbehaves by stealing sea-candy, he does learn his lesson and is joined by Ellie, the little girl whose room he had stumbled into. Ellie had been hurt (we assume fatally) in an accident, but does not seem to be a water baby; she "goes home" every Sunday, which makes Tom both curious and jealous. When he asks how he can earn the same privilege, the fairy sisters explain that he needs to do something he would not naturally like to do—in Tom's case, helping his hated former master Grimes. Mr. Grimes had also fallen in the river (while poaching) and had since been taken to The Other-end-of-Nowhere.

From this point on the plot becomes Tom's quest to find Grimes and achieve the water-baby equivalent of earning an angel's wings. After journeying to the Shiny Wall and meeting "Mother Carey," he continues through various allegorical "lands." Eventually Tom finds Mr. Grimes, imprisoned in a chimney (the theme of suitable punishment comes up throughout the book). Tom succeeds in his mission and is rewarded as promised, returning to the water-babies' home and Ellie—and he discovers that he and Ellie have become adults.

Is the book about natural history? Should young readers be expected to take great interest in the birds, fish, and sea organisms?

> *How easily a man might, if he would, wash his soul clean for a while from all the turmoil and intrigue, the vanity and vexation of spirit of that "too populous wilderness," by going out to be alone a while with God in heaven, and with that earth which He has given to the children of men..." (Charles Kingsley,* Glaucus: Wonders of the Shore*)*

The Water-Babies contains so many descriptions of river and ocean creatures, and puts so much emphasis on kindness to animals and respect for nature, that some people think of it as a natural-history rather than a literature choice. However, it is more of a didactic (learn-your-lesson) story, on two levels: first, aimed at getting children to do-as-they-would-be-done-by; but also as a platform for Kingsley to air his views on social reform, the issue of science (and pseudo-science) vs. faith, and a few other things that were aimed at parents and the general public rather than the child reader.

One writer has called *The Water-Babies* "science-supported fantasy," and that seems like a good way to describe it.

> *Those who wish honestly to learn the laws of Madam How, which we call Nature, by looking honestly at what she does, which we call Fact, have only to begin by looking at the very smallest thing, pin's head or pebble, at their feet, and it may lead them—whither, they cannot tell. (Charles Kingsley,* Madam How and Lady Why*)*

There is some very strange stuff in this book, such as talking birds and policemen's billy clubs that bounce around by themselves; in fact, some of its nonsense bits remind us of *Alice in Wonderland*.

The Water-Babies was published around the same time as Lewis Carroll's *Alice's Adventures in Wonderland*, and, like *Alice*, contains more nonsense (and also interest in things like numbers and looking-glass reversals) than earlier children's books. It predates *The Adventures of Pinocchio* and George MacDonald's children's fantasies, but shares some strong themes and imagery with those books. Think of noses that grow and Tom's prickles; the Blue Fairy and Mrs. Bedonebyasyoudid; and also the North Wind and Princess Irene's great-great-grandmother in George MacDonald's stories.

Sorting out how Kingsley's fairy-tale world works is somewhat confusing. Nobody seems to actually die (and stay dead) in this story; even the blubber-eating birds are old whalers being punished for their greed. This rather loose arrangement is similar to that in Andersen's "The Little Mermaid," with different kinds of beings in different stages of existence, and sometimes in different physical places as well (such as The Other-end-of-Nowhere). Time also shifts and passes in confusing ways—years can go by in a few minutes. You can't always make sense of it—you just have to enjoy the ride.

Is the book an allegory?

No, as Kingsley repeatedly reminds us—it is a fairy tale. However, being Charles Kingsley, he cannot help but poke fun at and sometimes strongly criticize things he disagrees with. Kingsley had more than a few opinions about various cultural, religious and ethnic groups, as well as quack medicine, bad children's books, junk food, and too-tight boots, and did not hesitate to include those in his books. In the case of mistreated child workers such as chimney sweeps, his criticism did, in fact, lead to new laws protecting them.

Why alter the book?

To eliminate ethnic and religious slurs.
To avoid some of Kingsley's more baffling Victorian references.
To give a bit of advance warning when a ramble is coming up.
To update some spelling and punctuation, as well as a few words that have changed meaning since Kingsley's time.

In some ways, *The Water-Babies* was never meant for children at all. It can be read as a thinly-disguised commentary on the still-quite-new idea of evolution (to which Kingsley was not entirely averse), and on the seemingly limitless progress of mankind; but also on the misuses of science and technology. As Charlotte Mason's teachers were reminded to "mix it with brains," Kingsley's slogan might have been "mix it with imagination." At one point in the story he refers to *Gulliver's Travels*, which, similarly, was written as satire of some very specific types of eighteenth-century people; but since much of that would have gone over children's heads, they simply enjoyed as much of the story as they understood, and took much of the rest as nonsense. Again, similarly, one might take *Alice's Adventures in Wonderland* as a wonderful story for its own sake; or as a deep dive into the eclectic mind of Lewis Carroll.

However, we don't (or shouldn't) present children with abridged versions of *Alice*, so why so with *The Water-Babies*?

I realize it is presumptuous to try to improve on Kingsley, although certainly I am not the first to try to shorten the story somewhat. For an older child who can do his own skipping-where-necessary, and who can handle Kingsley's surprising rudeness toward almost everything neither of his country nor of his church, certainly it would be preferable to enjoy The Real Thing. Adults who desire to follow Kingsley down his many philosophical and scientific rabbit holes are advised to find themselves an unabridged copy of *The Water-Babies*, cringeworthy though a few of the references may be. Our purpose here is to tell as much of the story as seems advisable for AO Year Three (or Form I) students, and their parents/teachers.

Eight Chapters, Many Readings

If you're reading straight through the book, you might read a chapter, or half a chapter, at a time. However, you could choose to go more slowly, especially with younger students. For that reason, the book has been divided into thirty-one suggested "Readings." You can tell where the original eight chapters are divided by the "Poetic Interludes" that come before each one.

Why No Illustrations?

The first reason, besides not being able to use copyrighted illustrations, is the issue of how one portrays the naked water-babies: some readers appreciate not having so many little backsides cluttering up the text. Another is that many of us are already overstimulated with pictures these days, and sometimes it is better to use our own imaginations to populate the story.

The exception will be in readings where, for instance, an aquatic creature is mentioned (like the *Limnias melicerta*), and it would be helpful and enlightening to look for a photo, either online or in reference books.

However, a browse through an illustrated edition (maybe after reading the edited version together) would not be a bad thing to do. I would give an especially high rating to the 1915 illustrations by cartoonist W. Heath Robinson, which are everything we could want them to be: modest, humorous, plentiful, and full of graceful Art Nouveau touches. His illustration of the turnips is, in itself, worth looking up.

Certain Vocabulary Words We Try Not to Use

> **Stupid:** Kingsley uses this adjective regularly; in this version it has been edited out where possible. In the usage of the time, "stupid" did not always reflect on one's intelligence, but could mean anything from foolish and unwilling to listen to wisdom, to merely dull and tedious. One might say that the hot day was making them feel "stupid," meaning sluggish and sleepy.
>
> **Heathen:** Here we get into some deep water. Someone regarded as a "heathen" is one who does not follow a generally accepted religious belief or practice. Because the word is contentious, it has been edited out where it did not seem necessary.
>
> *"Matthew Cuthbert, it's about time somebody adopted that child and taught her something. She's next door to a perfect heathen. Will you believe that she never said a prayer in her life till tonight?"*
> (L. M. Montgomery, *Anne of Green Gables* [AO Free Reading, Year Five])

A Few Questions for Older People to Consider

1. One of the most frequently repeated metaphors in the book is water, and its relationship to dirt/cleansing and death/rebirth. Does Kingsley's use of water tie in well with the (traditional) Christian uses of this image (cleansing, baptism), or is he doing something different with it?

2. Another frequent theme is that of physical transformation: boy into water-baby, insects shedding their skins, the DoAsYouLikes becoming ape-like creatures, and the ugly fairy becoming beautiful. Why do you think this is such a common theme in fairy-tales and other children's books?

3. Kingsley differentiates between those who abuse children out of malice, and those who neglect or mistreat them out of ignorance. Do you agree that there is a difference?

4. Finally: why does Kingsley seem to undercut himself by reminding us that it's "only" a fairy tale and that we mustn't believe it—even if it's true?

>**Elim Garak:** My dear Doctor, they're all true.
>**Dr. Julian Bashir:** Even the lies?
>**Elim Garak:** *Especially* the lies.
>(*Star Trek: Deep Space Nine*, "The Wire")

Poetic Interlude #1

Before beginning each chapter, Kingsley provides a bit of poetry, that might or might not give a clue to what is coming up next. This first "Interlude" is from William Wordsworth's "Lines Written in Early Spring." (This poem can also be found in AO's collection of poems for Year Four.]

I heard a thousand blended notes,
While in a grove I sate reclined;
In that sweet mood when pleasant thoughts
Bring sad thoughts to the mind.

To her fair works did Nature link
The human soul that through me ran;
And much it grieved my heart to think,
What man has made of man.

Reading #1

Introduction

Charles Kingsley begins this story by telling us almost everything we might want to know about Tom's early life as a chimney sweep. What might not be quite clear is that Tom has no family, and seems to live quite on his own. At that time, it was not uncommon for very poor people to sleep in rough, falling-down buildings, such as those that likely would have been found on Tom's "court."

The other two things that young readers might need to know are when and where the story takes place. *The Water-Babies* was first published as a magazine serial (a story that goes on from issue to issue) during 1862-1863, and then it was published as a book in 1863. So it's likely that the "real life" parts of the story are set around that time. The "where" is in the northern part of England, probably Yorkshire, and you will notice a few different words and ways of talking that sound like that part of the country. (One of the Free Reading books for AO Year Four (Form II) is *The Secret Garden*, by Frances Hodgson Burnett, which is also set in Yorkshire.)

Vocabulary

There are certainly a lot of potential vocabulary pitfalls in this first reading! However, please remember that the words are here only for reference, and are not meant to be taught via flashcard, worksheet, or any other such means. You might want to explain just a few words ahead of time that might help your students make better sense of the reading.

court: short street

flue: a large pipe (or open space) going up inside a chimney

public-house: place to drink alcohol (now often shortened to "pub"); tavern

ankle-jacks: boots

groom: boy employed to take care of horses

the Place: Harthover Place, the great estate owned by Sir John Harthover

drab: fabric of a dull brown colour

gaiters: leg coverings

breeches: trousers

under a flag of truce: agreeing to act peaceably

The Water-Babies

public schools: private schools where wealthy boys were taught to be gentlemen

awful: awe-inspiring

collier: one who works in a coal mine

poach: to steal fish or game belonging to someone else; one who does so is a **poacher**

squire: a country gentleman; usually the main landowner in a town or county

fifteen stone: 210 pounds (about 95 kg)

thrashed: beaten

a "buirdly awd chap": a burly or muscular fellow

gradely: pretty

pert: perky, lively

gamecock: a rooster bred for fighting

pitmen: miners

turnpike: a toll gate, where travelers would be charged to use a road (though these had largely gone out of fashion with the arrival of the railroads, so it is unclear whether Mr. Grimes had to pay to go through the gate)

matins: morning prayers

sedges: grasslike plants, often growing near rivers

he never had been so far into the country before: This seems odd, since Tom knows about the deer and pheasants at the Place, and it is implied that his earlier arrests might have been due to helping Grimes poach salmon. However, we can take it that he has never had such a leisurely jaunt there, especially during daylight hours.

crimson madder: a shade of red, produced by dyeing cloth with the madder plant

petticoat: under-skirt

nosegay: small bunch of flowers

beadle: an officer of the law

two years ago come Martinmas: Martinmas is the feast day of St. Martin, on November 11th. This story opens in midsummer, so she is saying "it will be two years ago this November."

cowed: frightened by her threats

foul: dirty, polluted

Places

Galway: a city and county in **Ireland**. At the time of this writing, many of its people had been impoverished by the Great Famine.

Vendale: a place we will hear more about in **Reading #4**

Reading

Part One

Once upon a time there was a little chimney-sweep, and his name was Tom.

That is a short name, and you have heard it before, so you will not have much trouble in remembering it.

He lived in a great town in the North country, where there were plenty of chimneys to sweep, and plenty of money for Tom to earn and his master to spend. He could not read nor write, and did not care to do either; and he never washed himself, for there was no water up the **court** where he lived. He had never been taught to say his prayers. He never had heard of God, or of Christ, except in words which you never have heard, and which it would have been well if he had never heard.

He cried half his time, and laughed the other half. He cried when he had to climb the dark **flues**, rubbing his poor knees and elbows raw; and when the soot got into his eyes, which it did every day in the week; and when his master beat him, which he did every day in the week; and when he had not enough to eat, which happened every day in the week likewise. And he laughed the other half of the day, when he was tossing half pennies with the other boys, or playing leap-frog over the posts, or bowling stones at the horses' legs as they trotted by, which last was excellent fun, when there was a wall at hand behind which to hide.

As for chimney-sweeping, and being hungry, and being beaten, he took all that for the way of the world, like the rain and snow and thunder, and stood manfully with his back to it till it was over, as his old donkey did to a hailstorm; and then shook his ears and was as jolly as ever; and thought of the fine times coming, when he would be a man, and a master sweep, and sit in the **public-house** with a quart of beer and a long pipe, and play cards for silver money, and wear velveteens and **ankle-jacks**, and keep a white bulldog with one grey ear, and carry her puppies in his pocket, just like a man. And he would have apprentices, one, two, three, if he could. How he would bully them, and knock them about, just as his master did to him; and make them carry home the soot sacks, while he rode before them on his donkey, with a pipe in his mouth and a flower in his buttonhole, like a king at the head of his army.

[*omission for content*]

One day a smart little **groom** rode into the court where Tom lived. Tom was just hiding behind a wall, to heave half a brick at his horse's legs as is the custom of that country when they welcome strangers; but the groom saw him, and halloed to him to know where Mr. Grimes, the chimney-sweep, lived. Now, Mr. Grimes was Tom's own master, and Tom was a good man of business, and always civil to customers, so he put the half-brick down quietly behind the wall, and proceeded to take orders.

Mr. Grimes was to come up next morning to Sir John Harthover's, at **the Place**, for his old chimney-sweep was gone to prison, and the chimneys wanted sweeping. And so he rode away, not giving Tom time to ask what the sweep had gone to prison for, which was a matter of interest to Tom, as he had been in prison once or twice himself. Moreover, the groom looked so very neat and clean, with his drab **gaiters**, drab **breeches**, drab jacket, snow-white tie with a smart pin in it, and clean round ruddy face, that Tom was offended and disgusted at his appearance, and considered him a stuck-up fellow, who gave himself airs because he wore smart clothes, and other people paid for them; and went behind the wall to fetch the half-brick after all; but did not, remembering that he had come in the way of business, and was, as it were, **under a flag of truce**.

His master was so delighted at his new customer that he knocked Tom down out of hand, and drank more beer that night than he usually did in two, in order to be sure of getting up in time next morning; for the more a man's head aches when he wakes, the more glad he is to turn out, and have a breath of fresh air. And, when he did get up at four the next morning, he knocked Tom down again, in order to teach him (as young gentlemen used to be taught at **public schools**) that he must be an extra good boy that day, as they were going to a very great house, and might make a very good thing of it, if they could but give satisfaction.

And Tom thought so likewise, and, indeed, would have done and behaved his best, even without being knocked down. For, of all places upon earth, Harthover Place (which he had never seen) was the most wonderful, and, of all men on earth, Sir John (whom he *had* seen, having been sent to jail by him twice) was the most **awful**.

Part Two

Harthover Place was really a grand place, even for the rich North country; with a [very large house]; a park full of deer, which Tom believed to be monsters who were in the habit of eating children; miles of game-preserves, in which Mr. Grimes and the **collier** lads **poached** at times, on which occasions Tom saw pheasants, and wondered what they tasted like; [and] a noble salmon-river, in which Mr. Grimes and his friends would have liked to poach; but then they must have got into cold water, and that they did not like at all. In short, Harthover was a grand place, and Sir John a grand old man, whom even Mr. Grimes respected; for not only could he send Mr. Grimes to prison when he deserved it, as he did once or twice a week; not only did he own all the land about for miles; not only was he a jolly, honest, sensible **squire**, as ever kept a pack of hounds, who would do what he thought right by his neighbours, as well as get what he thought right for himself; but, what was more, he weighed full **fifteen stone**, was nobody knew how many inches round the chest, and could have **thrashed** Mr. Grimes himself in fair fight, which very few folk round there could do, and which would not have been right for him to do, as a great many things are not which one both can do, and would like very much to do. So Mr. Grimes touched his hat to him when he rode through the town, and called him **a "buirdly awd chap,"** and his young ladies "**gradely** lasses," which are two high compliments in the North country; and thought that that made up for his poaching Sir John's pheasants; whereby you may perceive that Mr. Grimes had not been to a properly-inspected Government National School.

Now, I dare say, you never got up at three o'clock on a midsummer morning. Some people get up then because they want to catch salmon; and some because they want to climb Alps; and a great many more because they must, like Tom. But I assure you that three o'clock on a midsummer morning is the pleasantest time of all the twenty-four hours, and all the three hundred and sixty-five days; and why everyone does not get up then, I never could tell, save that they are all determined to spoil their nerves and their complexions by doing all night what they might just as well do all day. But Tom, instead of going out to dinner at half-past eight at night, and to a ball at ten, and finishing off somewhere between twelve and four, went to bed at seven (when his master went to the public-house), and slept like a dead pig; for which reason he was as **pert** as a **gamecock** (who always gets up early to wake the maids), and just ready to get up when the fine gentlemen and ladies were just ready to go to bed.

So he and his master set out. Grimes rode the donkey in front, and Tom and the brushes walked behind: out of the court, and up the street, past the closed window-shutters, and the winking weary policemen, and the roofs all shining grey in the grey dawn. They passed through the **pitmen's** village, all shut up and silent now, and through the **turnpike**; and then they were out in the real country, and plodding along the black dusty road, between black slag walls, with no sound but the groaning and thumping of the pit-engine in the next field.

But soon the road grew white, and the walls likewise; and at the wall's foot grew long grass and [bright] flowers, all drenched with dew; and instead of the groaning of the pit-engine, they heard the skylark saying his **matins** high up in the air, and the pit-bird warbling in the **sedges**, as he had warbled all night long.

All else was silent. For old Mrs. Earth was still fast asleep; and, like many pretty people, she looked still prettier asleep than awake. The great elm-trees in the gold-green meadows were fast asleep above, and the cows fast asleep beneath them; nay, the few clouds which were about were fast asleep likewise, and so tired that they had lain down on the earth to rest, in long white flakes and bars, among the stems of the elm-trees, and along the tops of the alders by the stream, waiting for the sun to bid them rise and go about their day's business in the clear blue overhead.

On they went; and Tom looked, and looked, for **he never had been so far into the country before**; and longed to get over a gate, and pick buttercups, and look for birds' nests in the hedge; but Mr. Grimes was a man of business, and would not have heard of that.

Part Three

Soon they came up with a poor Irishwoman, trudging along with a bundle at her back. She had a grey shawl over her head, and a **crimson madder petticoat**; so you may be sure she came from **Galway**. She had neither shoes nor stockings, and limped along as if she were tired and footsore; but she was a very tall handsome woman, with bright grey eyes, and heavy black hair hanging about her cheeks. And she took Mr. Grimes' fancy so much, that when he came alongside he called out to her: "This is a hard road for a gradely foot like that. Will ye up, lass, and ride behind me?"

But, perhaps, she did not admire Mr. Grimes' look and voice; for she answered quietly: "No, thank you; I'd sooner walk with your little lad here."

"You may please yourself," growled Grimes, and went on smoking.

So she walked beside Tom, and talked to him, and asked him where he lived, and what he knew, and all about himself, till Tom thought he had never met such a pleasant-spoken woman. And she asked him, at last, whether he said his prayers! and seemed sad when he told her that he knew no prayers to say.

Then he asked her where she lived, and she said far away by the sea. And Tom asked her about the sea; and she told him how it rolled and roared over the rocks in winter nights, and lay still in the bright summer days, for the children to bathe and play in it; and many a story more, till Tom longed to go and see the sea, and bathe in it likewise.

Part Four

Adding one more bit to the reading makes it a bit long, but it seems right to finish this scene before Grimes and Tom have to go off and sweep chimneys at the Place.

At last, at the bottom of a hill, they came to a spring; [not such a little spring as we have in the south of England], but a real North country limestone fountain, like one of those in Sicily or Greece, where [those in olden times] fancied the nymphs sat cooling themselves [on a] hot summer's day, while the shepherds peeped at them from behind the bushes. Out of a low cave of rock, at the foot of a limestone crag, the great fountain rose, quelling, and bubbling, and gurgling, so clear that you could not tell where the water ended and the air began; and ran away under the road, a stream large enough to turn a mill; among blue geranium, and golden globe-flower, and wild raspberry, and the bird-cherry with its tassels of snow.

And there Grimes stopped, and looked; and Tom looked too.

Tom was wondering whether anything lived in that dark cave, and came out at night to fly in the meadows. But Grimes was not wondering at all. Without a word, he got off his donkey, and clambered over the low road wall, and knelt down, and began dipping his ugly head into the spring—and very dirty he made it.

Tom was picking the flowers as fast as he could. The Irishwoman helped him, and showed him how to tie them up; and a very pretty **nosegay** they had made between them. But when he saw Grimes actually wash, he stopped, quite astonished; and when Grimes had finished, and began shaking his ears to dry them, he said: "Why, master, I never saw you do that before."

"Nor will again, most likely. 'Twasn't for cleanliness I did it, but for coolness. I'd be ashamed to want washing every week or so *[omission]*."

"I wish I might go and dip my head in," said poor little Tom. "It must be as good as putting it under the town-pump; and there is no **beadle** here to drive a chap away."

"Thou come along," said Grimes; "what dost want with washing thyself? Thou did not drink half a gallon of beer last night, like me."

"I don't care for you," said naughty Tom, and ran down to the stream, and began washing his face. Grimes was very sulky, because the woman preferred Tom's company to his; so he dashed at him with horrid words, and tore him up from his knees, and began beating him. But Tom was accustomed to that, and got his head safe between Mr. Grimes' legs, and kicked his shins with all his might.

"Are you not ashamed of yourself, Thomas Grimes?" cried the Irishwoman over the wall.

Grimes looked up, startled at her knowing his name; but all he answered was, "No, nor never was yet"; and went on beating Tom.

"True for you. If you ever had been ashamed of yourself, you would have gone over into **Vendale** long ago."

"What do you know about Vendale?" shouted Grimes; but he left off beating Tom.

"I know about Vendale, and about you, too. I know, for instance, what happened in Aldermire Copse, by night, **two years ago come Martinmas**."

"You do?" shouted Grimes; and leaving Tom, he climbed up over the wall, and faced the woman. Tom thought he was going to strike her; but she looked him too full and fierce in the face for that.

"Yes; I was there," said the Irishwoman quietly.

"You are no Irishwoman, by your speech," said Grimes, after many bad words.

"Never mind who I am. I saw what I saw; and if you strike that boy again, I can tell what I know."

Grimes seemed quite **cowed,** and got on his donkey without another word.

"Stop!" said the Irishwoman. "I have one more word for you both; for you will both see me again before all is over. Those that wish to be clean, clean they will be; and those that wish to be **foul**, foul they will be. Remember."

And she turned away, and through a gate into the meadow. Grimes stood still a moment, like a man who had been stunned. Then he rushed after her, shouting, "You come back."

But when he got into the meadow, the woman was not there. Had she hidden away? There was no place to hide in. But Grimes looked about, and Tom also, for he was as puzzled as Grimes himself at her disappearing so suddenly; but look where they would, she was not there.

Grimes came back again, as silent as a post, for he was a little frightened; and, getting on his donkey, filled a fresh pipe, and smoked away, leaving Tom in peace.

The Water-Babies

Narration and Discussion

Tell what you know so far about Tom the chimney-sweep.

In this reading we meet an "Irishwoman," although Grimes accuses her of not being quite what she seems. Do you think he is right?

For further thought: Find as many places as you can in this passage that mention washing/cleanliness and dirt (hint: even names are meaningful). This is a theme that is going to build throughout the story.

For even further thought: Wordsworth says, "And much it grieved my heart to think, / What man has made of man." Why do you think Kingsley chose these lines? Are there things that should still grieve us "to think what man has made of man?"

> Both infamy and fame mean being thought about and talked about by a large number of people; and we know how this natural desire is worked by the daily press; how we get, now a film actress, now a burglar, a spy, a hero, or a scientist set before us to be our admiration and our praise. (Charlotte Mason, Philosophy of Education, pp. 84-85)

Reading #2

Introduction

Tom goes to work cleaning out the giant chimneys at Harthover Place—and gets lost.

Vocabulary

lodge-gates: A small house, or **lodge**, where a gate-keeper would live.

bogy: This word usually means something frightening but unreal, like a hobgoblin; but the **bogies** that Tom sees here are sculptures on top of the gate-posts, a bit like **gargoyles**.

crest: badge, symbol

Wars of the Roses: wars fought for the English throne in the fifteenth century

prudent: wise

avenue: in this context, an **avenue** is a path or driveway leading up to a house

civilly: politely

rhododendrons, azaleas: flowering shrubs

mind that: pay attention, remember that

till they ran one into another: Those who have read Beatrix Potter's *The Tale of Samuel Whiskers* will remember that Tom Kitten got lost in a similar maze of old chimneys.

quality: rich people

kinsman: relative

ewer: water jug

fender: the frame around a fireplace

nurse: nursemaid, nanny

stupid: foolish and careless. See **Special Vocabulary Notes** in the Introduction for more discussion of this word.

Reading

Part One

And now they had gone three miles and more, and came to Sir John's **lodge-gates**.

Very grand lodges they were, with very grand iron gates and stone gate-posts, and on the top of each a most dreadful **bogy**, all teeth, horns, and tail, which was the **crest** which Sir John's ancestors wore in the **Wars of the Roses**; and very **prudent** men they were to wear it, for all their enemies must have run for their lives at the very first sight of them.

Grimes rang at the gate, and out came a keeper on the spot, and opened.

"I was told to expect thee," he said. "Now thou'lt be so good as to keep to the main **avenue**, and not let me find a hare or a rabbit on thee when thou comest back. I shall look sharp for one, I tell thee."

"Not if it's in the bottom of the soot-bag," quoth Grimes, and at that he laughed; and the keeper laughed and said:

"If that's thy sort, I may as well walk up with thee to the hall."

"I think thou best had," [said Grimes]. "It's thy business to see after thy game, man, and not mine."

So the keeper went with them; and, to Tom's surprise, he and Grimes chatted together all the way quite pleasantly. He did not know that a keeper is only a poacher turned outside in, and a poacher a keeper turned inside out.

They walked up a great lime avenue, a full mile long, and between their stems Tom peeped trembling at the horns of the sleeping deer, which stood up among the ferns.

Tom had never seen such enormous trees, and as he looked up he fancied that the blue sky rested on their heads. But he was puzzled very much by a strange murmuring noise, which followed them all the way. So much puzzled, that at last he took courage to ask the keeper what it was. He spoke very **civilly**, and called him Sir, for he was horribly afraid of him, which pleased the keeper, and he told him that they were the bees about the lime flowers.

"What are bees?" asked Tom.

"What make honey."

"What is honey?" asked Tom.

"Thou hold thy noise," said Grimes.

"Let the boy be," said the keeper. "He's a civil young chap now, and that's more than he'll be long if he bides with thee."

Grimes laughed, for he took that for a compliment.

"I wish I were a keeper," said Tom, "to live in such a beautiful place, and wear green velveteens and have a real dog-whistle at my button, like you."

The keeper laughed; he was a kind-hearted fellow enough.

"Let well alone, lad, and ill too at times. Thy life's safer than mine at all events, eh, Mr. Grimes?"

And Grimes laughed again, and then the two men began talking quite low.

Tom could hear, though, that it was about some poaching fight; and at last Grimes said surlily, "Hast thou anything against me?"

"Not now."

"Then don't ask me any questions till thou hast, for I am a man of honour." And at that they both laughed again, and thought it a very good joke.

Part Two

And by this time they were come up to the great iron gates in front of the house; and Tom stared through them at the **rhododendrons** and **azaleas**, which were all in flower; and then at the house itself, and wondered how many chimneys there were in it, and how long ago it was built, and what was the man's name that built it, and whether he got much money for his job?

These last were very difficult questions to answer. For Harthover had been built at ninety different times, and in nineteen different styles, and looked as if somebody had built a whole street of houses of every imaginable shape, and then stirred them together with a spoon.

[Omission: a list of the periods represented in Harthover, and the good-advice-givers who tried to get Sir John to fix up the old muddle.]

So they were all setting upon poor Sir John, year after year, and trying to talk him into spending a hundred thousand pounds or so, in building to please them and not himself. But he always put them off, like a canny North-countryman as he was. One wanted him to build a Gothic house, but he said he was no Goth; and another to build an Elizabethan, but he said he lived under good Queen Victoria, and not good Queen Bess; and another was bold enough to tell him that his house was ugly, but he said he lived inside it, and not outside; and another, that there was no unity in it, but he said that that was just why he liked the old place. For he liked to see how each Sir John, and Sir Hugh, and Sir Ralph, and Sir Randal, had left his mark upon the place, each after his own taste; and he had no more notion of disturbing his ancestors' work than of disturbing their graves. For now the house looked like a real live house, that had a history, and had grown and grown as the world grew; and that it was only an upstart fellow who did not know who his own grandfather was, who would change it for some spick-and-span new Gothic or Elizabethan thing, which looked as if it had been all spawned in a night, as mushrooms are. From which you may collect (if you have wit enough) that Sir John was a very sound-headed, sound-hearted squire, and just the man to keep the countryside in order, and show good sport with his hounds.

But Tom and his master did not go in through the great iron gates, as if they had been Dukes or Bishops, but round the back way, and a very long way round it was; and into a little back-door, where the ash-boy let them in, yawning horribly; and then in a passage the housekeeper met them, in such a flowered chintz dressing-gown, that Tom mistook her for My Lady herself, and she gave Grimes solemn orders about "You will take care of this, and take care of that," as if he was going up the chimneys, and not Tom. And Grimes listened, and said every now and then, under his voice, "You'll **mind that**, you little beggar?" and Tom did mind, all at least that he could. And then the housekeeper turned them into a grand room, all covered up in sheets of brown paper, and bade them begin, in a lofty and tremendous voice; and so after a whimper or two, and a kick from his master, into the grate Tom went, and up the chimney, while a housemaid stayed in the room to watch the furniture; to whom Mr. Grimes paid many playful and chivalrous compliments, but met with very slight encouragement in return.

How many chimneys Tom swept I cannot say; but he swept so many that he got quite tired, and puzzled too, for they were not like the town flues to which he was accustomed, but such as you would find—if you would only get up them and look, which perhaps you would not like to do—in old country-houses, large and crooked chimneys, which had been altered again and again, **till they ran one into another**. So Tom fairly lost his way in them; not that he cared much for that, though he was in pitchy darkness, for he was as much at home in a chimney as a mole is underground; but at last, coming down as he thought the right chimney, he came down the wrong one, and found himself standing on the hearthrug in a room the like of which he had never seen before.

Part Three

Tom had never seen the like. He had never been in gentlefolks' rooms but when the carpets were all up, and the curtains down, and the furniture huddled together under a cloth, and the pictures covered with aprons and dusters; and he had often enough wondered what the rooms were like when they were all ready for the **quality** to sit in. And now he saw, and he thought the sight very pretty.

The room was all dressed in white—white window-curtains, white bed-curtains, white furniture, and white walls, with just a few lines of pink here and there. The carpet was [patterned with] little flowers; and the walls were hung with pictures in gilt frames, which amused Tom very much. There were pictures of ladies and gentlemen, and pictures of horses and dogs. The horses he liked; but the dogs he did not care for much, for there were no bulldogs among them, not even a terrier. But the two pictures which took his fancy most were, [first], a man in long garments, with little children and their mothers round him, who was laying his hand upon the children's heads. That was a very pretty picture, Tom thought, to hang in a lady's room. For he could see that it was a lady's room by the dresses which lay about.

The other picture was that of a man nailed to a cross, which surprised Tom much. He fancied that he had seen something like it in a shop-window. But why was it there? "Poor man," thought Tom, "and he looks so kind and quiet. But why should the lady have such a sad picture as that in her room? Perhaps it was some **kinsman** of hers [who had been killed in such a way], and she kept it there for a remembrance." And Tom felt sad, and awed, and turned to look at something else.

The next thing he saw, and that too puzzled him, was a washing-stand, with **ewers** and basins, and soap and brushes, and towels, and a large bath full of clean water—what a heap of things all for washing! "She must be a very dirty lady," thought Tom, "by my master's rule, to want as much scrubbing as all that. But she must be very cunning to put the dirt out of the way so well afterwards, for I don't see a speck about the room, not even on the very towels."

And then, looking toward the bed, he saw that dirty lady, and held his breath with astonishment. Under the snow-white coverlet, upon the snow-white pillow, lay the most beautiful little girl that Tom had ever seen. Her cheeks were almost as white as the pillow, and her hair was like threads of gold spread all about over the bed. She might have been as old as Tom, or maybe a year or two older; but Tom did not think of that. He thought only of her delicate skin and golden hair, and wondered whether she was a real live person, or one of the wax dolls he had seen in the shops. But when he saw her breathe, he made up his mind that she was alive, and stood staring at her, as if she had been an angel out of heaven.

No. She cannot be dirty. She never could have been dirty, thought Tom to himself. And then he thought, "And are all people like that when they are washed?" And he looked at his own wrist, and tried to rub the soot off, and wondered whether it ever would come off. "Certainly I should look much prettier then, if I grew at all like her."

And looking round, he suddenly saw, standing close to him, a little ugly, [blackened], ragged figure *[omission]*. He turned on it angrily. What did such a [creature] want in that sweet young lady's room? And behold, it was himself, reflected in a great mirror the like of which Tom had never seen before.

And Tom, for the first time in his life, found out that he was dirty; and burst into tears with shame and anger; and turned to sneak up the chimney again and hide; and upset the **fender** and threw the fire-irons down, with a noise as of ten thousand tin kettles tied to ten thousand mad dogs' tails.

Up jumped the little white lady in her bed, and, seeing Tom, screamed as shrill as any peacock. In rushed a stout old **nurse** from the next room, and seeing Tom likewise, made up her mind that he had come to rob, plunder, destroy, and burn; and dashed at him, as he lay over the fender, so fast that she caught him by the jacket.

But she did not hold him. Tom had been in a policeman's hands many a time, and out of them too, what is more; and he would have been ashamed to face his friends for ever if he had been **stupid** enough to be caught by an old woman; so he doubled under the good lady's arm, across the room, and [was] out of the window in a moment.

Narration and Discussion

Why did the keeper not think that Tom should want to have a job like his?

Explain how Tom ended up in the little girl's bedroom.

For further thought #1: As mentioned in **Reading #1**, the story contains many references to washing and dirt. Tom lives in a town where, we assume, he has seen all kinds of people, not just poor and dirty ones; yet when he sees the girl in her very white bedroom, it is as if he has never seen "clean" before. Why is it that his eyes are being opened in this new way? (Did it have anything to do with what the Irishwoman said?)

For further thought #2: Do you recognize the descriptions of any of the pictures in the girl's bedroom? Do you think they might be important later on?

Reading #3

Introduction

Tom runs away—and then runs some more.

Vocabulary

scythe: cutting tool

The Water-Babies

shin: front part of the lower leg

churn: a container in which to make butter

hack: short for **hackney,** a riding horse

stoat: a small animal like a weasel

marten: yet another weasel-like animal

night-wig: Something which seems to exist only in this book.

she came in nowhere, and is consequently not placed: referring to winners and losers as if it had been a horse-race

magpies and jays: particularly noisy birds

screaking: screeching

copper: penny, small coin

coach-wheels: cartwheels

birch: a kind of tree. Kingsley also uses the word to mean "beat," as a schoolmaster or work-master (like Grimes) might do to someone with a birch rod.

till the cock-robins covered him with leaves: refers to the English children's story "Babes in the Wood"

grouse-moor: A **moor** is a piece of open, high and hilly land. A large part of northern England is made up of moors. **Grouse** are wild birds which live (and are hunted) on such places.

fell: another word for a moor

heather: one of the most common plants on a **moor**

bog: a wetland area, often (in this area) made of peat moss

cunning: clever, sly

stag: an adult male deer

throw the hounds out: trick his pursuers into thinking he had gone another way

plantation: literally, a planted area of the estate

a great brown, sharp-nosed creature: a mother fox or vixen

air danced reels: this is called "heat haze" or "heat shimmer," when the hot air rising mixes with cooler air and its increased density bends the light, creating visible wavy lines in the air. If that sounds too complicated, just remember to look on a hot, sunny day if you are near something that reflects heat, like a paved roadway--see if you can see a kind of shimmer in the air above it.

limekiln: a kiln (or oven) in which limestone is burned (so something giving off a great deal of heat)

heath: plants on the moor

a bit and a sup: something to eat

weir: dam, or some other structure holding back water in a river

ouzel: a bird like a blackbird

infinite main: ocean

Places

Exmoor: a moorland area in southwest England

Reading

Part One

He did not need to drop out, though he would have done so bravely enough. Nor even to let himself down a spout, which would have been an old game to him; for once he got up by a spout to the church roof, he said to take jackdaws' eggs, but the policeman said to steal lead; and, when he was seen on high, sat there till the sun got too hot; and came down by another spout, leaving the policemen to go back to the stationhouse and eat their dinners.

But all under the window spread a tree, with great leaves and sweet white flowers, almost as big as his head. It was magnolia, I suppose; but Tom knew nothing about that, and cared less; for down the tree he went, like a cat, and across the garden lawn, and over the iron railings, and up the park towards the wood, leaving the old nurse to scream "murder and fire" at the window.

The under-gardener, mowing, saw Tom, and threw down his **scythe**; caught his leg in it, and cut his **shin** open, whereby he kept his bed for a week; but in his hurry he never knew it, and gave chase to poor Tom.

The dairymaid heard the noise, got the **churn** between her knees, and tumbled over it, spilling all the cream; and yet she jumped up, and gave chase to Tom.

A groom cleaning Sir John's **hack** at the stables let him [the horse] go loose, whereby he kicked himself lame in five minutes; but he [the groom] ran out and gave chase to Tom.

Grimes upset the soot-sack in the new-graveled yard, and spoilt it all utterly; but he ran out and gave chase to Tom.

The old steward opened the park-gate in such a hurry, that he hung up his pony's chin upon the spikes, and, for aught I know, it hangs there still; but he jumped off, and gave chase to Tom.

The ploughman left his horses at the headland, and one jumped over the fence, and pulled the other into the ditch, plough and all; but he ran on, and gave chase to Tom.

The keeper, who was taking a **stoat** out of a trap, let the stoat go, and caught his own finger; but he jumped up, and ran after Tom; and considering what he said, and how he looked, I should have been sorry for Tom if he had caught him.

Sir John looked out of his study window (for he was an early old gentleman) and up at the nurse, and a **marten** dropped mud in his eye, so that he had at last to send for the doctor; and yet he ran out, and gave chase to Tom.

The Irishwoman, too, was walking up to the house to beg,—she must have got round by some byway,—but she threw away her bundle, and gave chase to Tom likewise. Only My Lady did not give chase; for when she had put her head out of the window, her **night-wig** fell into the garden, and she had to ring up her lady's-maid, and send her down for it privately, which quite put her out of the running, so that **she came in nowhere, and is consequently not placed**.

In a word, never was there heard at Hall Place—not even when the fox was killed in the conservatory, among acres of broken glass, and tons of smashed flower-pots—such a noise, row, hubbub, babel, shindy, hullabaloo, stramash, charivari, and total contempt of dignity, repose, and order, as that day, when Grimes, the gardener, the groom, the dairymaid, Sir John, the steward, the ploughman, the keeper, and the Irishwoman, all ran up the park, shouting "Stop thief," in the belief that Tom had at least a thousand pounds' worth of jewels in his empty pockets; and the very **magpies and jays** followed Tom up, **screaking** and screaming, as if he were a hunted fox *[omission]*.

And all the while poor Tom paddled up the park with his little bare feet, like a small *[omission]* gorilla fleeing to [a father gorilla in] the forest [who would take care of his attackers]. However, Tom did not remember ever having had a father; so he did not look for one, and expected to have to take care of himself; while as for running, he could keep up for a couple of miles with any stagecoach, if there was the chance of a **copper** or a cigar-end, and turn **coach-wheels** on his hands and feet ten times following, which is more than you can do. Wherefore his pursuers found it very difficult to catch him; and we will hope that they did not catch him at all.

Part Two

Tom, of course, made for the woods. He had never been in a wood in his life; but he was sharp enough to know that he might hide in a bush, or swarm up a tree, and, altogether, had more chance there than in the open. If he had not known that, he would have been foolisher than a mouse or a minnow.

But when he got into the wood, he found it a very different sort of place from what he had fancied. He pushed into a thick cover of rhododendrons, and found himself at once caught in a trap. The boughs laid hold of his legs and arms, poked him in his face and his stomach, made him shut his eyes tight (though that was no great loss, for he could not see at best a yard before his nose); and when he got through the rhododendrons, the hassock-grass and sedges tumbled him over, and cut his poor little fingers afterwards most spitefully; and the **birches** "birched" him soundly *[omission]*.

"I must get out of this," thought Tom, "or I shall stay here till somebody comes to help me—which is just what I don't want."

But how to get out was the difficult matter. And indeed I don't think he would ever have got out at all, but have stayed there **till the cock-robins covered him with leaves**, if he had not suddenly run his head against a wall.

Now running your head against a wall is not pleasant, especially if it is a loose wall, with the stones all set on edge, and a sharp cornered one hits you between the eyes and makes you see all manner of beautiful stars. The stars are very beautiful, certainly; but unfortunately they go in the twenty-thousandth part of a split second, and the pain which comes after them does not. And so Tom hurt his head; but he was a brave boy, and did not mind that a penny. He guessed that over the wall the cover would end; and up it he went, and over like a squirrel. And there he was, out on the great **grouse-moors**, which the country folk called Harthover **Fell—heather** and **bog** and rock, stretching away and up, up to the very sky.

Now, Tom was a cunning little fellow—as **cunning** as an old Exmoor **stag**. Why not? Though he was but ten years old, he had lived longer than most stags, and had more wits to start with into the bargain. He knew as well as a stag that if he backed he might **throw the hounds out.** So the first thing he did when he was over the wall was to make the neatest double sharp to his right, and run along under the wall for nearly half a mile.

Whereby Sir John, and the keeper, and the steward, and the gardener, and the ploughman, and the dairymaid, and all the hue-and-cry together, went on ahead half a mile in the very opposite direction, and inside the wall, leaving him a mile off on the outside; while Tom heard their shouts die away in the woods and chuckled to himself merrily.

At last he came to a dip in the land, and went to the bottom of it, and then he turned bravely away from the wall and up the moor; for he knew that he had put a hill between him and his enemies, and could go on without their seeing him.

But the Irishwoman, alone of them all, had seen which way Tom went. She had kept ahead of everyone the whole time; and yet she neither walked nor ran. She went along quite smoothly and gracefully, while her feet twinkled past each other so fast that you could not see which was foremost; till every one asked the other who the strange woman was; and all agreed, for want of anything better to say, that she must be in league with Tom.

But when she came to the **plantation**, they lost sight of her; and they could do no less. For she went quietly over the wall after Tom, and followed him wherever he went. Sir John and the rest saw no more of her; and out of sight was out of mind.

Part Three

So Tom went on and on, he hardly knew why; but he liked the great wide strange place, and the cool fresh bracing air. But he went more and more slowly as he got higher up the hill; for now the ground grew very bad indeed. Instead of soft turf and springy heather, he met great patches of flat limestone rock, just like ill-made pavements, with deep cracks between the stones and ledges, filled with ferns; so he had to hop from stone to stone, and now and then he slipped in between, and hurt his little bare toes, though they were tolerably tough ones; but still he would go on and up, he could not tell why.

What would Tom have said if he had seen, walking over the moor behind him, the very same Irishwoman who had taken his part upon the road? But whether it was that he looked too little behind him, or whether it was that she kept out of sight behind the rocks and knolls, he never saw her, though she saw him.

And now he began to get a little hungry, and very thirsty; for he had run a long way, and the sun had risen high in heaven, and the rock was as hot as an oven, and the **air danced reels** over it, as it does over a **limekiln**, till everything round seemed quivering and melting in the glare.

But he could see nothing to eat anywhere, and still less to drink. The **heath** was full of bilberries and whimberries; but they were only in flower yet, for it was June. And as for water, who can find that on the top of a limestone rock?

Now and then he passed by a deep dark swallow-hole, going down into the earth, as if it was the chimney of some dwarf's house underground; and more than once, as he passed, he could hear water falling, trickling, tinkling, many many feet below. How he longed to get down to it, and cool his poor baked lips! But, brave little chimney-sweep as he was, he dared not climb down such chimneys as those.

So he went on and on, till his head spun round with the heat, and he thought he heard church-bells ringing, a long way off.

"Ah!" he thought, "where there is a church there will be houses and people; and, perhaps, someone will give me **a bit and a sup**." So he set off again, to look for the church; for he was sure that he heard the bells quite plain.

And in a minute more, when he looked round, he stopped again, and said, "Why, what a big place the world is!" And so it was; for, from the top of the mountain he could see—what could he not see?

Behind him, far below, was Harthover, and the dark woods, and the shining salmon river; and on his left, far below, was the town, and the smoking chimneys of the collieries; and far, far away, the river widened to the shining sea; and [he saw] little white specks, which were ships *[omission]*. Before him lay, spread out like a map, great plains, and farms, and villages, amid dark knots of trees. They all seemed at his very feet; but he had sense to see that they were long miles away.

And to his right rose moor after moor, hill after hill, till they faded away, blue into blue sky. But between him and those moors, and really at his very feet, lay something, to which, as soon as Tom saw it, he determined to go, for that was the place for him.

A deep, deep green and rocky valley, very narrow, and filled with wood; but through the wood, hundreds of feet below him, he could see a clear stream *[omission]*. Oh, if he could but get down to that stream!

Then, by the stream, he saw the roof of a little cottage, and a little garden set out in squares and beds. And there was a tiny little red thing moving in the garden, no bigger than a fly. As Tom looked down, he saw that it was a woman in a red petticoat. Ah! perhaps she would give him something to eat.

And there were the church-bells ringing again. Surely there must be a village down there. Well, nobody would know him, or what had happened at the Place. The news could not have got there yet, even if Sir John had set all the policemen in the county after him; and he could get down there in five minutes.

Part Four

Tom was quite right about the hue-and-cry not having got thither; for he had come, without knowing it, the best part of ten miles from Harthover; but he was wrong about getting down in five minutes, for the cottage was more than a mile off, and a good thousand feet below.

However, down he went, like a brave little man as he was, though he was very footsore, and tired, and hungry, and thirsty; while the church-bells rang so loud, he began to think that they must be inside his own head, and the river chimed and tinkled far below; and this was the song which it sang:

    Clear and cool, clear and cool,
  By laughing shallow, and dreaming pool;
    Cool and clear, cool and clear,
  By shining shingle, and foaming weir;
  Under the crag where the ouzel sings,
  And the ivied wall where the church-bell rings,
    Undefiled, for the undefiled;
  Play by me, bathe in me, mother and child.

    Dank and foul, dank and foul,
  By the smoky town in its murky cowl;
    Foul and dank, foul and dank,
  By wharf and sewer and slimy bank;
  Darker and darker the farther I go,
  Baser and baser the richer I grow;
    Who dare sport with the sin-defiled?

The Water-Babies

> Shrink from me, turn from me, mother and child.
>
> Strong and free, strong and free,
> The floodgates are open, away to the sea,
> Free and strong, free and strong,
> Cleansing my streams as I hurry along,
> To the golden sands, and the leaping bar,
> And the taintless tide that awaits me afar.
> As I lose myself in the infinite main,
> Like a soul that has sinned and is pardoned again.
> Undefiled, for the undefiled;
> Play by me, bathe in me, mother and child.

So Tom went down; and all the while he never saw the Irishwoman going down behind him.

Narration and Discussion

Why didn't Tom just go back to the house and say that he hadn't stolen anything?

Why do you think the Irishwoman is continuing to follow Tom? Why does she not try to catch up with him or speak to him?

Do you like the river's song, or do you think it sounds dangerous? (Special note: There is a 1978 recording called *Lionel Jeffries' Water Babies*, which can be found online. This song comes about six minutes from the beginning.)

What is the highest place you have ever been? What did you see?

Poetic Interlude #2

The poetic lines for Chapter II come from "The Ministry of Angels," by Edmund Spenser.

And is there care in heaven? and is there love
In heavenly spirits to these creatures base
That may compassion of their evils move?
There is:—else much more wretched were the case
Of men than beasts: But oh! the exceeding grace
Of Highest God that loves His creatures so,
And all His works with mercy doth embrace,
That blessed Angels He sends to and fro,
To serve to wicked man, to serve His wicked foe!

The Water-Babies

Reading #4

Introduction

Tom finally finds a place to rest, but the heat (and possibly banging his head) have left him unwell.

Vocabulary

- **down:** a grass-covered hill, usually composed of chalk. Charles Kingsley lived in the south of England, where most of the "downs" are, and he seems to have used the word that came to mind. In the north, it would be more typical to call such a chalk hill a "wold."

- **bogies:** This word was mentioned earlier; here it means something like "bad spirits."

- **stout:** strong

- **staunch:** loyal

- **gnat:** a small two-winged fly resembling a mosquito

- **midge:** also a small two-winged fly, but from a different family

- **clematis:** a climbing, flowering plant

- **Chris-cross-row:** or "Christ-cross row"; refers to an old school book which was used to teach children the alphabet

- **beck:** brook, stream

- **clemmed:** hungry, famished

- **drought:** thirst

- **bairn:** child

- **draught:** swallow

- **outhouse:** shed, outbuilding

Places

Kingsley names a number of hills and other places where you could search for the valley of **Vendale**; however, as they are scattered across England and even into Scotland, I believe he is having a bit of geographical fun with us.

High Craven: part of the Craven Dales in Yorkshire

Bolland Forest: or Forest of Bowland. This is mostly in the county of Lancashire, but part of it is in Yorkshire.

Ingleborough: a mountain peak in Yorkshire

Nine Standards: Nine Standards Rigg is the summit (high point) of **Hartley Fell** in the **Pennine Hills**, in the north of England

Cross Fell: the highest point in England outside of the Lake District

Scaw Fell: or Scafell Pike. A mountain peak in the Lake District National Park (about a half hour's drive from Ambleside)

Carlisle: city in the north of England, near the Scottish border

Annan Water: the River Annan, in southwest Scotland

Berwick Law: a hill in Scotland

Lewthwaite Crag: apparently a real place but called Malham Cove

Reading

Part One

A mile off, and a thousand feet down.

So Tom found it; though it seemed as if he could have chucked a pebble on to the back of the woman in the red petticoat who was weeding in the garden, or even across the dale to the rocks beyond. For the bottom of the valley was just one field broad, and on the other side ran the stream; and above it, grey crag, grey **down**, grey stair, grey moor walled up to heaven.

A quiet, silent, rich, happy place; a narrow crack cut deep into the earth; so deep, and so out of the way, that the bad **bogies** can hardly find it out. The name of the place is Vendale; and if you want to see it for yourself, you must go up into the **High Craven**, and search from **Bolland Forest** north by **Ingleborough**, to the **Nine Standards** and **Cross Fell**; and if you have not found it, you must turn south, and search the Lake Mountains, down to **Scaw Fell** and the sea; and then, if you have not found it, you must go northward again by merry **Carlisle**, and search the Cheviots all across, from **Annan Water** to **Berwick Law**; and then, whether you have found Vendale or not, you will have found such a country, and such a people, as ought to make you proud of being a British boy.

So Tom went to go down; and first he went down three hundred feet of steep heather, mixed up with loose brown gritstone, as rough as a file; which was not pleasant to his poor little heels, as he came bump, stump, jump, down the steep. And still he thought he could throw a stone into the garden.

Then he went down three hundred feet of limestone terraces, one below the other, as straight as if a carpenter had ruled them with his ruler and then cut them out with his chisel. There was no heath there, but—

First, a little grass slope, covered with the prettiest flowers, rockrose and saxifrage, and thyme and basil, and all sorts of sweet herbs.

Then bump down a two-foot step of limestone.

Then another bit of grass and flowers.

Then bump down a one-foot step.

Then another bit of grass and flowers for fifty yards, as steep as the house-roof, where he had to slide down on his dear little tail.

Then another step of stone, ten feet high; and there he had to stop himself, and crawl along the edge to find a crack; for if he had rolled over, he would have rolled right into the old woman's garden, and frightened her out of her wits.

Then, when he had found a dark narrow crack, full of green-stalked fern *[omission]*, and had crawled down through it, with knees and elbows, as he would down a chimney, there was another grass slope, and another step, and so on, till—oh, dear me! I wish it was all over; and so did he. And yet he thought he could throw a stone into the old woman's garden.

At last he came to a bank of beautiful shrubs; white-beam with its great silver-backed leaves, and mountain-ash, and oak; and below them cliff and crag, cliff and crag, with great beds of crown-ferns and wood-sedge; while through the shrubs he could see the stream sparkling, and hear it murmur on the white pebbles. He did not know that it was three hundred feet below.

You would have been giddy, perhaps, at looking down: but Tom was not. He was a brave little chimney-sweep; and when he found himself on the top of a high cliff, instead of sitting down and crying *[omission]*, he said, "Ah, this will just suit me!" though he was very tired; and down he went, by stock and stone, sedge and ledge, bush and rush *[omission]*.

And all the while he never saw the Irishwoman coming down behind him.

Part Two

But he was getting terribly tired now. The burning sun on the fells had sucked him up; but the damp heat of the woody crag sucked him up still more; and the perspiration ran out of the ends of his fingers and toes, and washed him cleaner than he had been for a whole year. But, of course, he dirtied everything terribly as he went. There has been a great black smudge all down the crag ever since *[omission]*.

At last he got to the bottom. But, behold, it was not the bottom—as people usually find when they are coming down a mountain. For at the foot of the crag were heaps and heaps of fallen limestone *[omission]*; and before Tom got through [those], he was out in the bright sunshine again; and then he felt, once for all and suddenly, as people generally do, that he was b-e-a-t, beat.

You must expect to be beat a few times in your life, little man, if you live such a life as a man ought to live, let you be as strong and healthy as you may; and when you are, you will find it a very ugly feeling. I hope that that day you may have a **stout**, **staunch** friend by you who is not beat; for, if you have not, you had best lie where you are, and wait for better times, as poor Tom did.

He could not get on. The sun was burning, and yet he felt chill all over. He was quite empty, and yet he felt quite sick. There was but two hundred yards of smooth pasture between him and the cottage, and yet he could not walk down it. He could hear the stream murmuring only one field beyond it, and yet it seemed to him as if it was a hundred miles off.

He lay down on the grass till the beetles ran over him, and the flies settled on his nose. I don't know when he would have got up again, if the **gnats** and the **midges** had not taken compassion on him. But the gnats blew their trumpets so loud in his ear, and the midges nibbled so at his hands and face wherever they could find a place free from soot, that at last he woke up, and stumbled away, down over a low wall, and into a narrow road, and up to the cottage door.

Part Three

And a neat pretty cottage it was, with clipped yew hedges all round the garden, and yews inside too, cut into peacocks and trumpets and teapots and all kinds of [strange] shapes. And out of the open door came a noise like that of the frogs *[omission]* when they know that it is going to be scorching hot tomorrow—and how they know that I don't know, and you don't know, and nobody knows.

He came slowly up to the open door, which was all hung round with **clematis** and roses; and then peeped in, half afraid. And there sat by the empty fireplace, which was filled with a pot of sweet herbs, the nicest old woman that ever was seen, in her red petticoat, and short dimity bedgown, and clean white cap, with a black silk handkerchief over it, tied under her chin. At her feet sat the grandfather of all the cats; and opposite her sat, on two benches, twelve or fourteen neat, rosy, chubby little children, learning their **Chris-cross-row**; and gabble enough they made about it.

Such a pleasant cottage it was, with a shiny clean stone floor, and curious old prints on the walls, and an old black oak sideboard full of bright pewter and brass dishes, and a cuckoo clock in the corner, which began shouting as soon as Tom appeared: not that it was frightened at Tom, but that it was just eleven o'clock.

All the children started at Tom's [torn, dirty] figure. The girls began to cry, and the boys began to laugh, and all pointed at him rudely enough; but Tom was too tired to care for that.

"What art thou, and what dost want?" cried the old dame. "A chimney-sweep! Away with thee! I'll have no sweeps here."

"Water," said poor little Tom, quite faint.

"Water? There's plenty i' the **beck**," she said, quite sharply.

"But I can't get there; I'm most **clemmed** with hunger and **drought**." And Tom sank down upon the door-step, and laid his head against the post.

And the old dame looked at him through her spectacles one minute, and two, and three; and then she said, "He's sick; and a **bairn**'s a bairn, sweep or none."

"Water," said Tom.

"God forgive me!" and she put by her spectacles, and rose, and came to Tom. "Water's bad for thee; I'll give thee milk." And she *[omission]* brought a cup of milk and a bit of bread.

Tom drank the milk off at one **draught**, and then looked up, revived.

"Where didst come from?" said the dame.

"Over Fell, there," said Tom, and pointed up into the sky.

"Over Harthover? and down **Lewthwaite Crag**? Art sure thou art not lying?"

"Why should I?" said Tom, and leant his head against the post.

"And how got ye up there?"

"I came over from the Place"; and Tom was so tired and desperate he had no heart or time to think of a story, so he told all the truth in a few words.

"Bless thy little heart! And thou hast not been stealing, then?"

"No."

"Bless thy little heart! and I'll warrant not. Why, God's guided the bairn, because he was innocent! Away from the Place, and over Harthover Fell, and down Lewthwaite Crag! Who ever heard the like, if God hadn't led him? Why dost not eat thy bread?"

"I can't."

"It's good enough, for I made it myself."

"I can't," said Tom, and he laid his head on his knees, and then asked, "Is it Sunday?"

"No, then; why should it be?"

"Because I hear the church-bells ringing so."

"Bless thy pretty heart! The bairn's sick. Come wi' me, and I'll hap thee up somewhere. If thou wert a bit cleaner I'd put thee in my own bed, for the Lord's sake. But come along here."

But when Tom tried to get up, he was so tired and giddy that she had to help him and lead him. She put him in an **outhouse** upon soft sweet hay and an old rug, and bade him sleep off his walk, and she would come to him when school was over, in an hour's time.

Narration and Discussion

Would you like to go to the school in Vendale? Why or why not?

Why does the schoolmistress think Tom is not telling the truth?

What do you think is wrong with him?

Reading #5

Introduction

Tom, apparently delirious with fever, ends up in the Vendale stream. Also, we find out something more about the "Irishwoman."

Vocabulary

casement: a window that opens in an outward direction

Places

dear old North Devon: Kingsley is obviously a bit homesick for the place where he grew up.

Reading

Part One

And so she went in again, expecting Tom to fall fast asleep at once.

But Tom did not fall asleep. Instead he turned and tossed and kicked about in the strangest way, and felt so hot all over that he longed to get into the river and cool himself; and then he fell half asleep, and dreamt that he heard the little white lady crying to him, "Oh, you're so dirty; go and be washed"; and then that he heard the Irishwoman saying, "Those that wish to be clean, clean they will be."

And then he heard the church-bells ring so loud, close to him too, that he was sure it must be Sunday, in spite of what the old dame had said; and he would go to church, and see what a church was like inside, for he had never been in one, poor little fellow, in all his life. But the people would never let him come in, all over soot and dirt like that. He must go to the river and wash first.

And he said out loud again and again, though being half asleep he did not know it, "I must be clean, I must be clean."

And all of a sudden he found himself not in the outhouse on the hay, but in the middle of a meadow, over the road, with the stream just before him, saying continually, "I must be clean, I must be clean." He had got there on his own legs, between sleep and awake, as children will often get out of bed, and go about the room, when they are not quite well. But he was not a bit surprised, and went on to the bank of the brook, and lay down on the grass, and looked into the clear, clear limestone water, with every pebble at the bottom bright and clean, while the little silver trout dashed about in fright at the sight of his [dirty] face; and he dipped his hand in and found it so cool, cool, cool; and he said, "I will be a fish; I will swim in the water; I must be clean, I must be clean."

So he pulled off all his clothes in such haste that he tore some of them, which was easy enough with such ragged old things. And he put his poor hot sore feet into the water; and then his legs; and the farther he went in, the more the church-bells rang in his head.

"Ah," said Tom, "I must be quick and wash myself; the bells are ringing quite loud now; and they will stop soon, and then the door will be shut, and I shall never be able to get in at all."

Tom was mistaken: for in England the church doors are left open all service time, for any [peaceable person who likes to come in].But Tom did not know that, any more than he knew a great deal more which people ought to know.

And all the while he never saw the Irishwoman, not behind him this time, but before.

Part Two

For just before he came to the riverside, she had stepped down into the cool clear water; and her shawl and her petticoat floated off her, and the green water-weeds floated round her sides, and the white water-lilies floated round her head, and the fairies of the stream came up from the bottom and bore her away and down upon their arms; for she was the Queen of them all; and perhaps of more besides.

"Where have you been?" they asked her.

"I have been smoothing sick folks' pillows, and whispering sweet dreams into their ears; opening cottage **casements** to let out the stifling air; coaxing little children away from gutters, and foul pools where fever breeds [*omission*]; doing all I can to help those who will not help themselves: and little enough that is, and weary work for me. But I have brought you a new little brother, and watched him safe all the way here."

Then all the fairies laughed for joy at the thought that they had a little brother coming.

"But mind, maidens, he must not see you, or know that you are here. He is [still] like the beasts which perish; and from the beasts which perish he must learn. So you must not play with him, or speak to him, or let him see you: but only keep him from being harmed."

Then the fairies were sad, because they could not play with their new brother, but they always did what they were told. And their Queen floated away down the river; and whither she went, thither she came.

But all this Tom, of course, never saw or heard: and perhaps if he had it would have made little difference in the story; for he was so hot and thirsty, and longed so to be clean for once, that he tumbled himself as quick as he could into the clear cool stream.

And he had not been in it two minutes before he fell fast asleep, into the quietest, sunniest, coziest sleep that ever he had in his life; and he dreamt about the green meadows by which he had walked that morning, and the tall elm-trees, and the sleeping cows; and after that he dreamt of nothing at all.

The reason of his falling into such a delightful sleep is very simple; and yet hardly anyone has found it out. It was merely that the fairies took him.

Part Three: Interlude Between Kingsley and the Reader

Some people think that there are no fairies. But it is a wide world, and plenty of room in it for fairies, without people seeing them; unless, of course, they look in the right place. The most wonderful and the strongest things in the world, you know, are just the things which no one can see. There is life in you; and it is the life in you which makes you grow, and move, and think: and yet you can't see it. And there is steam in a steam-engine; and that is what makes it move: and yet you can't see it *[omission]*. At all events, we will make believe that there are fairies in the world. It will not be the last time by many a one that we shall have to make believe. And yet, after all, there is no need for that. There must be fairies; for this is a fairy tale: and how can one have a fairy tale if there are no fairies?

You don't see the logic of that?

Perhaps not. Then please not to see the logic of a great many arguments exactly like it, which you will hear before your beard is grey.

Part Four

The kind old dame came back at twelve, when school was over, to look at Tom: but there was no Tom there. She looked about for his footprints; but the ground was so hard that there was no slot, as they say in **dear old North Devon**. So the old dame went in again quite sulky, thinking that little Tom had tricked her with a false story, and shammed ill, and then run away again.

But she altered her mind the next day. For, when Sir John and the rest of them had run themselves out of breath, and lost Tom, they went back again, looking very foolish. And they looked more foolish still when Sir John heard more of the story from the nurse; and more foolish still, again, when they heard the whole story from Miss Ellie, the little lady in white. All she had seen was a poor little chimney-sweep, [covered in coal dust], crying and sobbing, and going to get up the chimney again. Of course, she was very much frightened: and no wonder. But that was all. The boy had taken nothing in the room; by the mark of his little sooty feet, they could see that he had never been off the hearthrug till the nurse caught hold of him. It was all a mistake.

So Sir John told Grimes to go home, and promised him five shillings if he would bring the boy quietly up to him, without beating him, that he might be sure of the truth. For he took for granted, and Grimes too, that Tom had made his way home.

But no Tom came back to Mr. Grimes that evening; and he went to the police-office, to tell them to look out for the boy. But no Tom was heard of. As for his having gone over those great fells to Vendale, they no more dreamed of that than of his having gone to the moon.

Narration and Discussion

This is one of the more difficult parts of the book to explain, especially since we do not yet have the full story of what has happened to Tom. Kingsley takes some pains to remind us that "this is a fairy tale," and, though we may believe that Tom has died in the river, in fairy tale terms he has simply been moved into a different place (we might say, a different state of being—and how very different, we shall soon see). One of Kingsley's very big ideas is about the beginnings of things; so, in that sense, Tom has not died at all so much as he has been given a chance to begin all over again.

In the meantime, we might think about what we have just discovered about the "Irishwoman," who is now shown to be the Queen of the "fairies of the stream," among other things. What do you think she might mean about Tom needing to learn "from the beasts which perish?"

For even further thought: As we have already mentioned, the themes of dirt, water, and cleansing are important to Kingsley. How does this passage add to those ideas?

Reading #6

Introduction

Sir John Harthover (an unexpectedly sympathetic character) tracks Tom to Vendale; but all he finds are his clothes.

And then Kingsley, in his most Kingsley voice, has a few things to say about what we think is true, and what might be even more true.

Vocabulary

over the hills and far away: out hunting (in this case, for Tom)

braces: suspenders

she was a tenant of his: Sir John owned her cottage

hearken: listen, pay attention

a bit of alder copse: a small group of alder trees

round the parotid region of his fauces: around his throat

external gills: gills (breathing organs) that are not inside (as in fishes), but outside. As an example of a creature with external gills, look for photographs of the **Axolotl**.

sucking: This appears to mean "in the larval stage," or "young"

eft: another word for a **newt** (a small amphibian). This becomes a running joke in the book, as Water-Baby Tom, with his **external gills**, is frequently mistaken for an **eft**.

until the coming of the Cocqcigrues (kok-se-groo): The Cocqcigrues are imaginary creatures, so waiting until they come means "forever." However, in this case, Kingsley seems to mean something more like "until the Judgement Day."

put it into spirits: preserved it in a jar

Aunt Agitate's Arguments, or Cousin Cramchild's Conversations: imaginary books, but based on certain real publications. See the note after this reading.

Queen of all the Fairies: Someone we have already met.

Reading

Part One

So Mr. Grimes came up to Harthover next day with a very sour face; but when he got there, Sir John was **over the hills and far away**; and Mr. Grimes had to sit in the outer servants' hall all day, and drink strong ale to wash away his sorrows; and they were washed away long before Sir John came back.

[Omission for length: Sir John and his hunting party (including a tracking dog) follow Tom's trail to the top of Lewthwaite Crag]

They could hardly believe that Tom would have gone so far; and when they looked at that awful cliff, they could never believe that he would have dared to face it. But if the dog said so, it must be true.

"Heaven forgive us!" said Sir John. "If we find him at all, we shall find him lying at the bottom." And he slapped his great hand upon his great thigh, and said— "Who will go down over Lewthwaite Crag, and see if that boy is alive? Oh that I were twenty years younger, and I would go down myself!" And so he would have done, as well as any sweep in the county. Then he said— "Twenty pounds to the man who brings me that boy alive!" and as was his way, what he said he meant.

Now among the lot was a little groom-boy, a very little groom indeed; and he was the same who had ridden up the court, and told Tom to come to the Hall; and he said— "Twenty pounds or none, I will go down over Lewthwaite Crag, if it's only for the poor boy's sake. For he was as civil a spoken little chap as ever climbed a flue."

So down over Lewthwaite Crag he went: a very smart groom he was at the top, and a very shabby one at the bottom; for he tore his gaiters, and he tore his breeches, and he tore his jacket, and he burst his **braces**, and he burst his boots, and he lost his hat, and what was worst of all, he lost his gold shirt pin, which he prized very much *[omission]*; but he never saw anything of Tom.

Part Two

And all the while Sir John and the rest were riding round, full three miles to the right, and back again, to get into Vendale, and to the foot of the crag.

When they came to the old dame's school, all the children came out to see. And the old dame came out too; and when she saw Sir John, she curtsied very low, for **she was a tenant of his**.

"Well, dame, and how are you?" said Sir John.

"Blessings on you as broad as your back, Harthover," says she—she didn't call him Sir John, but only Harthover, for that is the fashion in the North country— "and welcome into Vendale: but you're no hunting the fox this time of the year?"

"I am hunting, and strange game too," said he.

"Blessings on your heart, and what makes you look so sad the morn?"

"I'm looking for a lost child, a chimney-sweep, that is run away."

"Oh, Harthover, Harthover," says she, "ye were always a just man and a merciful; and ye'll no harm the poor little lad if I give you tidings of him?"

"Not I, not I, dame. I'm afraid we hunted him out of the house all on a miserable mistake, and the hound has brought him to the top of Lewthwaite Crag, and——"

Whereat the old dame broke out crying, without letting him finish his story. "So he told me the truth after all, poor little dear! Ah, first thoughts are best, and a body's heart'll guide them right, if they will but **hearken** to it." And then she told Sir John all.

"Bring the dog here, and lay him on," said Sir John, without another word, and he set his teeth very hard. And the dog opened at once; and went away at the back of the cottage, over the road, and over the meadow, and through **a bit of alder copse**; and there, upon an alder stump, they saw Tom's clothes lying. And then they knew as much about it all as there was any need to know.

Part Three

And Tom?

Ah, now comes the most wonderful part of this wonderful story. Tom, when he woke, for of course he woke—children always wake after they have slept exactly as long as is good for them—found himself swimming about in the stream, being about four inches, or—that I may be accurate—3.87902 inches long, and having **round the parotid region of his fauces** a set of **external gills** (I hope you understand all the big words) just like those of a **sucking eft**, which he mistook for a lace frill, till he pulled at them, found he hurt himself, and made up his mind that they were part of himself, and best left alone.

In fact, the fairies had turned him into a water-baby.

Part Four: Kingsley Speaks to the Reader

A water-baby? You never heard of a water-baby. Perhaps not. That is the very reason why this story was written. There are a great many things in the world which you never heard of; and a great many more which nobody ever heard of; and a great many things, too, which nobody will ever hear of, at least **until the coming of the Cocqcigrues**, when man shall be the measure of all things.

"But there are no such things as water-babies."

How do you know that? Have you been there to see? And if you had been there to see, and had seen none, that would not prove that there were none. And no one has a right to say that no water-babies exist, till they have seen no water-babies existing; which is quite a different thing, mind, from not seeing water-babies; and a thing nobody ever did, or perhaps ever will do.

"But surely if there were water-babies, somebody would have caught one at least?"

Well. How do you know that somebody has not?

"But they would have **put it into spirits**, or into the *Illustrated News*, or [sent it to the experts] to see what they would say about it."

Ah, my dear little man! that does not follow at all, as you will see before the end of the story.

"But a water-baby is contrary to nature."

Well, but, my dear little man, you must learn to talk about such things, when you grow older, in a very different way from that. You must not talk about "ain't" and "can't" when you speak of this great wonderful world round you, of which the wisest man knows only the very smallest corner, and is, as the great Sir Isaac Newton said, only a child picking up pebbles on the shore of a boundless ocean.

You must not say that this cannot be, or that that is contrary to nature. You do not know what Nature is, or what she can do; and nobody knows; not even Sir Roderick Murchison, or Professor Owen, or Professor Sedgwick, or Professor Huxley, or Mr. Darwin, or Professor Faraday, or Mr. Grove, or any other of the great men whom good boys are taught to respect. They are very wise men; and you must listen respectfully to all they say: but even if they should say, which I am sure they never would, "That cannot exist. That is contrary to nature," you must wait a little, and see; for perhaps even they may be wrong. It is only children who read **Aunt Agitate's Arguments, or Cousin Cramchild's Conversations**; or lads who go to popular lectures, and see a man pointing at a few big ugly pictures on the wall, or making nasty smells with bottles and squirts, for an hour or two, and calling that anatomy or chemistry—who talk about "cannot exist," and "contrary to nature." Wise men are afraid to say that there is anything contrary to nature, except what is contrary to mathematical truth; for two and two cannot make five, and two straight lines cannot join twice, and a part cannot be as great as the whole, and so on (at least, so it seems at present): but the wiser men are, the less they talk about "cannot." That is a very rash, dangerous word, that "cannot"; and if people use it too often, the **Queen of all the Fairies**, who makes the clouds thunder and the fleas bite, and takes just as much trouble about one as about the other, is apt to astonish them suddenly by showing them, that though they say she cannot, yet she can, and what is more, will, whether they approve or not.

[omission for length]

Narration and Discussion

Imagine that you are 3.87902 inches tall (that's 9.8527108 cm). Do you have any figures or dolls about that size to help visualize this? What would things around you look like if you were that small?

Have you ever believed in something, and been told that that idea is just a story, or just for babies? How did you respond?

Aunt Agitate and Cousin Cramchild (some thoughts for adult readers)

In Kingsley's preface to his 1869 book *Madam How and Lady Why*, he recalls his childhood reading:

> *When I was your age, there were no such children's books as there are now. Those which we had were few and dull, and the pictures in them ugly and mean: while you have your choice of books without number, clear, amusing, and attractive, as well as really instructive, on subjects which were only talked of fifty years ago by a few learned people, and very little understood even by them.*

However, even as an adult, Kingsley was frustrated by many things being written in children's books and periodicals (magazines were popular with both adults and children, and, in fact, *The Water-Babies* first appeared as a serial story in *Macmillan's Magazine*). One of his particular annoyances was a common message that certain things "cannot exist" or are "contrary to nature"; he believed that such well-intended talk killed children's sense of wonder.

Those adults reading this who have also read C. S. Lewis's *The Abolition of Man* will understand the word "debunkers" to mean people, especially those considered intellectuals, who ridicule anything that doesn't fit their particular "scientific" narrative, and "scientific" there must be in quotes because, from Kingsley's point of view, those people are actually anti-science, in the same way as Lewis's "debunkers" are anti-thought (along with some other antis). Lewis's *Narnia* books are not suggested until AO Year Four, but some students in Year Three may already be familiar with examples of "debunking" that come up throughout those books—the clue is to listen for people who say that certain beliefs are only for babies, or (horrors) just fairy-tales.

Just before writing *The Water-Babies*, Charles Kingsley seems to have read one such "debunking" children's book, called *Peter Parley's Annual*, and that title likely inspired his imaginary (and alliterative) works *Aunt Agitate's Arguments* and *Cousin Cramchild's Conversations*. We might even look further into those names: to agitate something is to stir it up, disturb it, and perhaps Kingsley felt that Aunt Agitate should stop stirring up the mud in the pond (displacing the water-babies as she did so). Similarly, Cousin Cramchild needed to leave aside the dry "facts"; to stop trying to replace suns with lamps, and the magic songs of creation with mere animal roaring.

> *Now the trouble with trying to make yourself stupider than you really are is that you very often succeed. Uncle Andrew did. He soon did hear nothing but roaring in Aslan's song. Soon he couldn't have heard anything else even if he had wanted to. (C. S. Lewis,*
> The Magician's Nephew*)*

These two unhelpful relations will be mentioned again several times in this story. As you read the chapters in between, though, remember the two of them standing off to the side, ready to jeer. Consider what Kingsley was trying to say to them, and (more importantly) to his younger readers who hadn't yet (he hoped) been infected by that kind of empty thinking.

Reading #7

Introduction

In this ending to Kingsley's second chapter, we see the grief of Tom's friends, even those he had just met. (But Tom himself is just fine.)

Vocabulary

Pterodactyl: one of the first prehistoric reptiles to be discovered

dragonfly: a fast-flying, long-bodied insect, which we will hear more about soon

Cousin Cramchild: see notes in **Reading #6**. Cousin Cramchild has a slight resemblance to Cousin Eustace in *The Voyage of the Dawn-Treader*.

Proteus: or Olm; a cave-dwelling salamander with external gills

Syllis: a kind of marine worm

Distoma: also called the **liver fluke**; a parasite with an unusual form of reproduction

caddis: or **caddisfly**, a group of insects with aquatic larvae and terrestrial adults (i.e. the young live in the water and the adults live on land). Their larvae are known for their unusual skill in house building.

> *In the brook there were caddis houses. Rush had discovered these first. They were tiny cases, not much more than an inch long, and about as big around as a soda straw. They were constructed of bits of twig and shell, tiny pebbles, and choke cherry pits, all held together with a miraculous, silky cement that was created by the retiring little architect who lived inside. (Elizabeth Enright,* The Four-Story Mistake*)*

dalesmen: the inhabitants of the valley

the dame: the schoolmistress

stir abroad: leave the house

an old song: This poem by Charles Kingsley is also called "Young and Old." It is included in the *AO Year One Poetry Anthology*.

grig: This can mean either an eel or a cricket; at any rate, something small and lively.

People

M. Quatrefages: Jean Louis Armand de Quatrefages de Bréau was a French biologist.

Reading

Part One: More Conversation Between Kingsley and the Reader

And therefore it is, that there are dozens and hundreds of things in the world which we should certainly have said were contrary to nature, if we did not see them going on under our eyes all day long. If people had never seen little seeds grow into great plants and trees, of quite different shape from themselves, and these trees again produce fresh seeds, to grow into fresh trees, they would have said, "The thing cannot be; it is contrary to nature." And they would have been quite as right in saying so, as in saying that most other things cannot be.

[omission for length]

Did not learned men, too, hold, till within the last twenty-five years, that a flying dragon was an impossible monster? And do we not now know that there are hundreds of them found [as fossils] up and down the world? People call them **Pterodactyls**: but that is only because they are ashamed to call them flying dragons, after denying so long that flying dragons could exist *[omission]*. Wise men know that their business is to examine what is, and not to settle what is not. They know that there are elephants [though they have never seen one]; they know that there have been flying dragons; and the wiser they are, the less inclined they will be to say that there are no water-babies.

No water-babies, indeed? Why, wise men of old said that everything on earth had its double in the water; and you may see that that is, if not quite true, still quite as true as most other theories which you are likely to hear for many a day. There are land-babies—then why not water-babies? Are there not water-rats, water-flies, water-crickets, water-crabs, water-tortoises, water-scorpions, water-tigers and water-hogs, water-cats and water-dogs, sea-lions and sea-bears, sea-horses and sea-elephants, sea-mice and sea-urchins, sea-razors and sea-pens, sea-combs and sea-fans; and of plants, are there not water-grass, and water-crowfoot, water-milfoil, and so on, without end?

"But all these things are only nicknames; the water things are not really akin to the land things."

That's not always true. They are, in millions of cases, not only of the same family, but actually the same individual creatures. Do not even you know that a green drake, and an alder-fly, and a **dragonfly**, live under water till they change their skins, just as Tom changed his? And if a water animal can continually change into a land animal, why should not a land animal sometimes change into a water animal? Don't be put down by any of **Cousin Cramchild's** arguments, but stand up to him like a man, and answer him (quite respectfully, of course) thus:—

If Cousin Cramchild says, that if there are water-babies, they must grow into water-men, ask him how he knows that they do not? and then, how he knows that they must, any more than the **Proteus** of the Adelsberg caverns grows into a perfect newt.

If he says that it is too strange a transformation for a land-baby to turn into a water-baby, ask him if he ever heard of the transformation of **Syllis,** or the **Distomas,** or the common jelly-fish, of which **M. Quatrefages** says excellently well—

> Who would not exclaim that a miracle had come to pass, if he saw a reptile come out of the egg dropped by the hen in his poultry-yard, and the reptile give birth at once to an indefinite number of fishes and birds? Yet the history of the jelly-fish is quite as wonderful as that would be.

Ask him if he knows about all this; and if he does not, tell him to go and look for himself; and advise him (very respectfully, of course) to settle no more what strange things cannot happen, till he has seen what strange things do happen every day.

[omission for length]

Does not each of us, in coming into this world, go through a transformation just as wonderful as that of a sea-egg, or a butterfly? and do not reason and analogy, as well as Scripture, tell us that that transformation is not the last? and that, though what we shall be, we know not, yet we are here but as the crawling caterpillar, and shall be hereafter as the perfect fly. The old Greeks *[omission]* saw as much as that two thousand years ago; and I care very little for Cousin Cramchild, if he sees even less than they. And so forth, and so forth, till he is quite cross.

And then tell him that if there are no water-babies, at least there ought to be; and that, at least, he cannot answer *[omission]*.

Am I in earnest? Oh dear no! Don't you know that this is a fairy tale, and all fun and pretense; and that you are not to believe one word of it, even if it is true?

Part Two

But at all events, so it happened to Tom.

And, therefore, the keeper, and the groom, and Sir John made a great mistake, and were very unhappy (Sir John at least) without any reason, when they found [something] in the water, and said it was Tom's body, and that he had been drowned. They were utterly mistaken. Tom was quite alive; and cleaner, and merrier, than he ever had been. The fairies had washed him, you see, in the swift river, so thoroughly, that not only his dirt, but his whole husk and shell had been washed quite off him, and the pretty little real Tom was washed out of the inside of it, and swam away, as a **caddis** does when its case of stones and silk is bored through, and away it goes on its back, paddling to the shore, there to split its skin, and fly away as a caperer, on four fawn-coloured wings, with long legs and horns. They are foolish fellows, the caperers, and fly into the candle at night, if you leave the door open. We will hope Tom will be wiser, now he has got safe out of his sooty old shell.

But good Sir John did not understand all this *[omission]*; and he took it into his head that Tom was drowned. When they looked into the empty pockets of his shell, and found no jewels there, nor money—nothing but three marbles, and a brass button with a string to it—then Sir John did something as like crying as ever he did in his life, and blamed himself more bitterly than he need have done. So he cried, and the groom-boy cried, and the huntsman cried, and the dame cried, and the little girl cried, and the dairymaid cried, and the old nurse cried (for it was somewhat her fault), and My Lady cried, for though people have wigs, that is no reason why they should not have hearts.

But the keeper did not cry, though he had been so good-natured to Tom the morning before; for he was so dried up with running after poachers, that you could no more get tears out of him than milk out of leather.

And Grimes did not cry, for Sir John gave him ten pounds, and he drank it all in a week.

Sir John sent, far and wide, to find Tom's father and mother: but [that was impossible]. And the little girl would not play with her dolls for a whole week, and never forgot poor little Tom.

Part Three

And soon My Lady put a pretty little tombstone over Tom's shell in the little churchyard in Vendale, where the old **dalesmen** all sleep side by side between the limestone crags. And **the dame** decked it with garlands every Sunday, till she grew so old that she could not **stir abroad**; then the little children decked it for her. And always she sang **an old old song**, as she sat spinning what she called her wedding-dress.

The children could not understand it, but they liked it none the less for that; for it was very sweet, and very sad; and that was enough for them. And these are the words of it:—

> When all the world is young, lad,
>> And all the trees are green;
>
> And every goose a swan, lad,
>> And every lass a queen;
>
> Then hey for boot and horse, lad,
>> And round the world away;
>
> Young blood must have its course, lad,
>> And every dog his day.
>
> When all the world is old, lad,
>> And all the trees are brown;
>
> And all the sport is stale, lad,
>> And all the wheels run down;
>
> Creep home, and take your place there,
>> The spent and maimed among:
>
> God grant you find one face there,
>> You loved when all was young.

Those are the words: but they are only the body of it: the soul of the song was the dear old woman's sweet face, and sweet voice, and the sweet old air to which she sang; and that, alas! one cannot put on paper. And at last she grew so stiff and lame, that the angels were forced to carry her; and they helped her on with her wedding-dress, and carried her up over Harthover Fells, and a long way beyond that too; and there was a new schoolmistress in Vendale *[omission]*.

And all the while Tom was swimming about in the river, with a pretty little lace-collar of gills about his neck, as lively as a **grig**, and as clean as a fresh-run salmon.

Epilogue

Now if you don't like my story, then go to the schoolroom and learn your multiplication-table, and see if you like that better. Some people, no doubt, would do so. So much the better for us, if not for them. It takes all sorts, they say, to make a world.

Narration and Discussion

Why do you think an important man like Sir John tried so hard to find Tom when he was lost, and even to track down his parents?

What do you think the old woman's song was about?

Why does Kingsley say that it is really no more miraculous for Tom to turn into a water-baby, than it is for many of the everyday "miracles" of nature to happen? What amazing things in the natural world have you seen or read about?

Poetic Interlude #3

The verse for the next chapter comes from the end of The Rime of the Ancient Mariner, *by Samuel Taylor Coleridge. [This bit of the poem is also found in AO's poetry anthology for Year One students.]*

> He prayeth well who loveth well
> Both men and bird and beast;
> He prayeth best who loveth best
> All things both great and small:
> For the dear God who loveth us,
> He made and loveth all.

The Water-Babies

Reading #8

Introduction

Tom, for the first time in his life, is clean, seems to have enough to eat, and nobody is beating him or making him climb chimneys. But his new life in the stream is not entirely happy.

Vocabulary

amphibious: explained in the text

sand-pipe: also called the sandy-cased caddis

spoon-bonnet: a hat popular in the 1860's, with a wide front brim

one wonderful little fellow: the rotifer *Limnias melicerta*. (You can find photos of this intrepid builder online.)

a certain old lady who is coming: We will hear more about her soon.

howked: to **howk** usually means to dig something out of a hole, so possibly Tom was trying to pry the creatures out of their places. It could also mean "to hit," which would also make sense.

People

There was a wise man once: the poet William Wordsworth

Reading

Part One: In which Kingsley continues to converse with the reader

Tom was now quite **amphibious**.
   You do not know what that means?
   You had better, then, ask the nearest [school-teacher], who may possibly answer you smartly enough, thus—

> "Amphibious. Adjective, derived from two Greek words, *amphi*, a fish, and *bios*, a beast. An animal supposed by our ignorant ancestors to be compounded of a fish and a beast; which therefore, like the hippopotamus, can't live on the land, and dies in the water."

Sailors and Seababies

However that may be, Tom was amphibious: and what is better still, he was clean. For the first time in his life, he felt how comfortable it was to have nothing on him but himself. But he only enjoyed it: he did not know it, or think about it; just as you enjoy life and health, and yet never think about being alive and healthy; and may it be long before you have to think about it!

He did not remember having ever been dirty. Indeed, he did not remember any of his old troubles, being tired, or hungry, or beaten, or sent up dark chimneys. Since that sweet sleep, he had forgotten all about his master, and Harthover Place, and the little white girl, and in a word, all that had happened to him when he lived before; and what was best of all, he had forgotten all the bad words which he had learned from Grimes, and the rude boys with whom he used to play. That is not strange: for you know, when you came into this world, and became a land-baby, you remembered nothing. So why should he, when he became a water-baby?

Then have [we] lived before?

My dear child, who can tell? One can only tell that, by remembering something which happened where we lived before; and as we remember nothing, we know nothing about it; and no book, and no man, can never tell us certainly.

There was a wise man once, a very wise man, and a very good man, who wrote a poem about the feelings which some children have about having lived before; and this is what he said—

> Our birth is but a sleep and a forgetting;
> The Soul that rises with us, our life's Star,
>   Hath had elsewhere its setting
>   And cometh from afar;
>   Not in entire forgetfulness,
>   And not in utter nakedness,
> But trailing clouds of glory do we come
>   From God, who is our home...

There, you can know no more than that. But if I was you, I would believe that. For then the great fairy Science, who is likely to be queen of all the fairies for many a year to come, can only do you good, and never do you harm; and instead of fancying, with some people, that your body makes your soul, as if a steam-engine could make its own coke; or, with some people, that your soul has nothing to do with your body, but is only stuck into it like a pin into a pin-cushion, to fall out with the first shake—you will believe the one true,

orthodox,	logical,
rational,	irrefragable,
philosophical,	nominalistic,

realistic,	productive,
inductive,	salutary,
deductive,	comfortable,
seductive,	

and on-all-accounts-to-be-received doctrine of this wonderful fairy tale; which is, that your soul makes your body, just as a snail makes his shell.

For the rest, it is enough for us to be sure that whether or not we lived before, we shall live again; though not, I hope, as poor little *[omission]* Tom did. For he went downward into the water; but we, I hope, shall go upward to a very different place.

Part Two

But Tom was very happy in the water. He had been sadly overworked in the land-world; and so now, to make up for that, he had nothing but holidays in the water-world for a long, long time to come. He had nothing to do now but enjoy himself, and look at all the pretty things which are to be seen in the cool clear water-world, where the sun is never too hot, and the frost is never too cold.

And what did he live on?

Water-cresses, perhaps; or perhaps water-gruel, and water-milk; too many land-babies do so likewise. But we do not know what one-tenth of the water-things eat; so we are not answerable for the water-babies.

Sometimes he went along the smooth gravel water-ways, looking at the crickets which ran in and out among the stones, as rabbits do on land; or he climbed over the ledges of rock, and saw the **sand-pipes** hanging in thousands, with every one of them a pretty little head and legs peeping out; or he went into a still corner, and watched the caddises eating dead sticks as greedily as you would eat plum-pudding, and building their houses with silk and glue. Very fanciful ladies they were; none of them would keep to the same materials for a day. One would begin with some pebbles; then she would stick on a piece of green wood; then she found a shell, and stuck it on too; and the poor shell was alive, and did not like at all being taken to build houses with: but the caddis did not let him have any voice in the matter, being rude and selfish, as vain people are apt to be; then she stuck on a piece of rotten wood, then a very smart pink stone, and so on, till she was patched all over *[omission]*. Then she found a long straw, five times as long as herself, and said, "Hurrah! my sister has a tail, and I'll have one too"; and she stuck it on her back, and marched about with it quite proud, though it was very inconvenient indeed. And, at that, tails became all the fashion among the caddis-baits in that pool, as they were at the end of the Long Pond last May, and they all toddled about with long straws sticking out behind, getting between each other's legs, and tumbling over each other, and looking so ridiculous, that Tom laughed at them till he cried, as we did. But they were quite right, you know; for people must always follow the fashion, even if it be **spoon-bonnets**.

Then sometimes he came to a deep still reach; and there he saw the water-forests. They would have looked to you only little weeds: but Tom, you must remember, was so little that everything looked a hundred times as big to him as it does to you, just as things do to a minnow, who sees and catches the little water-creatures which you can only see in a microscope.

And in the water-forest he saw the water-monkeys and water-squirrels (they had all six legs, though; everything almost has six legs in the water, except efts and water-babies); and nimbly enough they ran among the branches. There were water-flowers there too, in thousands; and Tom tried to pick them: but as soon as he touched them, they drew themselves in and turned into knots of jelly; and then Tom saw that they were all alive—bells, and stars, and wheels, and flowers, of all beautiful shapes and colours; and all alive and busy, just as Tom was. So now he found that there was a great deal more in the world than he had fancied at first sight.

There was **one wonderful little fellow**, too, who peeped out of the top of a house built of round bricks. He had two big wheels, and one little one, all over teeth, spinning round and round like the wheels in a thrashing-machine; and Tom stood and stared at him, to see what he was going to make with his machinery. And what do you think he was doing? Brick-making. With his two big wheels he swept together all the mud which floated in the water: all that was nice in it he put into his stomach and ate; and all the mud he put into the little wheel on his breast, which really was a round hole set with teeth; and there he spun it into a neat hard round brick; and then he took it and stuck it on the top of his house-wall, and set to work to make another. Now was not he a clever little fellow?

Tom thought so; but when he wanted to talk to him the brick-maker was much too busy and proud of his work to take notice of him.

Part Three

Now you must know that all the things under the water talk; only not such a language as ours, but such as horses, and dogs, and cows, and birds talk to each other; and Tom soon learned to understand them and talk to them; so that he might have had very pleasant company if he had only been a good boy. But I am sorry to say, he was too like some other little boys, very fond of hunting and tormenting creatures for mere sport. Some people say that boys cannot help it; that it is nature, and only a proof that we are all originally descended from beasts of prey.

But whether it is nature or not, little boys can help it, and must help it. For if they have naughty, low, mischievous tricks in their nature, as monkeys have, that is no reason why they should give way to those tricks like monkeys, who know no better. And therefore they must not torment dumb creatures; for if they do, **a certain old lady who is coming** will surely give them exactly what they deserve.

But Tom did not know that; and he pecked and **howked** the poor water-things about sadly, till they were all afraid of him, and got out of his way, or crept into their shells; so he had no one to speak to or play with. The water-fairies, of course, were very sorry to see him so unhappy, and longed to take him, and tell him how naughty he was, and teach him to be good, and to play and romp with him too: but they had been forbidden to do that. Tom had to learn his lesson for himself by sound and sharp experience, as many another foolish person has to do, though there may be many a kind heart yearning over them all the while, and longing to teach them what they can only teach themselves.

Narration and Discussion

Why does Tom not remember his previous life on land? Is that a good thing?

Describe some of Tom's new acquaintances. (Remember that he is less than four inches tall, so even small creatures would seem large to him.)

For further thought: As mentioned before, Kingsley was very interested in the idea of things as they were at their beginning; and the creatures Tom meets during his early days as a Water-Baby are very simple, even primitive ones. He watches them, but they don't talk back to him, or at least not much—Kingsley says that's because Tom teases them and they are afraid of him. The fairies are not allowed to advise him on how to do better (and hopefully move up the underwater social scale a bit). Do you think he will be able to figure it out on his own?

For even further thought: Kingsley says, "For then you will believe the one true doctrine of this wonderful fairy tale; which is, that your soul makes your body, just as a snail makes his shell." What do you think he means?

Reading #9

Introduction

After a few false starts, Tom begins to make some underwater friends.

Vocabulary

caddis: see the notes in **Reading #8**

hover: This is an unusual noun that may refer specifically to a group of trout, gathered together motionlessly in a river or stream. Since the next thing that happens is that a trout **floushes** out at Tom, this definition appears to be the correct one.

floush or **flouse:** splash

a very ugly dirty creature: a dragonfly larva. (Fun fact: dragonfly larvae can take up to five years to reach adulthood.)

split: part of the metamorphosis into an adult dragonfly

gauze: a thin, translucent material

dock: a wild plant that can be eaten or used for medicine

hare and hounds: a racing game

alderflies: a type of fly that lives near water

caperer: a large sedge fly, enjoyed by trout

duns: mayflies in the last stage before full maturity

spinners: "spent" mayflies that have returned to the water to die

claret: dark red (like wine)

People

Blondin: Charles Blondin, a French tightrope walker

Léotard: Jules Léotard, a French trapeze artist

Reading

Part One

At last one day [Tom] found a **caddis**, and wanted it to peep out of its house: but its house-door was shut. He had never seen a caddis with a house-door before: so what must he do, the meddlesome little fellow, but pull it open, to see what the poor lady was doing inside. What a shame! How should you like to have any one breaking your bedroom-door in, to see how you looked when you were in bed?

So Tom broke to pieces the door, which was the prettiest little grating of silk, stuck all over with shining bits of crystal; and when he looked in, the caddis poked out her head, and it had turned into just the shape of a bird's. But when Tom spoke to her she could not answer; for her mouth and face were tight tied up in a new night-cap of neat pink skin.

However, if she didn't answer, all the other caddises did; for they held up their hands and shrieked *[omission]*: "Oh, you nasty horrid boy; there you are at it again! And she had just laid herself up for a fortnight's sleep, and then she would have come out with such beautiful wings, and flown about, and laid such lots of eggs: and now you have broken her door, and she can't mend it because her mouth is tied up for a fortnight, and she will die. Who sent you here to worry us out of our lives?"

So Tom swam away. He was very much ashamed of himself, and felt all the naughtier; as little boys do when they have done wrong and won't say so.

Part Two

Then he came to a pool full of little trout, and began tormenting them, and trying to catch them: but they slipped through his fingers, and jumped clean out of the water in their fright. But as Tom chased them, he came close to a great dark **hover** under an alder root, and out **floushed** a huge old brown trout ten times as big as he was, and ran right against him, and knocked all the breath out of his body; and I don't know which was the more frightened of the two.

Part Three

Then he went on sulky and lonely, as he deserved to be; and under a bank he saw **a very ugly dirty creature** sitting, about half as big as himself, which had six legs, and a big stomach, and a most ridiculous head with two great eyes and a face just like a donkey's.

"Oh," said Tom, "you are an ugly fellow to be sure!" and he began making faces at him; and put his nose close to him, and halloed at him, like a very rude boy. When, hey presto! all the thing's donkey-face came off in a moment, and out popped a long arm with a pair of pincers at the end of it, and caught Tom by the nose. It did not hurt him much; but it held him quite tight.

"Yah, ah! Oh, let me go!" cried Tom.

"Then let me go," said the creature. "I want to be quiet. I want to **split**."

Tom promised to let him alone, and he let go.

"Why do you want to split?" said Tom.

"Because my brothers and sisters have all split, and turned into beautiful creatures with wings; and I want to split too. Don't speak to me. I am sure I shall split. I will split!"

Tom stood still, and watched him. And he swelled himself, and puffed, and stretched himself out stiff, and at last—crack, puff, bang—he opened all down his back, and then up to the top of his head.

And out of his inside came the most slender, elegant, soft creature, as soft and smooth as Tom: but very pale and weak, like a little child who has been ill a long time in a dark room. It moved its legs very feebly; and looked about it half ashamed, like a girl when she goes for the first time into a ballroom; and then it began walking slowly up a grass stem to the top of the water.

Tom was so astonished that he never said a word: but he stared with all his eyes. And he went up to the top of the water too, and peeped out to see what would happen.

And as the creature sat in the warm bright sun, a wonderful change came over it. It grew strong and firm; the most lovely colours began to show on its body, blue and yellow and black, spots and bars and rings; out of its back rose four great wings of bright brown **gauze**; and its eyes grew so large that they filled all its head, and shone like ten thousand diamonds.

"Oh, you beautiful creature!" said Tom; and he put out his hand to catch it.

But the thing whirred up into the air, and hung poised on its wings a moment, and then settled down again by Tom quite fearless.

"No!" it said, "you cannot catch me. I am a dragonfly now, the king of all the flies; and I shall dance in the sunshine, and hawk over the river, and catch gnats, and have a beautiful wife like myself. I know what I shall do. Hurrah!" And he flew away into the air, and began catching gnats.

"Oh! come back, come back," cried Tom, "you beautiful creature. I have no one to play with, and I am so lonely here. If you will but come back I will never try to catch you."

"I don't care whether you do or not," said the dragonfly; "for you can't. But when I have had my dinner, and looked a little about this pretty place, I will come back, and have a little chat about all I have seen in my travels. Why, what a huge tree this is! and what huge leaves on it!" It was only a big **dock [plant]**; but you know the dragonfly had never seen any but little water-trees; starwort, and milfoil, and water-crowfoot, and such like; so it did look very big to him. Besides, he was very short-sighted, as all dragonflies are; and never could see a yard before his nose; any more than a great many other folks, who are not half as handsome as he.

Part Four

The dragonfly did come back, and chatted away with Tom. He was a little conceited about his fine colours and his large wings; but you know, he had been a poor dirty ugly creature all his life before; so there were great excuses for him. He was very fond of talking about all the wonderful things he saw in the trees and the meadows; and Tom liked to listen to him, for he had forgotten all about them. So in a little while they became great friends.

And I am very glad to say, that Tom learned such a lesson that day, that he did not torment creatures for a long time after. And then the caddises grew quite tame, and used to tell him strange stories about the way they built their houses, and changed their skins, and turned at last into winged flies; till Tom began to long to change his skin, and have wings like them some day.

And the trout and he made it up (for trout very soon forget if they have been frightened and hurt). So Tom used to play with them at **hare and hounds**, and great fun they had; and he used to try to leap out of the water, head over heels, as they did before a shower came on; but somehow he never could manage it.

He liked most, though, to see them rising at the flies, as they sailed round and round under the shadow of the great oak, where the beetles fell flop into the water, and the green caterpillars let themselves down from the boughs by silk ropes for no reason at all; and then changed their foolish minds for no reason at all either; and hauled themselves up again into the tree, rolling up the rope in a ball between their paws; which is a very clever rope dancer's trick; and neither **Blondin** nor **Léotard** could do it: but why they should take so much trouble about it no one can tell; for they cannot get their living, as Blondin and Léotard do, by trying to break their necks on a string.

And very often Tom caught them just as they touched the water; and caught the **alderflies**, and the **caperers**, and the cock-tailed **duns** and **spinners**, yellow and brown, **claret** and grey, and gave them to his friends the trout.

Perhaps he was not quite kind to the flies [by doing that]; but one must do a good turn to one's friends when one can.

Narration and Discussion

How does Tom get to be friends with the dragonfly?

What have you seen (yourself) in nature that makes you wish you could imitate it?

Reading #10

Introduction

Tom meets up with small and large creatures, and begins to wonder if there is more to life than just swimming (or flying).

Vocabulary

a new sort: Probably a **mayfly**, since they are notably short-lived as adults.

cock (verb): to tilt up, in an impudent way. We do not use this word much now as a verb, but it does come up in the adjective "cocky."

impudence: boldness, cheek

conjurors: magicians

Handsome is that handsome does: what one does is more important than one's appearance. (More commonly, "handsome is as handsome does.")

eft: a newt. See note in **Reading #7**.

bogies: spooky things

freshet: a surge of water from the sea, often after a rain

grinning like a Cheshire cat: this phrase dates back to the 18th century, but Kingsley's use of it here may have inspired Lewis Carroll's Cheshire Cat in *Alice's Adventures in Wonderland* (1865).

out of the sea: probably refers to the North Sea

sentimental: emotional and sad

burn: brook, stream

Reading

Part One

And at last he gave up catching even the flies; for he made acquaintance with one by accident and found him a very merry little fellow. And this was the way it happened; and it is all quite true.

He was basking at the top of the water one hot day in July, catching duns and feeding the trout, when he saw **a new sort**, a dark grey little fellow with a brown head. He was a very little fellow indeed: but he made the most of himself, as people ought to do. He **cocked** up his head, and he cocked up his wings, and he cocked up his tail, and he cocked up the two whisks at his tail-end, and, in short, he looked the cockiest little man of all little men. And so he proved to be; for instead of getting away, he hopped upon Tom's finger, and sat there [as bold as you please]; and he cried out in the tiniest, shrillest, squeakiest little voice you ever heard,

"Much obliged to you, indeed; but I don't want it yet."

"Want what?" said Tom, quite taken aback by his **impudence**.

"Your leg, which you are kind enough to hold out for me to sit on. I must just go and see after my wife for a few minutes. Dear me! what a troublesome business a family is!" (though the idle little rogue did nothing at all, but left his poor wife to lay all the eggs by herself). "When I come back, I shall be glad of it, if you'll be so good as to keep it sticking out just so"; and off he flew.

Tom thought him a very cool sort of personage; and still more so, when, in five minutes, he came back, and said— "Ah, you were tired waiting? Well, your other leg will do as well."

And he popped himself down on Tom's knee, and began chatting away in his squeaking voice.

"So you live under the water? It's a low place. I lived there for some time; and was very shabby and dirty. But I didn't choose that that should last. So I turned respectable, and came up to the top, and put on this grey suit. It's a very business-like suit, you think, don't you?"

"Very neat and quiet indeed," said Tom.

"Yes, one must be quiet and neat and respectable, and all that sort of thing for a little, when one becomes a family man. But I'm tired of it, that's the truth. I've done quite enough business, I consider, in the last week, to last me my life. So I shall put on a ball dress, and [go out and see the world, and have a dance or two]. Why shouldn't one be jolly if one can?"

"And what will become of your wife?"

"Oh! she is a [dull creature], and thinks about nothing but eggs. If she chooses to come, why she may; and if not, why I go without her;—and here I go."

And, as he spoke, he turned quite pale, and then quite white.

"Why, you're ill!" said Tom. But he did not answer.

"You're dead," said Tom, looking at him as he stood on his knee as white as a ghost.

"No, I ain't!" answered a little squeaking voice over his head. "This is me up here, in my ball-dress; and that's my skin. Ha, ha! you could not do such a trick as that!"

And no more Tom could, nor Houdin, nor Robin, nor Frikell, all the **conjurors** in the world. For the little rogue had jumped clean out of his own skin, and left it standing on Tom's knee: eyes, wings, legs, tail, exactly as if it had been alive.

"Ha, ha!" he said, and he jerked and skipped up and down, never stopping an instant [omission]. "Ain't I a pretty fellow now?"

And so he was; for his body was white, and his tail orange, and his eyes all the colours of a peacock's tail. And what was the oddest of all, the whisks at the end of his tail had grown five times as long as they were before.

"Ah!" said he, "now I will see the [world]. My living won't cost me much, for I have no mouth, you see, and no inside; so I can never be hungry nor have the stomach-ache neither." No more he had. He had grown as dry and hard and empty as a quill, as such silly shallow-hearted fellows deserve to grow.

But, instead of being ashamed of his emptiness, he was quite proud of it, as a good many fine gentlemen are, and began flirting and flipping up and down, and singing—

> My wife shall dance, and I shall sing,
>
> So merrily pass the day;
>
> For I hold it for quite the wisest thing,
>
> To drive dull care away.

And he danced up and down for three days and three nights, till he grew so tired, that he tumbled into the water, and floated down. But what became of him Tom never knew, and he himself never minded; for Tom heard him singing to the last, as he floated down—

> To drive dull care away-ay-ay!

And if he did not care, why nobody else cared either.

Part Two

But one day Tom had a new adventure. He was sitting on a water-lily leaf, he and his friend the dragonfly, watching the gnats dance. The dragonfly had eaten as many as he wanted, and was sitting quite still and sleepy, for it was very hot and bright. The gnats (who did not care the least for their poor brothers' death) danced a foot over his head quite happily, and a large black fly settled within an inch of his nose, and began washing his own face and combing his hair with his paws: but the dragonfly never stirred, and kept on chatting to Tom about the times when he lived under the water.

Suddenly, Tom heard the strangest noise up the stream; cooing, and grunting, and whining, and squeaking *[omission]*. He looked up the water, and there he saw a sight as strange as the noise; a great ball rolling over and over down the stream, seeming one moment of soft brown fur, and the next of shining glass: and yet it was not a ball; for sometimes it broke up and streamed away in pieces, and then it joined again; and all the while the noise came out of it louder and louder.

Tom asked the dragonfly what it could be: but, of course, with his short sight, he could not even see it, though it was not ten yards away.

So he took the neatest little header into the water, and started off to see for himself; and, when he came near, the ball turned out to be four or five beautiful creatures, many times larger than Tom, who were swimming about, and rolling, and diving, and twisting, and wrestling, and cuddling, and kissing, and biting, and scratching, in the most charming fashion that ever was seen. And if you don't believe me, you may go to the Zoological Gardens *[omission]*, and then say, if otters at play in the water are not the merriest, lithest, gracefullest creatures you ever saw.

But, when the biggest of them saw Tom, she darted out from the rest, and cried in the water-language sharply enough, "Quick, children, here is something to eat, indeed!" and came at poor Tom, showing such a wicked pair of eyes, and such a set of sharp teeth in a grinning mouth, that Tom, who had thought her very handsome, said to himself, "**Handsome is that handsome does**," and slipped in between the water-lily roots as fast as he could, and then turned round and made faces at her.

"Come out," said the wicked old otter, "or it will be worse for you."

But Tom looked at her from between two thick roots, and shook them with all his might, making horrible faces all the while, just as he used to grin through the railings at the old women, when he lived before. It was not quite well bred, no doubt; but you know, Tom had not finished his education yet.

"Come away, children," said the otter in disgust, "it is not worth eating, after all. It is only a nasty **eft**, which nothing eats, not even those vulgar pike in the pond."

"I am not an eft!" said Tom; "efts have tails."

"You are an eft," said the otter, very positively; "I see your two hands quite plain, and I know you have a tail."

"I tell you I have not," said Tom. "Look here!" and he turned his pretty little self quite round; and, sure enough, he had no more tail than you.

The otter might have got out of it by saying that Tom was a frog: but, like a great many other people, when she had once said a thing, she stood to it, right or wrong; so she answered: "I say you are an eft, and therefore you are, and not fit food for gentlefolk like me and my children. You may stay here till the salmon eat you (she knew the salmon would not, but she wanted to frighten poor Tom). Ha! ha! they will eat you, and we will eat them"; and the otter laughed such a wicked cruel laugh—as you may hear them do sometimes; and the first time that you hear it you will probably think it is **bogies**.

"What are salmon?" asked Tom.

"Fish, you eft, great fish, nice fish to eat. They are the lords of the fish, and we are lords of the salmon"; and she laughed again. "We hunt them up and down the pools, and drive them up into a corner, the silly things; they are so proud, and bully the little trout, and the minnows, till they see us coming, and then they are so meek all at once; and we catch them, but we disdain to eat them all; we just bite out their soft throats and suck their sweet juice—Oh, so good!"—(and she licked her wicked lips)— "and then throw them away, and go and catch another. They are coming soon, children, coming soon; I can smell the rain coming up off the sea, and then hurrah for a **freshet**, and salmon, and plenty of eating all day long." And the otter grew so proud that she turned head over heels twice, and then stood upright half out of the water, **grinning like a Cheshire cat.**

"And where do they come from?" asked Tom, who kept himself very close, for he was considerably frightened.

"**Out of the sea**, eft, the great wide sea, where they might stay and be safe if they liked. But out of the sea the silly things come, into the great river down below, and we come up to watch for them; and when they go down again we go down and follow them. And there we fish for the bass and the pollock, and have jolly days along the shore, and toss and roll in the breakers, and sleep snug in the warm dry crags. Ah, that is a merry life too, children, if it were not for those horrid men."

"What are men?" asked Tom; but somehow he seemed to know before he asked.

"Two-legged things, eft: and, now I come to look at you, they are actually something like you, if you had not a tail" (she was determined that Tom should have a tail), "only a great deal bigger, worse luck for us; and they catch the fish with hooks and lines, which get into our feet sometimes, and set pots along the rocks to catch lobsters. They speared my poor dear husband as he went out to find something for me to eat. I was laid up among the crags then, and we were very low in the world, for the sea was so rough that no fish would come in shore. But they speared him, poor fellow, and I saw them carrying him away upon a pole. Ah, he lost his life for your sakes, my children, poor dear obedient creature that he was."

And the otter grew so **sentimental** (for otters can be very sentimental when they choose, like a good many people who are both cruel and greedy, and no good to anybody at all) that she sailed solemnly away down the **burn**, and Tom saw her no more for that time. And lucky it was for her that she did so; for no sooner was she gone, than down the bank came seven little rough terrier dogs, snuffing and yapping, and grubbing and splashing, in full cry after the otter.

Tom hid among the water-lilies till [the dogs] were gone; for he could not guess that they were the water-fairies come to help him. But he could not help thinking of what the otter had said about the great river and the broad sea.

And, as he thought, he longed to go and see them. He could not tell why; but the more he thought, the more he grew discontented with the narrow little stream in which he lived, and all his companions there; and wanted to get out into the wide wide world, and enjoy all the wonderful sights of which he was sure it was full.

Narration and Discussion

How does Tom know he is not an eft? What does he think he is?

Kingsley says about the mayfly, "And if he did not care, why nobody else cared either." Do you think he is right? Does that remind you of any other stories?

Reading #11

Introduction

Discontented with life in the stream, Tom sets off for bigger places.

Vocabulary

> **stupid:** sleepy and slow. See **Special Vocabulary Notes** in the Introduction for more discussion of this word.
>
> **omnium-gatherums:** a collection of miscellaneous things
>
> **strids:** passages
>
> **cataracts:** waterfalls
>
> **breakers:** waves

Reading

Part One

[So Tom] set off to go down the stream. But the stream was very low; and when he came to the shallows he could not keep under water, for there was no water left to keep under. So the sun burned his back and made him sick; and he went back again and lay quiet in the pool for a whole week more.

And then, on the evening of a very hot day, he saw a sight.

He had been [feeling] very **stupid** all day, and so had the trout; for they would not move an inch to take a fly, though there were thousands on the water, but lay dozing at the bottom under the shade of the stones; and Tom lay dozing too, and was glad to cuddle their smooth cool sides, for the water was quite warm and unpleasant.

But toward evening it grew suddenly dark, and Tom looked up and saw a blanket of black clouds lying right across the valley above his head, resting on the crags right and left. He felt not quite frightened, but very still; for everything was still. There was not a whisper of wind, nor a chirp of a bird to be heard; and next a few great drops of rain fell plop into the water, and one hit Tom on the nose, and made him pop his head down quickly enough.

And then the thunder roared, and the lightning flashed, and leapt across Vendale and back again, from cloud to cloud, and cliff to cliff, till the very rocks in the stream seemed to shake: and Tom looked up at it through the water, and thought it the finest thing he ever saw in his life.

But out of the water he dared not put his head; for the rain came down by bucketsful, and the hail hammered like shot on the stream, and churned it into foam; and soon the stream rose, and rushed down, higher and higher, and fouler and fouler, full of beetles, and sticks; and straws, and worms, and addle-eggs, and wood-lice, and leeches, and odds and ends, and **omnium-gatherums**, and this, that, and the other, enough to fill nine museums. Tom could hardly stand against the stream, and hid behind a rock. But the trout did not; for out they rushed from among the stones, and began gobbling the beetles and leeches in the most greedy and quarrelsome way, and swimming about with great worms hanging out of their mouths, tugging and kicking to get them away from each other.

Part Two

And now, by the flashes of the lightning, Tom saw a new sight—all the bottom of the stream alive with great eels, turning and twisting along, all downstream and away. They had been hiding for weeks past in the cracks of the rocks, and in burrows in the mud; and Tom had hardly ever seen them, except now and then at night: but now they were all out, and went hurrying past him so fiercely and wildly that he was quite frightened. And as they hurried past he could hear them say to each other, "We must run, we must run. What a jolly thunderstorm! Down to the sea, down to the sea!"

And then the otter came by with all her brood, twining and sweeping along as fast as the eels themselves; and she spied Tom as she came by, and said: "Now is your time, eft, if you want to see the world. Come along, children, never mind those nasty eels: we shall breakfast on salmon tomorrow. Down to the sea, down to the sea!"

Then came a flash brighter than all the rest, and by the light of it—in the thousandth part of a second they were gone again—but he had seen them, he was certain of it— three beautiful little white girls, with their arms twined round each other's necks, floating down the torrent, as they sang, "Down to the sea, down to the sea!"

"Oh stay! Wait for me!" cried Tom; but they were gone: yet he could hear their voices clear and sweet through the roar of thunder and water and wind, singing as they died away, "Down to the sea!"

"Down to the sea?" said Tom; "everything is going to the sea, and I will go too. Good-bye, trout." But the trout were so busy gobbling worms that they never turned to answer him; so that Tom was spared the pain of bidding them farewell.

And now, down the rushing stream, guided by the bright flashes of the storm; past tall birch-fringed rocks, which shone out one moment as clear as day, and the next were dark as night; past dark hovers under swirling banks, from which great trout rushed out on Tom, thinking him to be good to eat, and turned back sulkily, for the fairies sent them home again with a tremendous scolding, for daring to meddle with a water-baby; on through narrow **strids** and roaring **cataracts**, where Tom was deafened and blinded for a moment by the rushing waters; along deep reaches, where the white water-lilies tossed and flapped beneath the wind and hail; past sleeping villages; under dark bridge-arches, and away and away to the sea. And Tom could not stop, and did not care to stop; he would see the great world below, and the salmon, and the **breakers**, and the wide wide sea.

Part Three

And when the daylight came, Tom found himself out in the river *[omission]* at Harthover *[omission]*. A full hundred yards broad it was, sliding on from broad pool to broad shallow, and broad shallow to broad pool, over great fields of shingle, under oak and ash coverts, past low cliffs of sandstone, past green meadows, and fair parks, and a great house of grey stone, and brown moors above, and here and there against the sky the smoking chimney of a colliery.

But Tom thought nothing about what the river was like. All his fancy was, to get down to the wide wide sea. And after a while he came to a place where the river spread out into broad still shallow reaches, so wide that little Tom, as he put his head out of the water, could hardly see across.

And there he stopped. He got a little frightened. "This must be the sea," he thought. "What a wide place it is! If I go on into it I shall surely lose my way, or some strange thing will bite me. I will stop here and look out for the otter, or the eels, or someone to tell me where I shall go."

So he went back a little way, and crept into a crack of the rock, just where the river opened out into the wide shallows, and watched for someone to tell him his way: but the otter and the eels were gone on, miles and miles down the stream.

There he waited, and slept too, for he was quite tired with his night's journey.

Narration and Discussion

Could you draw an imaginary map of where Tom has gone? Where is it that he wants to go next?

Do you think it will be a good plan for Tom to search for the otter?

Reading #12

Introduction

Tom chats with a salmon, and discovers that there are other beings like himself.

Vocabulary

amber hue: golden colour

ten times as big as the biggest trout, and a hundred times as big as Tom: If Tom is about four inches tall, and we're comparing by length, that would make this fish four hundred inches long, or 33 1/3 feet, or over 11 yards (10 m) long. Do salmon really grow that long? Chinook/King salmon are the largest salmon, and they grow up to 58 inches (1.5 m) long. What about the trout? The kind of brook trout Tom knew probably weighed no more than 5 pounds and would be about 15 inches (38 cm) long. Conclusion? It seems that Kingsley was exaggerating a bit for effect. But anyway, it was a big fish.

sculling: propelling himself along as if he were rowing a boat

stake-nets: exactly as they sound: nets put up on rows of stakes, to catch fish

degraded: brought down low

little folks: This usually refers to children, but in this case it seems to mean people of lower social status than the "great folks."

Reading

Part One

When Tom woke, the stream was clearing to a beautiful **amber hue**, though it was still very high. And after a while he saw a sight which made him jump up; for he knew in a moment it was one of the things which he had come to look for.

Such a fish! **ten times as big as the biggest trout, and a hundred times as big as Tom**, **sculling** up the stream past him, as easily as Tom had sculled down. Such a fish! shining silver from head to tail, and here and there a crimson dot; with a grand hooked nose and grand curling lip, and a grand bright eye, looking round him as proudly as a king, and surveying the water right and left as if all belonged to him. Surely he must be the salmon, the king of all the fish.

Tom was so frightened that he longed to creep into a hole; but he need not have been; for salmon are all true gentlemen, and, like true gentlemen, they look noble and proud enough, and yet, like true gentlemen, they never harm or quarrel with any one, but go about their own business, and leave rude fellows to themselves.

The salmon looked at him full in the face, and then went on without minding him, with a swish or two of his tail which made the stream boil again. And in a few minutes came another, and then four or five, and so on; and all passed Tom, rushing and plunging up the cataract with strong strokes of their silver tails, now and then leaping clean out of water and up over a rock, shining gloriously for a moment in the bright sun; while Tom was so delighted that he could have watched them all day long.

Part Two

And at last one came up bigger than all the rest; but he came slowly, and stopped, and looked back, and seemed very anxious and busy. And Tom saw that he was helping another salmon, an especially handsome one, who had not a single spot upon it, but was clothed in pure silver from nose to tail.

"My dear," said the great fish to his companion, "you really look dreadfully tired, and you must not over-exert yourself at first. Do rest yourself behind this rock;" and he shoved her gently with his nose, to the rock where Tom sat.

You must know that this was the salmon's wife. For salmon, like other true gentlemen, always choose their lady, and love her, and are true to her, and take care of her and work for her, and fight for her, as every true gentleman ought; and are not like vulgar chub and roach and pike, who have no high feelings, and take no care of their wives.

Then he saw Tom, and looked at him very fiercely one moment, as if he was going to bite him. "What do you want here?" he said, very fiercely.

"Oh, don't hurt me!" cried Tom. "I only want to look at you; you are so handsome."

"Ah!" said the salmon, very stately but very civilly. "I really beg your pardon; I see what you are, my little dear. I have met one or two creatures like you before, and found them very agreeable and well-behaved. Indeed, one of them showed me a great kindness lately, which I hope to be able to repay. I hope we shall not be in your way here. As soon as this lady is rested, we shall proceed on our journey."

What a well-bred old salmon he was!

"So you have seen things like me before?" asked Tom.

"Several times, my dear. Indeed, it was only last night that one at the river's mouth came and warned me and my wife of some new **stake-nets** which had got into the stream, I cannot tell how, since last winter, and showed us the way round them, in the most charmingly obliging way."

"So there are babies in the sea?" cried Tom, and clapped his little hands. "Then I shall have someone to play with there? How delightful!"

"Were there no babies up this stream?" asked the lady salmon.

"No! and I grew so lonely. I thought I saw three last night; but they were gone in an instant, down to the sea. So I went too; for I had nothing to play with but caddises and dragonflies and trout."

"Ugh!" cried the lady, "what low company!"

"My dear, if he has been in low company, he has certainly not learnt their low manners," said the salmon.

"No, indeed, poor little dear: but how sad for him to live among such people as caddises, who have actually six legs, the nasty things; and dragonflies, too! why they are not even good to eat; for I tried them once, and they are all hard and empty; and, as for trout, everyone knows what they are." Whereon she curled up her lip, and her husband curled up his too, and looked dreadfully scornful *[omission]*.

"Why do you dislike the trout so?" asked Tom.

"My dear, we do not even mention them, if we can help it; for I am sorry to say they are relations of ours who do us no credit. A great many years ago they were just like us: but they were so lazy, and cowardly, and greedy, that instead of going down to the sea every year to see the world and grow strong and fat, they chose to stay and poke about in the little streams and eat worms and grubs; and they are very properly punished for it; for they have grown ugly and brown and spotted and small; and are actually so **degraded** in their tastes, that they will eat our children."

"And then they pretend to scrape acquaintance with us again," said the lady. "Why, I have actually known one of them propose to a lady salmon, the impudent little creature."

"I should hope," said the gentleman, "that there are very few ladies of our race who would degrade themselves by listening to such a creature for an instant. If I saw such a thing happen, I should consider it my duty to put them both to death upon the spot." So the old salmon said *[omission]*; and what is more, he would have done it too. For you must know, no enemies are so bitter against each other as those who are of the same race; and a salmon looks on a trout as some great folks look on some **little folks**, as something just too much like himself to be tolerated.

Narration and Discussion

Why is Tom so excited to hear that the salmon has met creatures like him before?

According to the salmon, what happened to their relations?

For further thought: It seems likely that Kingsley's young listener might have wondered about that last sentence, and Kingsley might have responded with a "Don't worry about it until you're older." But what do you think he meant?

Poetic Interlude #4

The verses for this chapter are from the poem "The Tables Turned," by William Wordsworth.

Sweet is the lore which Nature brings;
Our meddling intellect
Mis-shapes the beauteous forms of things
We murder to dissect.

Enough of science and of art:
Close up these barren leaves;
Come forth, and bring with you a heart
That watches and receives.

The Water-Babies

Reading #13

Introduction

Tom suddenly encounters an old enemy.

Vocabulary

snipe: a wading bird

torch: a light carried in the hand. Since this was long before battery-powered flashlights (torches) were available, this torch might have been a lantern on a pole, or even something simpler like a long stick with burning material on one end.

muckle fellow: large one

made himself easy: relaxed

hawser: a rope for towing or tying up a ship

Reading

Part One

So the salmon went up, after Tom had warned them of the wicked old otter; and Tom went down, but slowly and cautiously, coasting along the shore. He was many days about it, for it was many miles down to the sea; and perhaps he would never have found his way, if the fairies had not guided him, without his seeing their fair faces, or feeling their gentle hands.

And, as he went, he had a very strange adventure. It was a clear still September night, and the moon shone so brightly down through the water, that he could not sleep, though he shut his eyes as tight as possible.

So at last he came up to the top, and sat upon a little point of rock, and looked up at the broad yellow moon, and wondered what she was, and thought that she looked at him.

And he watched the moonlight on the rippling river, and the black heads of the firs, and the silver-frosted lawns, and listened to the owl's hoot, and the **snipe**'s bleat, and the fox's bark, and the otter's laugh; and smelt the soft perfume of the birches, and the wafts of heather honey off the grouse moor far above; and felt very happy, though he could not well tell why. You, of course, would have been very cold sitting there on a September night, without the least bit of clothes on your wet back; but Tom was a water-baby, and therefore felt cold no more than a fish.

Suddenly, he saw a beautiful sight. A bright red light moved along the river-side, and threw down into the water a long tap-root of flame. Tom, curious little rogue that he was, must needs go and see what it was; so he swam to the shore, and met the light as it stopped over a shallow run at the edge of a low rock. And there, underneath the light, lay five or six great salmon, looking up at the flame with their great goggle eyes, and wagging their tails, as if they were very much pleased at it.

Tom came to the top, to look at this wonderful light nearer, and made a splash. And he heard a voice say: "There was a fish rose."

He did not know what the words meant: but he seemed to know the sound of them, and to know the voice which spoke them; and he saw on the bank three great two-legged creatures, one of whom held the light, flaring and sputtering, and another a long pole. And he knew that they were men, and was frightened, and crept into a hole in the rock, from which he could see what went on.

Part Two

The man with the **torch** bent down over the water, and looked earnestly in; and then he said: "Tak' that **muckle fellow**, lad; he's ower fifteen punds; and haud your hand steady."

Tom felt that there was some danger coming, and longed to warn the foolish salmon, who kept staring up at the light as if he was bewitched. But before he could make up his mind, down came the pole through the water; there was a fearful splash and struggle, and Tom saw that the poor salmon was speared right through, and was lifted out of the water.

And then, from behind, there sprang on these three men three other men; and there were shouts, and blows, and words which Tom recollected to have heard before; and he shuddered and turned sick at them now, for he felt somehow that they were strange, and ugly, and wrong, and horrible.

And it all began to come back to him. They were men; and they were fighting; savage, desperate, up-and-down fighting, such as Tom had seen too many times before. And he stopped his little ears, and longed to swim away; and was very glad that he was a water-baby, and had nothing to do any more with horrid dirty men, with foul clothes on their backs, and foul words on their lips; but he dared not stir out of his hole: while the rock shook over his head with the trampling and struggling of the keepers and the poachers.

All of a sudden there was a tremendous splash, and a frightful flash, and a hissing, and all was still. For into the water, close to Tom, fell one of the men; he who held the light in his hand. Into the swift river he sank, and rolled over and over in the current. Tom heard the men above run along, seemingly looking for him; but he drifted down into the deep hole below, and there lay quite still, and they could not find him.

Tom waited a long time, till all was quiet; and then he peeped out, and saw the man lying. At last he screwed up his courage and swam down to him. "Perhaps," he thought, "the water has made him fall asleep, as it did me."

Then he went nearer. He grew more and more curious, he could not tell why. He must go and look at him. He would go very quietly, of course; so he swam round and round him, closer and closer; and, as he did not stir, at last he came quite close and looked him in the face. The moon shone so bright that Tom could see every feature; and, as he saw, he recollected, bit by bit, it was his old master, Grimes.

Tom turned tail, and swam away as fast as he could.

"Oh dear me!" he thought, "now he will turn into a water-baby. What a nasty troublesome one he will be! And perhaps he will find me out, and beat me again."

So he went up the river again a little way, and lay there the rest of the night under an alder root; but, when morning came, he longed to go down again to the big pool, and see whether Mr. Grimes had turned into a water-baby yet. So he went very carefully, peeping round all the rocks, and hiding under all the roots.

Mr. Grimes lay there still; he had not turned into a water-baby.

Part Three

In the afternoon Tom went back again. He could not rest till he had found out what had become of Mr. Grimes. But this time Mr. Grimes was gone; and Tom made up his mind that he was turned into a water-baby.

He might have **made himself easy,** poor little man; Mr. Grimes did not turn into a water-baby, or anything like one at all. But he did not make himself easy; and a long time he was fearful lest he should meet Grimes suddenly in some deep pool. He could not know that the fairies had carried him away, and put him, where they put everything which falls into the water, exactly where it ought to be *[omission]*.

Then Tom went on down [the river], for he was afraid of staying near Grimes; and as he went, all the vale looked sad. The red and yellow leaves showered down into the river; the flies and beetles were all dead and gone; the chill autumn fog lay low upon the hills, and sometimes spread itself so thickly on the river that he could not see his way. But he felt his way instead, following the flow of the stream, day after day, past great bridges, past boats and barges, past the great town, with its wharfs, and mills, and tall smoking chimneys, and ships which rode at anchor in the stream; and now and then he ran against their **hawsers**, and wondered what they were, and peeped out, and saw the sailors lounging on board smoking their pipes; and ducked under again, for he was terribly afraid of being caught by "man" and turned into a chimney-sweep once more.

He did not know that the fairies were close to him always, shutting the sailors' eyes lest they should see him, and turning him aside from millraces, and sewer-mouths, and all foul and dangerous things.

Narration and Discussion

What do you think has happened to Mr. Grimes?

Why do you think the vale suddenly "looked sad" after Tom's meeting with Grimes?

Sailors and Seababies

Reading #14

Introduction

Tom meets many new creatures, including a somewhat-friendly lobster; but he is still longing to make contact with other water-babies.

Vocabulary

>**buoy:** a bright object that is anchored in water as a marker for ships, or to show danger
>
>**as if his veins had run champagne:** as if his blood were full of soda bubbles
>
>**bass, mullet:** sea fish
>
>**terns:** sea birds, like gulls
>
>**sea-pie:** a kind of magpie (bird)
>
>**turbot:** a fish with a flat body
>
>**pollock:** a fish in the cod family
>
>**purple sea-snails:** probably the species *Janthina janthina*
>
>**a beautiful creature:** Kingsley often keeps us guessing about the identity of his fish and fowl. Is this one possibly a lancetfish? Or a kind of eel with teeth?
>
>**barnacle:** a shelled crustacean known for attaching itself to things (like boats)
>
>**Victoria Cross:** a British medal for extreme bravery
>
>**breastbone:** Children long ago used to make a kind of jumping toy out of a bone, wax and a stick; see Hans Christian Andersen's story "The Jumper."

Places

>**Chesapeake (Bay):** located on the east coast of the United States
>
>**Carolinas:** the states of North and South Carolina, in the United States

Reading

Part One

Poor [Tom], it was a dreary journey for him; and more than once he longed to be back in Vendale, playing with the trout in the bright summer sun. But it could not be. What has been once can never come over again. And people can be little babies, even water-babies, only once in their lives.

Besides, people who make up their minds to go and see the world, as Tom did, must needs find it a weary journey. Lucky for them if they do not lose heart and stop half-way, instead of going on bravely to the end as Tom did *[omission]*. But Tom was always a brave, determined little [boy], who never knew when he was beaten; and on and on he held, till he saw a long way off the red **buoy** through the fog. And then he found, to his surprise, the stream turned round, and running up inland.

It was the tide, of course: but Tom knew nothing of the tide. He only knew that in a minute more the water, which had been fresh, turned salt all round him. And then there came a change over him. He felt as strong, and light, and fresh, **as if his veins had run champagne**; and gave, he did not know why, three skips out of the water, a yard high, and head over heels, just as the salmon do when they first touch the noble rich salt water, which, as some wise men tell us, is the mother of all living things.

He did not care now for the tide being against him. The red buoy was in sight, dancing in the open sea; and to the buoy he would go, and to it he went. He passed great shoals of **bass** and **mullet**, leaping and rushing in after the shrimps, but he never heeded them, or they him.

And once he passed a great black shining seal, who was coming in after the mullet. The seal put his head and shoulders out of water, and stared at him *[omission]*. And Tom, instead of being frightened, said, "How d'ye do, sir; what a beautiful place the sea is!" And the old seal, instead of trying to bite him, looked at him with his soft sleepy winking eyes, and said, "Good tide to you, my little man; are you looking for your brothers and sisters? I passed them all at play outside."

"Oh, then," said Tom, "I shall have playfellows at last," and he swam on to the buoy, and got upon it (for he was quite out of breath) and sat there, and looked round for water-babies: but there were none to be seen.

The sea-breeze came in freshly with the tide and blew the fog away; and the little waves danced for joy around the buoy, and the old buoy danced with them. The shadows of the clouds ran races over the bright blue bay, and yet never caught each other up; and the breakers plunged merrily upon the wide white sands, and jumped up over the rocks, to see what the green fields inside were like, and tumbled down and broke themselves all to pieces, and never minded it a bit, but mended themselves and jumped up again. And the **terns** hovered over Tom like huge white dragonflies with black heads, and the gulls laughed like girls at play, and the **sea-pies**, with their red bills and legs, flew to and fro from shore to shore, and whistled sweet and wild. And Tom looked and looked, and listened; and he would have been very happy, if he could only have seen the water-babies.

Part Two

Then when the tide turned, he left the buoy, and swam round and round in search of them: but in vain. Sometimes he thought he heard them laughing: but it was only the laughter of the ripples. And sometimes he thought he saw them at the bottom: but it was only white and pink shells.

And once he was sure he had found one, for he saw two bright eyes peeping out of the sand. So he dived down, and began scraping the sand away, and cried, "Don't hide; I do want someone to play with so much!" And out jumped a great **turbot** with his ugly eyes and mouth all awry, and flopped away along the bottom, knocking poor Tom over.

And he sat down at the bottom of the sea, and cried salt tears from sheer disappointment. To have come all this way, and faced so many dangers, and yet to find no water-babies! How hard! Well, it did seem hard: but people, even little babies, cannot have all they want without waiting for it, and working for it too, my little man, as you will find out some day.

Part Three

And Tom sat upon the buoy long days, long weeks, looking out to sea, and wondering when the water-babies would come back; and yet they never came. Then he began to ask all the strange things which came in out of the sea if they had seen any; and some said "Yes," and some said nothing at all. He asked the bass and the **pollock**; but they were so greedy after the shrimps that they did not care to answer him a word.

Then there came in a whole fleet of **purple sea-snails**, floating along, each on a sponge full of foam, and Tom said, "Where do you come from, you pretty creatures? and have you seen the water-babies?"

And the sea-snails answered, "Whence we come we know not; and whither we are going, who can tell? We float out our life in the mid-ocean, with the warm sunshine above our heads, and the warm gulf-stream below; and that is enough for us. Yes; perhaps we have seen the water-babies. We have seen many strange things as we sailed along." And they floated away, the [foolish] things, and all went ashore upon the sands.

Then there came in a great lazy sunfish, as big as a fat pig cut in half; and he seemed to have been cut in half too, and squeezed in a clothes-press till he was flat; but to all his big body and big fins he had only a little rabbit's mouth, no bigger than Tom's; and, when Tom questioned him, he answered in a little squeaky feeble voice: "I'm sure I don't know; I've lost my way. I meant to go to the **Chesapeake**, and I'm afraid I've got wrong somehow. Dear me! it was all by following that pleasant warm water. I'm sure I've lost my way." And, when Tom asked him again, he could only answer, "I've lost my way. Don't talk to me; I want to think."

But, like a good many other people, the more he tried to think the less he could think; and Tom saw him blundering about all day, till the coast-guardsmen saw his big fin above the water, and rowed out, and struck a boat-hook into him, and took him away. They took him up to the town and showed him for a penny a head, and made a good day's work of it. But of course Tom did not know that.

Then there came by a shoal of porpoises, rolling as they went—papas, and mammas, and little children—and all quite smooth and shiny, because the fairies French-polish them every morning; and they sighed so softly as they came by, that Tom took courage to speak to them: but all they answered was, "Hush, hush, hush"; for that was all they had learned to say.

[omission for length]

And then there came by **a beautiful creature**, like a ribbon of pure silver with a sharp head and very long teeth; but it seemed very sick and sad. Sometimes it rolled helpless on its side; and then it dashed away glittering like white fire; and then it lay sick again and motionless.

"Where do you come from?" asked Tom. "And why are you so sick and sad?"

"I come from the warm **Carolinas,** and the sandbanks fringed with pines; where the great owl-rays leap and flap, like giant bats, upon the tide. But I wandered north and north, upon the treacherous warm gulf-stream, till I met with the cold icebergs, afloat in the mid ocean. So I got tangled among the icebergs, and chilled with their frozen breath. But the water-babies helped me from among them, and set me free again. And now I am mending every day; but I am very sick and sad; and perhaps I shall never get home again to play with the owl-rays anymore."

"Oh!" cried Tom. "And you have seen water-babies? Have you seen any near here?"

"Yes; they helped me again last night, or I should have been eaten by a great black porpoise."

How vexatious! The water-babies close to him, and yet he could not find one.

Part Four

And then he left the buoy, and used to go along the sands and round the rocks, and come out in the night—**like the forsaken Merman in [Matthew] Arnold's beautiful, beautiful poem**, which you must learn by heart someday.

(The poem begins:

Come, dear children, let us away;

Down and away below!

Now my brothers call from the bay,

Now the great winds shoreward blow,

Now the salt tides seaward flow;

Now the wild white horses play,

Champ and chafe and toss in the spray.

Children dear, let us away!

This way, this way!)

[He would] sit upon a point of rock, among the shining seaweeds, in the low October tides, and cry and call for the water-babies; but he never heard a voice call in return. And at last, with his fretting and crying, he grew quite lean and thin.

But one day among the rocks he found a play-fellow. It was not a water-baby, alas! but it was a lobster; and a very distinguished lobster he was; for he had live **barnacles** on his claws, which is a great mark of distinction in lobsterdom, and no more to be bought for money than a good conscience or the **Victoria Cross**.

Tom had never seen a lobster before; and he was mightily taken with this one; for he thought him the most curious, odd, ridiculous creature he had ever seen; and there he was not far wrong; for all the ingenious men, and all the scientific men, and all the fanciful men, in the world *[omission]* could never invent, if all their wits were boiled into one, anything so curious, and so ridiculous, as a lobster.

He had one claw knobbed and the other jagged; and Tom delighted in watching him hold on to the seaweed with his knobbed claw, while he cut up salads with his jagged one, and then put them into his mouth, after smelling at them, like a monkey. And always the little barnacles threw out their casting-nets and swept the water, and came in for their share of whatever there was for dinner. But Tom was most astonished to see how he fired himself off—snap! Like the leap-frogs which you make out of a goose's **breastbone**. Certainly he took the most wonderful shots, and backwards, too. For, if he wanted to go into a narrow crack ten yards off, what do you think he did? If he had gone in head foremost, of course he could not have turned round. So he used to turn his tail to it, and lay his long horns, which carry his sixth sense in their tips (and nobody knows what that sixth sense is), straight down his back to guide him, and twist his eyes back till they almost came out of their sockets, and then made ready, present, fire, snap!—and away he went, pop into the hole; and peeped out and twiddled his whiskers, as much as to say, "You couldn't do that."

Tom asked him about water-babies. Yes, he said, he had seen them often. But he did not think much of them. They were meddlesome little creatures that went about helping fish and shells which got into scrapes. Well, for his part, [he said], he should be ashamed to be helped by little soft creatures that had not even a shell on their backs. He had lived quite long enough in the world to take care of himself.

He was a conceited fellow, the old lobster, and not very civil to Tom; and you will hear how he had to alter his mind before he was done, as conceited people generally have. But he was so funny, and Tom so lonely, that he could not quarrel with him; and they used to sit in holes in the rocks, and chat for hours.

Narration and Discussion

Why is Tom growing so thin?

Kingsley says about the sunfish: "But, like a good many other people, the more he tried to think the less he could think." What do you think?

Tell about your favourite character in this reading.

Reading #15

Introduction

In this story we meet Ellie again (the little girl from Harthover Place), and her strange companion, **Professor Ptthmllnsprts**.

Special note on the omissions in this section

This particular part of *The Water-Babies* goes off on absurd and wordy tangents, especially in the parts about **Professor Ptthmllnsprts** (see note under **People**).

> One hippopotami cannot get on a bus,
> Because one hippopotami is two hippopotamus…
>
> (Allan Sherman)

As Charles Kingsley himself might say, well, if you don't believe it, you may go and consult an unabridged edition of the book. In the other readings, I have noted [*omissions*] with brackets; but as they are so plentiful in this section, we will leave them aside to avoid tedium.

Vocabulary

>**give the birds their Christmas dinner of crumbs:** an old custom
>
>**The Triumph of Galatea:** This was, originally, a fresco done by the famous artist Raphael; but Raphael's painting (or even smaller versions of it) is not quite as Ellie describes it. Perhaps her picture was by another artist who used the same theme and title.
>
>**hippopotamus major:** There was a scientific debate going on in the early 1860's, that only human beings had a part of the brain called the *hippocampus minor*. Kingsley poked fun at this belief at a meeting of scientists, saying, "We were very much delighted, and I may say, quite interested, to find that we had all hippopotamuses in our brains." As he was also writing *The Water-Babies* at the time, he decided to incorporate the hippopotamus into the story.
>
>**corn:** a painful kind of sore on the foot
>
>**prove a universal negative:** A universal negative says that one kind of thing cannot be part of another group of things.

Sailors and Seababies

Aunt Agitate's Arguments: see previous readings

Holothurian: an echinoderm of the class Holothuroidea. (The Professor is, obviously, showing off.)

Synapta: Synapta maculate, the snake sea cucumber. (Ditto.)

Cephalopod: the class of mollusks that includes the octopus and squid

put him in spirits: preserved his body in a jar of chemicals

they all went home: that is, back to Harthover Place

People

Professor Ptthmllnsprts: Many scholarly papers have been written about the identity of the Professor, which would have no doubt amused Charles Kingsley. He is, pretty much without doubt, a composite of two evolutionary experts; but at least one commentator has pointed out that Kingsley, also being a collector of natural oddities, might have seen himself in the character as well, at least in the idea of taking Tom home and making a pet of him. The professor's name is just a slurred version of "Put Them All In Spirits."

Wise old [Roman]: Decimus Junius Juvenalis. See note **The Greatest Reverence**, below.

The Greatest Reverence: A Note for the Adults

Kingsley writes, "There was a wise old [Roman] once, who said, '*Maxima debetur pueris reverentia*,' [meaning] "The greatest reverence is due to children"; that is, that grown people should never say or do anything wrong before children, lest they should set them a bad example." Charlotte Mason also quotes this saying, although her word order is different:

> *Maxima reverentia debetur pueris* has a wider meaning than it
> generally receives. We take it as meaning that we should not do or
> say anything unseemly before the young, but does it not also include
> a profound and reverent study of the properties and possibilities
> present in a child? (*A Philosophy of Education*)

Apparently by Mason's day, this ancient saying had become a tired educational cliché. However, like Kingsley, Mason liked to look below the surface of things, and she turned this idea on its head. She fully agreed that the Mr. Grimes of the world needed to be stopped; but she was even more concerned about teachers (and parents) who might undermine children's character by subtly misusing their authority, using tactics such as suggestion, influence, or even "love."

Professor Ptthmllnsprts would fall into that misuse-of-authority category as well, due to his refusal to admit that there might be water-babies—even when he had one right in front of him—to such an insignificant, uneducated being as a little girl. But he, at least, was eventually punished for his crimes.

Do we need to call in "a very terrible old fairy" to correct the rest of the mis-users? (Who may, in fact, be us?) Well, in fact, we have a number of better and more pleasant ways, and one of them is to study Charlotte Mason's books, and then to apply her methods to the raising and education of children—and other people—including ourselves.

> The work of education is greatly simplified when we realize that children, apparently all children, want to know all human knowledge; they have an appetite for what is put before them, and, knowing this, our teaching becomes buoyant with the courage of our convictions. (*A Philosophy of Education*)

Reading

Prologue

And about this time there happened to Tom a very strange and important adventure—so important, indeed, that he was very near never finding the water-babies at all; and I am sure you would have been sorry for that.

I hope that you have not forgotten the little white lady all this while.

At least, here she comes, looking like a clean white good little darling, as she always was, and always will be.

For it befell in the pleasant short December days, when the wind always blows from the south-west, till Old Father Christmas comes and spreads the great white table-cloth, ready for little boys and girls to **give the birds their Christmas dinner of crumbs**—it befell (to go on) in the pleasant December days, that Sir John hunting all day, and dining at five, fell asleep every evening, and snored so terribly that all the windows in Harthover shook, and the soot fell down the chimneys *[omission]*.

[And the result of all that was that Sir John's wife, tired of the snoring and the soot, decided to take the children on a holiday to the seaside.]

Part One

Now it befell that, on the very shore, and over the very rocks, where Tom was sitting with his friend the lobster, there walked one day the little white lady, Ellie herself, and with her a very wise man indeed—**Professor Ptthmllnsprts**. He was, as I said, a very great naturalist, and he had come here to collect all the nasty things which he could find on the coast of England. He had met Sir John at Scarborough, or Fleetwood, or somewhere or other (if you don't care where, nobody else does), and had made acquaintance with him, and become very fond of his children.

So Ellie and he were walking on the rocks, and he was showing her about one in ten thousand of all the beautiful and curious things which are to be seen there. But little Ellie was not satisfied with them at all. She liked much better to play with live children, or even with dolls, which she could pretend were alive; and at last she said honestly, "I don't care about all these things, because they can't play with me, or talk to me. If there were little children now in the water, as there used to be, and I could see them, I should like that."

"Children in the water, you strange little duck?" said the professor.

"Yes," said Ellie. "I know there used to be children in the water, and mermaids too, and mermen. I saw them all in a picture at home, of a beautiful lady sailing in a car drawn by dolphins, and babies flying round her, and one sitting in her lap; and the mermaids swimming and playing, and the mermen trumpeting on conch-shells; and it is called '**The Triumph of Galatea**'; and there is a burning mountain in the picture behind. It hangs on the great staircase, and I have looked at it ever since I was a baby, and dreamt about it a hundred times; and it is so beautiful, that it must be true."

But the professor had not the least notion of allowing that things were true, merely because people thought them beautiful. [He] held that no man was forced to believe anything to be true, but what he could see, hear, taste, or handle.

Sidebar: One Hippopotami

[The professor] held very strange theories about a good many things. He had even got up once at the British Association, and declared that apes had **hippopotamus majors** in their brains just as men have. Which was a shocking thing to say; for, if it were so, what would become of the faith, hope, and charity of immortal millions? You may think that there are other more important differences between you and an ape, such as being able to speak, and make machines, and know right from wrong, and say your prayers, and other little matters of that kind; but that is a child's fancy, my dear. Nothing is to be depended on but the great hippopotamus test.

If you have a hippopotamus major in your brain, you are no ape, though you had four hands, no feet, and were more apish than the apes of all aperies.

But if a hippopotamus major is ever discovered in one single ape's brain, nothing will save your great-great-great-great-great-great-great-great-great-great-great-greater-greatest-grandmother from having been an ape too.

No, my dear little man; always remember that the one true, certain, final, and all-important difference between you and an ape is, that you have a hippopotamus major in your brain, and it has none; and that, therefore, to discover one in its brain will be a very wrong and dangerous thing, at which everyone will be very much shocked, as we may suppose they were at the professor.—Though really, after all, it don't much matter; because—as Lord Dundreary and others would put it—nobody but men have hippopotamuses in their brains; so, if a hippopotamus was discovered in an ape's brain, why it would not be one, you know, but something else.

[So the professor had written a paper proving that] there were not, never had been, and could not be, any rational or half-rational beings except men, anywhere, anywhen, or anyhow. And he had to get up very early in the morning to prove that, and to eat his breakfast overnight; but he did it, at least to his own satisfaction. From all which you may guess that the professor was not the least of little Ellie's opinion. So he gave her a succinct compendium of his famous paper at the British Association, in a form suited for the youthful mind. But [omission] instead of being convinced by Professor Ptthmllnsprts' arguments, she only asked the same question over again.

"But why are there not water-babies?"

I trust and hope that it was because the professor trod at that moment on the edge of a very sharp mussel, and hurt one of his **corns** sadly, that he answered quite sharply, forgetting that he was a scientific man, and therefore ought to have known that he couldn't know; and that he was a logician, and therefore ought to have known that he could not **prove a universal negative**—I say, I trust and hope it was because the mussel hurt his corn, that the professor answered quite sharply:

"Because there ain't."

Which was not even good English, my dear little boy; for, as you must know from ***Aunt Agitate's Arguments***, the professor ought to have said, if he was so angry as to say anything of the kind—Because there are not: or are none: or are none of them; or (if he had been reading *Aunt Agitate* too) because they do not exist.

Part Two

And he groped with his net under the weeds so violently, that, as it befell, he caught poor little Tom. He felt the net very heavy; and lifted it out quickly, with Tom all entangled in the meshes.

"Dear me!" he cried. "What a large pink **Holothurian**; with hands, too! It must be connected with **Synapta**." And he took him out.

"It has actually eyes" he cried. "Why, it must be a **Cephalopod**! This is most extraordinary!"

"No, I ain't!" cried Tom, as loud as he could; for he did not like to be called bad names.

"It is a water-baby!" cried Ellie; and of course it was.

"Water-fiddlesticks, my dear!" said the professor; and he turned away sharply. But there was no denying it. It was a water-baby: and he had said a moment ago that there were none. What was he to do?

He would have liked, of course, to have taken Tom home in a bucket. He would not have **put him in spirits**. Of course not. He would have kept him alive, and petted him (for he was a very kind old gentleman), and written a book about him, and given him two long names, of which the first would have said a little about Tom, and the second all about himself. But—what would all the learned men say to him after his speech at the British Association? And what would Ellie say, after what he had just told her?

There was a wise old [Roman] once, who said, "*Maxima debetur pueris reverentia*," [meaning] "The greatest reverence is due to children"; that is, that grown people should never say or do anything wrong before children, lest they should set them a bad example. But some people, and I am afraid the professor was one of them, interpret that in a strange, curious, one-sided, left-handed, topsy-turvy, inside-out, behind-before fashion; for they make it mean, that you must show your respect for children, by never confessing yourself in the wrong to them, even if you know that you are so, lest they should lose confidence in their elders.

Now, if the professor had said to Ellie, "Yes, my darling, it is a water-baby, and a very wonderful thing it is; and it shows how little I know of the wonders of nature, in spite of forty years' honest labour. I was just telling you that there could be no such creatures; and, behold! here is one come to confound my conceit and show me that Nature can do, and has done, beyond all that man's poor fancy can imagine. So, let us thank the Maker, and Inspirer, and Lord of Nature for all His wonderful and glorious works, and try and find out something about this one"; —I think that, if the professor had said that, little Ellie would have believed him more firmly, and respected him more deeply, and loved him better, than ever she had done before.

But he was of a different opinion. He hesitated a moment. He longed to keep Tom, and yet he half wished he never had caught him; and at last he quite longed to get rid of him. So he turned away and poked Tom with his finger, for want of anything better to do; and said carelessly, "My dear little maid, you must have dreamt of water-babies last night, your head is so full of them."

Part Three

Now Tom had been in the most horrible and unspeakable fright all the while; and had kept as quiet as he could, though he was called a Holothurian and a Cephalopod; for it was fixed in his little head that if a man with clothes on caught him, he might put clothes on him too, and make a dirty black chimney-sweep of him again. But, when the professor poked him, it was more than he could bear; and, between fright and rage, he [fought back] as valiantly as a mouse in a corner, and bit the professor's finger till it bled.

"Oh! ah! yah!" cried he; and glad of an excuse to be rid of Tom, dropped him on to the seaweed, and thence he dived into the water and was gone in a moment.

"But it was a water-baby, and I heard it speak!" cried Ellie. "Ah, it is gone!" And she jumped down off the rock to try and catch Tom before he slipped into the sea.

Too late! and what was worse, as she sprang down, she slipped, and fell some six feet, with her head on a sharp rock, and lay quite still.

The professor picked her up, and tried to waken her, and called to her, and cried over her, for he loved her very much: but she would not waken at all. So he took her up in his arms and carried her to her governess, and **they all went home**; and little Ellie was put to bed, and lay there quite still; only now and then she woke up and called out about the water-baby. But no one knew what she meant, and the professor did not tell, for he was ashamed to tell.

And, after a week, one moonlight night, the fairies came flying in at the window and brought her such a pretty pair of wings that she could not help putting them on; and she flew with them out of the window, and over the land, and over the sea, and up through the clouds, and nobody heard or saw anything of her for a very long while.

Editor's Note: Right now our readers are sitting in shock, as Kingsley appears to have killed off yet another major character; and he then continues his absurdities about Professor Ptthmllnsprts, although we are no longer in the mood to laugh at them. However, we will see Ellie again, and honestly quite soon; so bear with us while we finish off the tale of the professor (abbreviated for everyone's sake).

Part Four: The Punishment of Professor Ptthmllnsprts

And this is why they say that no one has ever yet seen a water-baby. For my part, I believe that the naturalists get dozens of them when they are out dredging; but they say nothing about them, and throw them overboard again, for fear of spoiling their theories.

But, you see the professor was found out, as everyone is in due time. A very terrible old fairy found the professor out and took him in hand very severely. But she says she is always most severe with the best people, because there is most chance of curing them. So she took the poor professor in hand: and because he was not content with things as they are, she filled his head with things as they are not, to try if he would like them better; and because he did not choose to believe in a water-baby when he saw it, she made him believe in worse things than water-babies—

in unicorns,
firedrakes,
manticoras,
basilisks,
amphisbaenas,
griffins,
phoenixes,
rocs,
orcs,
dog-headed men,
three-headed dogs,
three-bodied geryons,

and other pleasant creatures, which folks think never existed yet, and which folks hope never will exist, though they know nothing about the matter, and never will; and these creatures so upset, terrified, flustered, aggravated, confused, astounded, horrified, and totally flabbergasted the poor professor that the doctors said that he was out of his wits for three months; and perhaps they were right, as they are now and then.

But he became ever after a sadder and a wiser man; which is a very good thing to become, my dear little boy, even though one has to pay a heavy price for the blessing.

Narration and Discussion

Why didn't the professor want to admit that he was looking at a real-live water-baby?

Do you think his punishment was appropriate?

For further thought: Why do you think Kingsley chose the verse he did to begin this chapter?

Poetic Interlude #5

The verse for this chapter come from Wordsworth's poem "Ode to Duty." After you have read the next few readings, come back and look at the lines Kingsley chose. Can you guess who he might be describing? ("Benignant" means kindly.)

> Stern Lawgiver! yet thou dost wear
> The Godhead's most benignant grace;
> Nor know we anything so fair
> As is the smile upon thy face:
> Flowers laugh before thee on their beds
> And fragrance in thy footing treads;
> Thou dost preserve the stars from wrong;
> And the most ancient heavens, through Thee, are fresh and strong.

Reading #16

Introduction

Tom does his first unselfish deed—and suddenly finds that he is not alone after all.

Vocabulary

three-fathom water: Three fathoms are equivalent to 18 feet (5.48 m).

prawn: a small crustacean, similar to a shrimp

wrasses: a family of brightly-coloured fish

withe (or withy): willow stem

in the lock-up: in jail

lobster pot: lobster trap

the otter: See **Reading #11**

Dr. Dulcimer's famous suburban establishment…: an (imaginary) private school

People

Mrs. Bedonebyasyoudid: A character we have not met yet.

the old fairy with the birch rod: See above.

Polonius: a counsellor to the king in Shakespeare's play *Hamlet*

Jack Tars: sailors

Places

Plymouth: a port city in Devon (the area where Kingsley grew up)

the Mewstone: a small, uninhabited island near Plymouth

Reading

Prologue

But what became of little Tom?

He slipped away off the rocks into the water, as I said before. But he could not help thinking of little Ellie. He did not remember who she was; but he knew that she was a little girl, though she was a hundred times as big as he *[omission]*. He thought about her all that day, and longed to have had her to play with; but he had very soon to think of something else. And here is the account of what happened to him, as it was published next morning in the *Waterproof Gazette*, on the finest watered paper, for the use of the great fairy, **Mrs. Bedonebyasyoudid**, who reads the news very carefully every morning, and especially the police cases, as you will hear very soon.

Part One

[Tom] was going along the rocks in **three-fathom water**, watching the **pollock** catch **prawns**, and the **wrasses** nibble barnacles off the rocks, shells and all, when he saw a round cage of green **withes**; and inside it, looking very much ashamed of himself, sat his friend the lobster, twiddling his horns, instead of thumbs.

"What, have you been naughty, and have they put you **in the lock-up**?" asked Tom.

The lobster felt a little indignant at such a notion, but he was too much depressed in spirits to argue; so he only said, "I can't get out."

"Why did you get in?"

"After that nasty piece of dead fish." He had thought it looked and smelt very nice when he was outside, and so it did, for a lobster; but now he turned round and abused it because he was angry with himself.

"Where did you get in?"

"Through that round hole at the top."

"Then why don't you get out through it?"

"Because I can't." And the lobster twiddled his horns more fiercely than ever, but he was forced to confess. "I have jumped upwards, downwards, backwards, and sideways, at least four thousand times; and I can't get out. I always get up underneath there, and can't find the hole."

Tom looked at the trap, and having more wit than the lobster, he saw plainly enough what was the matter; as you may if you will look at a **lobster pot**.

"Stop a bit," said Tom. "Turn your tail up to me, and I'll pull you through hindforemost, and then you won't stick in the spikes."

But the lobster was so [foolish] and clumsy that he couldn't hit the hole.

Tom reached and clawed down the hole after him, till he caught hold of him; and then, as was to be expected, the clumsy lobster pulled him in head foremost.

"Hullo! here is a pretty business," said Tom. "Now take your great claws, and break the points off those spikes, and then we shall both get out easily."

"Dear me, I never thought of that," said the lobster; "and after all the experience of life that I have had!" You see, experience is of very little good unless a man, or a lobster, has wit enough to make use of it. For a good many people, like old **Polonius**, have seen all the world, and yet remain little better than children after all.

But they had not got half the spikes away when they saw a great dark cloud over them: and lo, and behold, it was **the otter**.

How she did grin and grin when she saw Tom. "Yar!" said she, "you little meddlesome wretch, I have you now! I will serve you out for telling the salmon where I was!" And she crawled all over the pot to get in.

Tom was horribly frightened, and still more frightened when she found the hole in the top, and squeezed herself right down through it, all eyes and teeth. But no sooner was her head inside than valiant Mr. Lobster caught her by the nose and held on. And there they were all three in the pot, rolling over and over, and very tight packing it was. And the lobster tore at the otter, and the otter tore at the lobster, and both squeezed and thumped poor Tom till he had no breath left in his body; and I don't know what would have happened to him if he had not at last got on the otter's back, and safe out of the hole.

He was right glad when he got out: but he would not desert his friend who had saved him; and the first time he saw his tail uppermost he caught hold of it, and pulled with all his might.

But the lobster would not let go.

"Come along," said Tom; "don't you see she is dead?" And so she was, quite drowned and dead. And that was the end of the wicked otter.

But the lobster would not let go.

"Come along, you [silly] old stick-in-the-mud," cried Tom, "or the fisherman will catch you!" And that was true, for Tom felt some one above beginning to haul up the pot.

But the lobster would not let go.

Tom saw the fisherman haul him up to the boat-side, and thought it was all up with him. But when Mr. Lobster saw the fisherman, he gave such a furious and tremendous snap, that he snapped out of his hand, and out of the pot, and safe into the sea. But he left his knobbed claw behind him; for it never came into his [foolish] head to let go after all, so he just shook his claw off as the easier method.

Part Two (Optional)

Kingsley veers off here to tell a story within the story.

Tom asked the lobster why he never thought of letting go. He said very determinedly that it was a point of honour among lobsters.

And so it is, as the **Mayor of Plymouth** found out once to his cost—eight or nine hundred years ago, of course; for if it had happened lately it would be personal to mention it.

For one day he was so tired with sitting on a hard chair, in a grand furred gown, with a gold chain round his neck, that he decided he would go and have an afternoon's fun, like any schoolboy, and catch lobsters with an iron hook. So to **the Mewstone** he went, and for lobsters he looked. And when he came to a certain crack in the rocks he was so excited that, instead of putting in his hook, he put in his hand; and Mr. Lobster was at home, and caught him by the finger, and held on.

"Yah!" said the mayor, and pulled as hard as he dared: but the more he pulled, the more the lobster pinched, till he was forced to be quiet.

Then he tried to get his hook in with his other hand; but the hole was too narrow.

Then he pulled again; but he could not stand the pain.

Then he shouted and bawled for help: but there was no one near *[omission]*. Then he began to turn a little pale; for the tide flowed, and still the lobster held on.

Then he turned quite white; for the tide was up to his knees, and still the lobster held on.

Then he thought of cutting off his finger; but he wanted two things to do it with—courage and a knife; and he had got neither.

Then he turned quite yellow; for the tide was up to his waist, and still the lobster held on.

Then he thought over all the naughty things he ever had done; all the sand which he had put in the sugar, and the sloe-leaves in the tea, and the water in the treacle, and the salt in the tobacco (because his brother was a brewer, and a man must help his own kin).

Then he turned quite blue; for the tide was up to his breast, and still the lobster held on.

Then, I have no doubt, he repented fully of all the said naughty things which he had done, and promised to mend his life, as too many do when they think they have no life left to mend. Whereby, as they fancy, they make a very cheap bargain. But **the old fairy with the birch rod** soon undeceives them.

And then he grew all colours at once, and turned up his eyes like a duck in thunder; for the water was up to his chin, and still the lobster held on.

And then came a man-of-war's boat round the Mewstone, and saw his head sticking up out of the water. One said it was a keg of brandy, and another that it was a coconut, and another that it was a buoy loose *[omission]*; but just then such a yell came out of a great hole in the middle of it that the midshipman in charge guessed what it was, and bade [them] pull up to it as fast as they could.

So somehow or other the **Jack Tars** got the lobster out, and set the mayor free, and put him ashore at the Barbican. He never went lobster-catching again; and we will hope he put no more salt in the tobacco, not even to sell his brother's beer. And that is the story of the Mayor of Plymouth, which has two advantages—first, that of being quite true; and second, that of having (as folks say all good stories ought to have) no moral whatsoever: no more, indeed, has any part of this book, because it is a fairy tale, you know.

Part Three

And now happened to Tom a most wonderful thing; for he had not left the lobster five minutes before he came upon a water-baby.

Sailors and Seababies

A real live water-baby, sitting on the white sand, very busy about a little point of rock. And when it saw Tom it looked up for a moment, and then cried, "Why, you are not one of us. You are a new baby! Oh, how delightful!" And it ran to Tom, and Tom ran to it, and they hugged and kissed each other for ever so long, they did not know why. But they did not want any introductions there under the water.

At last Tom said, "Oh, where have you been all this while? I have been looking for you so long, and I have been so lonely."

"We have been here for days and days. There are hundreds of us about the rocks. How was it you did not see us, or hear us when we sing and romp every evening before we go home?"

Tom looked at the baby again, and then he said: "Well, this is wonderful! I have seen things just like you again and again, but I thought you were shells, or sea-creatures. I never took you for water-babies like myself."

Now, was not that very odd? So odd, indeed, that you will, no doubt, want to know how it happened, and why Tom could never find a water-baby till after he had got the lobster out of the pot. And, if you will read this story nine times over, and then think for yourself, you will find out why. It is not good for little boys to be told everything, and never to be forced to use their own wits. They would learn, then, no more than they do at **Dr. Dulcimer's famous suburban establishment for the idler members of the youthful aristocracy**, where the masters learn the lessons and the boys hear them—which saves a great deal of trouble—for the time being.

Narration and Discussion

Tell the story of Tom's rescue of the lobster, as it might have been told in the *Waterproof Gazette*.

Kingsley says, "It is not good for little boys to be told everything, and never to be forced to use their own wits." Do you agree?

For further thought (mostly for the adults): Kingsley mentions a school "where the masters learn the lessons and the boys hear them—which saves a great deal of trouble—for the time being." What do you think Charlotte Mason might say about that?

Reading #17

Introduction

Tom finds the home of the water-babies, and we hear the story of St. Brendan.

The Water-Babies

Vocabulary

shillelagh: a thick stick, often used as a weapon

till the coming of the Cocqcigrues (kok-se-groo): Do you remember this phrase from **Reading #6?** We will hear it once more later on.

firth: a narrow inlet of the sea

basalt: a kind of volcanic rock

serpentine: a dark green mineral

sandstone: a sedimentary rock made up of grains of sand or quartz cemented together

grotto: a small cave

madrepore: a reef-building coral, or the polyp which produces it

People

St. Brendan: Brendan of Clonfert, the Irish saint also known as Brendan the Navigator. **Note on spelling:** Kingsley's text spells his name **Brandan**. I have changed it to **Brendan** as that seems to be the standard current spelling.

Fourier: Jean-Baptiste Joseph Fourier, French mathematician and physicist

Queen Amphitrite: In Greek mythology, Amphitrite was the queen of the sea, and the wife of Poseidon

Places

Staffa: an island of Scotland, known for its basalt formations

Kynance: a cove in Cornwall, England, known for its cliffs

Livermead: a spot near Torquay, in Devon (England), known for its red **sandstone**

Capri, **Adelsberg:** sites in Italy and Slovenia

Reading

Part One

"Now," said the baby, "come and help me, or I shall not have finished before my brothers and sisters come, and it is time to go home."

"What shall I help you at?"

"At this poor dear little rock; a great clumsy boulder came rolling by in the last storm, and knocked all its head off, and rubbed off all its flowers. And now I must plant it again with seaweeds, and coralline, and anemones, and I will make it the prettiest little rock-garden on all the shore."

So they worked away at the rock, and planted it, and smoothed the sand down round it, and capital fun they had till the tide began to turn. And then Tom heard all the other babies coming, laughing and singing and shouting and romping; and the noise they made was just like the noise of the ripple. So he knew that he had been hearing and seeing the water-babies all along; only he did not know them, because his eyes and ears were not opened.

And in they came, dozens and dozens of them, some bigger than Tom and some smaller, all in the neatest little white bathing dresses; and when they found that he was a new baby, they hugged him and kissed him, and then put him in the middle and danced round him on the sand, and there was no one ever so happy as poor little Tom.

"Now then," they cried all at once, "we must come away home, we must come away home, or the tide will leave us dry. We have mended all the broken seaweed, and put all the rock-pools in order, and planted all the shells again in the sand, and nobody will see where the ugly storm swept in last week."

And this is the reason why the rock-pools are always so neat and clean; because the water-babies come inshore after every storm to sweep them out, and comb them down, and put them all to rights again. Only where men are wasteful and dirty, and let sewers run into the sea instead of putting the stuff upon the fields like thrifty reasonable souls; or throw herrings' heads and dead dog-fish, or any other refuse, into the water; or in any way make a mess upon the clean shore—there the water-babies will not come, sometimes not for hundreds of years (for they cannot abide anything smelly or foul), but leave the sea-anemones and the crabs to clear away everything, till the good tidy sea has covered up all the dirt in soft mud and clean sand, where the water-babies can plant live cockles and whelks and razor-shells and sea-cucumbers and golden-combs, and make a pretty live garden again, after man's dirt is cleared away.

(And that, I suppose, is the reason why there are no water-babies at any watering-place which I have ever seen.)

Part Two (Optional)

Again, a story within the story.

And where is the home of the water-babies? In **St. Brendan's** fairy isle. Did you never hear of the blessed St. Brendan, how he preached to the wild Irish on the wild, wild Kerry coast, he and five other hermits, till they were weary and longed to rest?

For the [people there] would not listen to them, or come to confession and to mass, but liked better to brew *[omission]*, and dance *[omission]*, and knock each other over the head with **shillelaghs** *[omission]*, and steal each other's cattle, and burn each other's homes; till St. Brendan and his friends were weary of them, for they would not learn to be peaceable Christians at all.

So St. Brendan went out to the point of Old Dunmore, and looked over the tideway roaring round the Blasquets, at the end of all the world, and away into the ocean, and sighed— "Ah that I had wings as a dove!" And far away, before the setting sun, he saw a blue fairy sea, and golden fairy islands, and he said, "Those are the islands of the blessed." Then he and his friends got into a [boat], and sailed away and away to the westward *[omission for content]*.

And when St. Brendan and the hermits came to that fairy isle they found it overgrown with cedars and full of beautiful birds; and he sat down under the cedars and preached to all the birds in the air. And they liked his sermons so well that they told the fishes in the sea; and they came, and St. Brendan preached to them; and the fishes told the water-babies, who live in the caves under the isle; and they came up by hundreds every Sunday, and St. Brendan got quite a neat little Sunday-school. And there he taught the water-babies for a great many hundred years, till his eyes grew too dim to see, and his beard grew so long that he dared not walk for fear of treading on it, and then he might have tumbled down. And at last he and the five hermits fell fast asleep under the cedar-shades, and there they sleep unto this day. But the fairies took to the water-babies, and taught them their lessons themselves.

And some say that St. Brendan will awake and begin to teach the babies once more: but some think that he will sleep on, for better for worse, **till the coming of the Cocqcigrues**. But, on still clear summer evenings, when the sun sinks down into the sea, among golden cloud-capes and cloud-islands, and locks and **firths** of azure sky, the sailors fancy that they see, away to westward, St. Brendan's fairy isle *[omission]*.

Part Three

Now when Tom got there, he found that the isle stood all on pillars, and that its roots were full of caves. There were pillars of black **basalt**, like **Staffa**; and pillars of green and crimson **serpentine**, like **Kynance**; and pillars ribboned with red and white and yellow **sandstone**, like **Livermead**; and there were blue **grottoes** like **Capri**, and white grottoes like **Adelsberg**; all curtained and draped with seaweeds, purple and crimson, green and brown; and strewn with soft white sand, on which the water-babies sleep every night. But, to keep the place clean and sweet, the crabs picked up all the scraps off the floor and ate them like so many monkeys; while the rocks were covered with ten thousand sea-anemones, and corals and **madrepores**, who scavenged the water all day long, and kept it nice and pure.

But, to make up to them for having to do such nasty work, they were not left black and dirty, as poor chimney-sweeps and dustmen are. No; the fairies are more considerate and just than that, and have dressed them all in the most beautiful colours and patterns, till they look like vast flower-beds of [bright] blossoms. If you think I am talking nonsense, I can only say that it is true; and that an old gentleman named **Fourier** used to say that we ought to do the same by chimney-sweeps and dustmen, and honour them instead of despising them *[omission]*.

Sailors and Seababies

And there were the water-babies in thousands, more than Tom, or you either, could count.—All the little children whom the good fairies [care for], because their cruel mothers and fathers will not; all who are untaught and brought up [without knowledge of God], and all who come to grief by ill-usage or ignorance or neglect *[omission]*; they were all there, except, of course, the babes of Bethlehem who were killed by wicked King Herod; for they were taken straight to heaven long ago, as everybody knows, and we call them the Holy Innocents.

Narration and Discussion

This passage has lots of ideas that someone might agree with, or disagree with, or argue with. Tell about one thing that you think Kingsley got right, and something you are not sure about. Is there anything that you think he is quite wrong on?

Why do you think Kingsley differentiates between the mess and damage caused by boulders or storms, and that created by human pollution?

Creative narration: You are a water-baby. What's on your to-do list for today?

Reading #18

Introduction

Tom now meets someone who will teach him to "take care what he is at."

Vocabulary

- **water-snakes:** In an omitted passage, Kingsley described the island's "police force," run by a bunch of fierce water-snakes.

- **anemones** (a-nem-oh-nees): They have been mentioned already, but this seems to be a good place to explain the difference between land anemones (a plant) and sea anemones, which are actually part of the animal kingdom. They are related to the corals, jellyfish, and *Hydra*.

- **sea-bullseyes, sea-toffee:** bullseyes and toffee are types of candy

- **take them in:** fool them

- **birched:** beat them with her birch rod

- **butties:** men who hired labourers for coal mining

- **sea-nettles:** a kind of jellyfish

Reading

Part One

But I wish Tom had given up all his naughty tricks, and left off tormenting dumb animals now that he had plenty of playfellows to amuse him. Instead of that, I am sorry to say, he would meddle with the creatures, all but the **water-snakes**, for they would stand no nonsense.

So he tickled the madrepores, to make them [close up]; and frightened the crabs, to make them hide in the sand and peep out at him with the tips of their eyes; and put stones into the **anemones'** mouths, to make them fancy that their dinner was coming.

The other children warned him, and said, "Take care what you are at. Mrs. Bedonebyasyoudid is coming." But Tom never heeded them, being quite riotous with high spirits and good luck, till, one Friday morning early, Mrs. Bedonebyasyoudid came indeed.

A very tremendous lady she was; and when the children saw her they all stood in a row, very upright indeed, and smoothed down their bathing dresses, and put their hands behind them, just as if they were going to be examined by the inspector. And she had on a black bonnet, and a black shawl *[omission]*, and a pair of large green spectacles, and a great hooked nose, hooked so much that the bridge of it stood quite up above her eyebrows; and under her arm she carried a great birch-rod. Indeed, she was so ugly that Tom was tempted to make faces at her: but did not; for he did not admire the look of the birch-rod under her arm.

And she looked at the children one by one, and seemed very much pleased with them, though she never asked them one question about how they were behaving; and then began giving them all sorts of nice sea-things—sea-cakes, sea-apples, sea-oranges, **sea-bullseyes, sea-toffee**; and to the very best of all she gave sea-ices, made out of sea-cows' cream, which never melt under water *[omission]*.

Now little Tom watched all these sweet things given away, till his mouth watered, and his eyes grew as round as an owl's. For he hoped that his turn would come at last; and so it did. For the lady called him up, and held out her fingers with something in them, and popped it into his mouth; and, lo and behold, it was a nasty cold hard pebble.

"You are a very cruel woman," said he, and began to whimper.

"And you are a very cruel boy; who puts pebbles into the sea-anemones' mouths, to **take them in**, and make them fancy that they had caught a good dinner! As you did to them, so I must do to you."

"Who told you that?" said Tom.

"You did yourself, this very minute."

Tom had never opened his lips; so he was very much taken aback indeed.

"Yes; every one tells me exactly what they have done wrong; and that without knowing it themselves. So there is no use trying to hide anything from me. Now go, and be a good boy, and I will put no more pebbles in your mouth, if you put none in other creatures."

"I did not know there was any harm in it," said Tom.

"Then you know now. People continually say that to me; but I tell them, if you don't know that fire burns, that is no reason that it should not burn you; and if you don't know that dirt breeds fever, that is no reason why the fevers should not kill you. The lobster did not know that there was any harm in getting into the lobster-pot; but it caught him all the same."

"Dear me," thought Tom, "she knows everything!" And so she did, indeed.

"And so, if you do not know that things are wrong, that is no reason why you should not be punished for them; though not as much, not as much, my little man," (and the lady looked very kindly, after all), "as if you did know."

"Well, you are a little hard on a poor lad," said Tom.

"Not at all; I am the best friend you ever had in all your life. But I will tell you; I cannot help punishing people when they do wrong. I like it no more than they do; I am often very, very sorry for them, poor things: but I cannot help it. If I tried not to do it, I should do it all the same. For I work by machinery, just like an engine; and am full of wheels and springs inside; and am wound up very carefully, so that I cannot help going."

"Was it long ago since they wound you up?" asked Tom. For he thought, the cunning little fellow, "She will run down some day: or they may forget to wind her up, as old Grimes used to forget to wind up his watch when he came in from the public-house; and then I shall be safe."

"I was wound up once and for all, so long ago, that I forget all about it."

"Dear me," said Tom, "you must have been made a long time!"

"I never was made, my child; and I shall go for ever and ever; for I am as old as Eternity, and yet as young as Time." And there came over the lady's face a very curious expression—very solemn, and very sad; and yet very, very sweet. And she looked up and away, as if she were gazing through the sea, and through the sky, at something far, far off; and as she did so, there came such a quiet, tender, patient, hopeful smile over her face that Tom thought for the moment that she did not look ugly at all. And no more she did; for she was like a great many people who have not a pretty feature in their faces, and yet are lovely to behold, and draw little children's hearts to them at once; because though the house is plain enough, yet from the windows a beautiful and good spirit is looking forth.

And Tom smiled in her face, she looked so pleasant for the moment. And the strange fairy smiled too and said: "Yes. You thought me very ugly just now, did you not?" Tom hung down his head, and got very red about the ears.

"And I am very ugly. I am the ugliest fairy in the world; and I shall be, till people behave themselves as they ought to do. And then I shall grow as handsome as my sister, who is the loveliest fairy in the world; and her name is Mrs. Doasyouwouldbedoneby. So she begins where I end, and I begin where she ends; and those who will not listen to her must listen to me, as you will see. Now, all of you run away, except Tom; and he may stay and see what I am going to do. It will be a very good warning for him to begin with, before he goes to school.

"Now, Tom, every Friday I come down here and call up all who have ill-used little children and serve them as they served the children."

And at that Tom was frightened, and crept under a stone; which made the two crabs who lived there very angry, and frightened their friend the butterfish into flapping hysterics: but he would not move for them.

[Omission for length and content: Mrs. Bedonebyasyoudid summons the doctors who treat little children in foolish ways, and gives them a taste of their own medicine. She also gets her revenge on parents who make children wear uncomfortable clothes and shoes.]

Then she called up all the careless nurserymaids, and stuck pins into them all over, and wheeled them about in perambulators with tight straps across their stomachs and their heads and arms hanging over the side, till they [felt] quite sick *[omission]*.

[Then she] called up all the cruel schoolmasters—whole regiments and brigades of them; and when she saw them, she frowned most terribly, and set to work in earnest, as if the best part of the day's work was to come *[omission]*. And she boxed their ears, and thumped them over the head with rulers, and pandied their hands with canes, and told them that they told stories, and were this and that bad sort of people; and the more they were very indignant, and stood upon their honour, and declared they told the truth, the more she declared they were not, and that they were only telling lies; and at last she **birched** them all round soundly with her great birch-rod and [gave them each three thousand lines of memory work] to learn by heart before she came back next Friday. And at that they all cried and howled so, that their breaths came all up through the sea like bubbles out of soda-water; and that is one reason of the bubbles in the sea.

There are others: but that is the one which principally concerns little boys. And by that time she was so tired that she was glad to stop; and, indeed, she had done a very good day's work.

Part Three

Tom did not quite dislike the old lady; but he could not help thinking her a little spiteful—and no wonder if she was, poor old soul; for if she has to wait to grow handsome till people do as they would be done by, she will have to wait a very long time. Poor old Mrs. Bedonebyasyoudid! she has a great deal of hard work before her, and had better have been born a washerwoman, and stood over a tub all day; but, you see, people cannot always choose their own profession.

But Tom longed to ask her one question; and after all, whenever she looked at him, she did not look cross at all; and now and then there was a funny smile in her face, and she chuckled to herself in a way which gave Tom courage, and at last he said: "Pray, ma'am, may I ask you a question?"

"Certainly, my little dear."

"Why don't you bring all the bad masters here and serve them out too? The **butties** that knock about the poor collier-boys; and the nailers that file off their lads' noses and hammer their fingers; and all the master sweeps, like my master Grimes? I saw him fall into the water long ago; so I surely expected he would have been here. I'm sure he was bad enough to me."

Then the old lady looked so very stern that Tom was quite frightened, and sorry that he had been so bold. But she was not angry with him. She only answered, "I look after them all the week round; and they are in a very different place from this, because they knew that they were doing wrong." She spoke very quietly; but there was something in her voice which made Tom tingle from head to foot, as if he had got into a shoal of **sea-nettles**.

"But these people," she went on, "did not know that they were doing wrong: they were only [foolish] and impatient; and therefore I only punish them till they become patient, and learn to use their common sense like reasonable beings. But as for chimney-sweeps, and collier-boys, and nailer lads, my sister has set good people to stop all that sort of thing; and very much obliged to her I am; for if she could only stop the cruel masters from ill-using poor children, I should grow handsome at least a thousand years sooner. And now do you be a good boy, and do as you would be done by, which they did not; and then, when my sister, Madame Doasyouwouldbedoneby, comes on Sunday, perhaps she will take notice of you, and teach you how to behave. She understands that better than I do." And so she went.

Narration and Discussion

Why did Mrs. Bedonebyasyoudid put a pebble in Tom's mouth? Do you think that he will get sea-candies instead, next time she comes?

Reading #19

Introduction

In this short passage we meet the nicer-looking sister of Mrs. Bedonebyasyoudid.

Vocabulary

cuddly: Apparently the first recorded use of this word in English.

"The doll you lost!": This poem is included in the *AO Year One Poetry Anthology*.

***Aunt Agitate's Arguments*:** see previous notes

Reading

Tom was very glad to hear that there was no chance of meeting Grimes again, though he was a little sorry for him, considering that he used sometimes to give him the leavings of the beer: but he determined to be a very good boy all Saturday; and he was; for he never frightened one crab, nor tickled any live corals, nor put stones into the sea anemones' mouths, to make them fancy they had got a dinner; and when Sunday morning came, sure enough, Mrs. Doasyouwouldbedoneby came too. Whereat all the little children began dancing and clapping their hands, and Tom danced too with all his might.

And as for the pretty lady, I cannot tell you what the colour of her hair was, or of her eyes: no more could Tom; for, when any one looks at her, all they can think of is, that she has the sweetest, kindest, tenderest, funniest, merriest face they ever saw, or want to see. But Tom saw that she was a very tall woman, as tall as her sister; but instead of being gnarly [omission], and scaly, and prickly, like her, she was the most nice, soft [omission], **cuddly**, delicious creature who ever [held] a baby; and she understood babies thoroughly, for she had plenty of her own, whole rows and regiments of them, and has to this day.

And all her delight was, whenever she had a spare moment, to play with babies, in which she showed herself a woman of sense; for babies are the best company, and the pleasantest playfellows, in the world; at least, so all the wise people in the world think.

And therefore when the children saw her, they naturally all caught hold of her, and pulled her till she sat down on a stone, and climbed into her lap, and clung round her neck, and caught hold of her hands; and then they all put their thumbs into their mouths, and began cuddling and purring like so many kittens, as they ought to have done. While those who could get nowhere else sat down on the sand, and cuddled her [bare] feet [omission]. And Tom stood staring at them; for he could not understand what it was all about.

"And who are you, you little darling?" she said.

"Oh, that is the new baby!" they all cried, pulling their thumbs out of their mouths; "and he never had any mother," and they all put their thumbs back again, for they did not wish to lose any time.

"Then I will be his mother, and he shall have the very best place; so get out, all of you, this moment." And she took up two great armfuls of babies—nine hundred under one arm, and thirteen hundred under the other—and threw them away, right and left, into the water. But they [did not mind it], and did not even take their thumbs out of their mouths, but came paddling and wriggling back to her like so many tadpoles, till you could see nothing of her from head to foot for the swarm of little babies.

But she took Tom in her arms, and laid him in the softest place of all, and kissed him, and patted him, and talked to him, tenderly and low, such things as he had never heard before in his life; and Tom looked up into her eyes, and loved her, and loved, till he fell fast asleep from pure love.

And when he woke she was telling the children a story. And what story did she tell them? One story she told them, which begins every Christmas Eve, and yet never ends at all for ever and ever; and, as she went on, the children took their thumbs out of their mouths and listened quite seriously; but not sadly at all; for she never told them anything sad; and Tom listened too, and never grew tired of listening. And he listened

Sailors and Seababies

so long that he fell fast asleep again, and, when he woke, the lady was [holding] him still.

"Don't go away," said little Tom. "This is so nice. I never had any one to cuddle me before."

"Don't go away," said all the children; "you have not sung us one song."

"Well, I have time for only one. So what shall it be?"

"The doll you lost! The doll you lost!" cried all the babies at once.

So the strange fairy sang:—

> I once had a sweet little doll, dears,
>> The prettiest doll in the world;
> Her cheeks were so red and so white, dears,
>> And her hair was so charmingly curled.
> But I lost my poor little doll, dears,
>> As I played in the heath one day:
> And I cried for her more than a week, dears.
>> But I never could find where she lay.
>
> I found my poor little doll, dears,
>> As I played in the heath one day:
> Folks say she is terribly changed, dears,
>> For her paint is all washed away,
> And her arm trodden off by the cows, dears,
>> And her hair not the least bit curled:
> Yet for old sakes' sake she is still, dears,
>> The prettiest doll in the world.

What a silly song for a fairy to sing! And what silly water-babies to be quite delighted at it! Well, but you see they have not the advantage of **Aunt Agitate's Arguments** in the sea-land down below.

"Now," said the fairy to Tom, "will you be a good boy for my sake, and torment no more sea-beasts till I come back?"

"And you will cuddle me again?" said poor little Tom.

"Of course I will, you little duck. I should like to take you with me and cuddle you all the way, only I must not"; and away she went.

So Tom really tried to be a good boy, and tormented no sea-beasts after that as long as he lived; and he is quite alive, I assure you, still.

Oh, how good little boys ought to be who have kind, [gentle] mammas to cuddle them and tell them stories; and how afraid they ought to be of growing naughty, and bringing tears into their mammas' pretty eyes!

Narration and Discussion

We might think that Mrs. Bedonebyasyoudid, with her fearsome appearance and big stick, would be the instructor in behaviour. However, she tells Tom that when Mrs. Doasyouwouldbedoneby comes on Sunday, "perhaps she will take notice of you, and teach you how to behave." Why do you think that might be her job instead?

What is the story "which begins every Christmas Eve, and yet never ends at all for ever and ever?"

Does the song about the lost doll remind you of any other stories?

Poetic Interlude #6

The lines chosen for the next chapter are from Wordsworth's long poem "Ode: Intimations of Immortality from Recollections of Early Childhood." *They seem to be Wordsworth's way of saying, "Children, don't be in too much of a hurry to grow up."*

Thou little Child, yet glorious in the night
Of heaven-born freedom on thy being's height,
Why with such earnest pains dost thou provoke
The years to bring the inevitable yoke,
Thus blindly with thy blessedness at strife?
Full soon thy Soul shall have her earthly freight,
And custom lie upon thee with a weight,
Heavy as frost, and deep almost as life!

Reading #20

Introduction

This is, perhaps, one of the best-remembered passages in *The Water-Babies*: the case of the stolen sweets.

Vocabulary

waxed fat and kicked: Deuteronomy 32:15

sweetmeats: sweets, candies

Reading

[omission at the beginning of the chapter]

Now you may fancy that Tom was quite good, when he had everything that he could want or wish: but you would be very much mistaken. Being quite comfortable is a very good thing; but it does not make people good. Indeed, it sometimes makes them naughty, as it made the people in the Bible, who **waxed fat and kicked**, like horses overfed and underworked.

And I am very sorry to say that this happened to little Tom. For he grew so fond of the sea-bullseyes and sea-lollipops that his foolish little head could think of nothing else: and he was always longing for more, and wondering when the strange lady would come again and give him some, and what she would give him, and how much, and whether she would give him more than the others. And he thought of nothing but lollipops by day, and dreamt of nothing else by night—and what happened then?

That he began to watch the lady to see where she kept the sweet things: and began hiding, and sneaking, and following her about, and pretending to be looking the other way, or going after something else, till he found out that she kept them in a beautiful mother-of-pearl cabinet away in a deep crack of the rocks.

And he longed to go to the cabinet, and yet he was afraid; and then he longed again, and was less afraid; and at last, by continual thinking about it, he longed so violently that he was not afraid at all. And one night, when all the other children were asleep, and he could not sleep for thinking of lollipops, he crept away among the rocks, and got to the cabinet, and behold! it was open.

But, when he saw all the nice things inside, instead of being delighted, he was quite frightened, and wished he had never come there. And then he would only touch them, and he did; and then he would only taste one, and he did; and then he would only eat one, and he did; and then he would only eat two, and then three, and so on; and then he was terrified lest she should come and catch him, and began gobbling them down so fast that he did not taste them, or have any pleasure in them; and then he felt sick, and would have only one more; and then only one more again; and so on till he had eaten them all up.

And all the while, close behind him, stood Mrs. Bedonebyasyoudid.

Part Two

Some people may say, But why did she not keep her cupboard locked? Well, I know.— It may seem a very strange thing, but she never does keep her cupboard locked; every one may go and taste for themselves, and fare accordingly. It is very odd, but so it is; and I am quite sure that she knows best. Perhaps she wishes people to keep their fingers out of the fire, by having them burned.

She took off her spectacles, because she did not like to see too much; and in her pity she arched up her eyebrows into her very hair, and her eyes grew so wide that they would have taken in all the sorrows of the world, and filled with great big tears, as they too often did. But all she said was: "Ah, you poor little dear! you are just like all the rest." But she said it to herself, and Tom neither heard nor saw her.

Now, you must not fancy that she was sentimental at all. If you do, and think that she is going to let off you, or me, or any human being when we do wrong, because she is too tender-hearted to punish us, then you will find yourself very much mistaken, as many a man does every year and every day.

But what did the strange fairy do when she saw all her lollipops eaten? Did she fly at Tom, catch him by the scruff of the neck, hold him *[omission]*, hurry him, hit him, poke him, pull him, pinch him, pound him, put him in the corner, shake him, slap him, set him on a cold stone to reconsider himself, and so forth? Not a bit. You may watch her at work if you know where to find her. But you will never see her do that. For, if she had, she knew quite well Tom would have fought, and kicked, and bit, and said bad words, and turned again that moment into a naughty little *[omission]* chimney-sweep [who trusted no-one]. For, if she had, she would have tempted him to tell lies in his fright; and that would have been worse for him, if possible, than even becoming a [naughty] chimney-sweep again.

No. She leaves that for anxious parents and teachers (lazy ones, some call them), who, instead of giving children a fair trial, such as they would expect and demand for themselves, force them by fright to confess their own faults *[omission]*. Some folks may say, "Ah! but the Fairy does not need to do that if she knows everything already." True. But, if she did not know, she would not surely behave worse than a British judge and jury; and no more should parents and teachers either.

So she just said nothing at all about the matter, not even when Tom came next day with the rest for sweet things. He was horribly afraid of coming: but he was still more afraid of staying away, lest anyone should suspect him. He was dreadfully afraid, too, lest there should be no sweets—as was to be expected, he having eaten them all—and lest then the fairy should inquire who had taken them. But, behold! She pulled out just as many as ever, which astonished Tom, and frightened him still more.

And, when the fairy looked him full in the face, he shook from head to foot:

however she gave him his share like the rest, and he thought within himself that she could not have found him out. But, when he put the sweets into his mouth, he hated the taste of them; and they made him so sick that he had to get away as fast as he could; and terribly sick he was, and very cross and unhappy, all the week after.

Then, when next week came, he had his share again; and again the fairy looked him full in the face; but more sadly than she had ever looked. And he could not bear the sweets: but took them again in spite of himself.

Part Three

And [on Sunday], when Mrs. Doasyouwouldbedoneby came, he wanted to be cuddled like the rest; but she said very seriously:

"I should like to cuddle you; but I cannot, you are so [tough] and prickly."

And Tom looked at himself: and he was all over prickles, just like a sea-egg. Which was quite natural; for you must know and believe that people's souls make their bodies just as a snail makes its shell (I am not joking, my little man; I am in serious, solemn earnest). And therefore, when Tom's soul grew all prickly with naughty tempers, his body could not help growing prickly too, so that nobody would cuddle him, or play with him, or even like to look at him.

What could Tom do now but go away and hide in a corner and cry? For nobody would play with him, and he knew full well why. And he was so miserable all that week that when the ugly fairy came and looked at him once more full in the face, more seriously and sadly than ever, he could stand it no longer, and thrust the **sweetmeats** away, saying, "No, I don't want any: I can't bear them now," and then burst out crying, poor little man, and told Mrs. Bedonebyasyoudid every word as it happened.

He was horribly frightened when he had done so; for he expected her to punish him very severely. But, instead, she only took him up and kissed him, which was not quite pleasant, for her chin was very bristly indeed; but he was so lonely-hearted, he thought that rough kissing was better than none.

"I will forgive you, little man," she said. "I always forgive every one the moment they tell me the truth of their own accord."

"Then you will take away all these nasty prickles?"

"That is a very different matter. You put them there yourself, and only you can take them away."

"But how can I do that?" asked Tom, crying afresh.

"Well, I think it is time for you to go to school; so I shall fetch you a schoolmistress, who will teach you how to get rid of your prickles." And so she went away.

Narration and Discussion

Kingsley says, "Being quite comfortable is a very good thing; but it does not make people good. Indeed, it sometimes makes them naughty…" Do you agree?

Sailors and Seababies

Why did Tom's prickles not disappear, even though he was sorry for stealing?

Who do you think Tom's schoolmistress might be?

Creative narration #1: As Mrs. Bedonebyasyoudid is said to enjoy reading crime stories in the *Waterproof Gazette*, tell the story as it might have been reported there.

Creative narration #2: Retell the story of Tom and the lollipops in any creative format you like.

For further thought: In Charlotte Mason's book *Ourselves*, a book which students will begin reading in AO Year Seven (Form III), she gives some advice that might have helped Tom. She points out that hunger is, in itself, a very helpful thing; if we never felt hungry, we wouldn't eat. However, healthy hunger, which is a good servant, has an "evil twin" called Gluttony, which aims at being the "master." Does this sound like advice that Mrs. Doasyouwouldbedoneby might have given?

> Gluttony leads his victim to the confectioner's windows and makes him think how nice this or that would taste: all his pocket-money goes in tarts, sweets, and toffee... He does not think much about his lessons, because he has a penny in his pocket and is considering what is the nicest thing he can buy for it; or, if he is older, perhaps he has a pound, but his thought is still the same, and Gluttony gets it all... As for nice things, of course we all want nice things now and then; but let us eat what is given to us of the chocolate or fruit at table, and not think any more about it...The best plan is to want to spend your money upon something else—some sort of collection, perhaps; or to save up to buy a present or a fishing-rod or anything worth having. Gluttony lets you alone when you cease to think of him and his good things. (*Ourselves* Book I, pp. 12-14)

Reading #21

Introduction

As Tom begins his "schooling," also discovers that there is something important he has to do. The trouble is, he doesn't want to do it. At all. Not ever.

Vocabulary

she always went away home: As Ellie tries to explain to Tom, "home" is a very beautiful place, but she cannot describe it very well. Based on what happened at the seashore, and on her appearance ("with long robes floating all around her"), it seems

You are the very same little chimney-sweep who came into my bedroom: It is interesting that Ellie recognizes Tom, since when she saw him in her bedroom, he was so dirty, and, also, since he is now a much-changed Water-Baby. We must suppose that something of his essential Tom-ness has always been there.

Other-end-of-Nowhere: The Other-end-of-Nowhere seems to be a place of "letting the punishment fit the crime."

I'll go: We have not been told where Tom must go, but only that it will be somewhere he does not like, to do what he does not like, and help somebody he does not like.

Reading

Part One

Tom was frightened at the notion of a schoolmistress; for he thought she would certainly come with a birch-rod or a cane; but he comforted himself, at last, that she might be something like the old woman in Vendale—which she was not in the least; for, when the fairy brought her, she was the most beautiful little girl that ever was seen, with long curls floating behind her like a golden cloud, and long robes floating all round her like a silver one.

"There he is," said the fairy; "and you must teach him to be good, whether you like or not."

"I know," said the little girl; but she did not seem quite to like, for she put her finger in her mouth, and looked at Tom under her brows; and Tom put his finger in his mouth, and looked at her under his brows, for he was horribly ashamed of himself.

The little girl seemed hardly to know how to begin; and perhaps she would never have begun at all if poor Tom had not burst out crying, and begged her to teach him to be good and help him to cure his prickles; and at that she grew so tender-hearted that she began teaching him as prettily as ever [a] child was taught in the world.

And what did the little girl teach Tom? She taught him, first, what you have been taught ever since you said your first prayers at your mother's knees; but she taught him much more simply. For the lessons in that world, my child, have no such hard words in them as the lessons in this, and therefore the water-babies like them better than you like your lessons, and long to learn them more and more; and grown men cannot puzzle nor quarrel over their meaning, as they do here on land; for those lessons all rise clear and pure *[omission]* out of the everlasting ground of all life and truth.

So she taught Tom every day in the week; only on Sundays **she always went away home**, and the kind fairy took her place. And before she had taught Tom many Sundays, his prickles had vanished quite away, and he was smooth and clean again.

"Dear me!" said the little girl; "why, I know you now. **You are the very same little chimney-sweep who came into my bedroom.**"

"Dear me!" cried Tom. "And I know you, too, now. You are the very little white lady whom I saw in bed." And he [omission] longed to hug and kiss her; but did not, remembering that she was a lady born; so he only jumped round and round her till he was quite tired. And then they began telling each other all their story—how he had got into the water, and she had fallen over the rock; and how he had swum down to the sea, and how she had flown out of the window; and how this, that, and the other, till it was all talked out: and then they both began over again, and I can't say which of the two talked fastest.

And then they set to work at their lessons again, and both liked them so well that they went on well till seven full years were past and gone.

Part Two

You may fancy that Tom was quite content and happy all those seven years; but the truth is, he was not. He had always one thing on his mind, and that was—where little Ellie went, when she went home on Sundays.

To a very beautiful place, she said.

But what was the beautiful place like, and where was it?

Ah! that is just what she could not say. And it is strange, but true, that no one can say; and that those who have been oftenest in it, or even nearest to it, can say least about it, and make people understand least what it is like. There are a good many folks about the **Other-end-of-Nowhere** [*a place we will hear more about later*], who pretend to know it from north to south as well as if they had been penny postmen there; but, as they are safe at the Other-end-of-Nowhere, nine hundred and ninety-nine million miles away, what they say cannot concern us.

But the dear, sweet, loving, wise, good, self-sacrificing people, who really go there, can never tell you anything about it, save that it is the most beautiful place in all the world; and, if you ask them more, they grow modest, and hold their peace, for fear of being laughed at; and quite right they are. So all that good little Ellie could say was, that it was worth all the rest of the world put together. And of course that only made Tom the more anxious to go likewise.

"Miss Ellie," he said at last, "I will know why I cannot go with you when you go home on Sundays, or I shall have no peace, and give you none either."

"You must ask the fairies that."

So when the fairy, Mrs. Bedonebyasyoudid, came next, Tom asked her.

"Little boys who are only fit to play with sea-beasts cannot go there," she said. "Those who go there must go first where they do not like, and do what they do not like, and help somebody they do not like."

"Why, did Ellie do that?"

"Ask her."

And Ellie blushed, and said, "Yes, Tom, I did not like coming here at first; I was so much happier at home, where it is always Sunday. And I was afraid of you, Tom, at first, because—because—"

"Because I was all over prickles? But I am not prickly now, am I, Miss Ellie?"

"No," said Ellie. "I like you very much now; and I like coming here, too."

"And perhaps," said the fairy, "you will learn to like going where you don't like, and helping someone that you don't like, as Ellie has." But Tom put his finger in his mouth, and hung his head down; for he did not see that at all.

So when Mrs. Doasyouwouldbedoneby came, Tom asked her; for he thought in his little head, "She is not so strict as her sister, and perhaps she may let me off more easily."

Ah, Tom, Tom, silly fellow! and yet I don't know why I should blame you, while so many grown people have got the very same notion in their heads. But, when they try it, they get just the same answer as Tom did. For, when he asked the second fairy, she told him just what the first did, and in the very same words.

Tom was very unhappy at that. And, when Ellie went home on Sunday, he fretted and cried all day, and did not care to listen to the fairy's stories about good children, though they were prettier than ever. Indeed, the more he overheard of them, the less he liked to listen, because they were all about children who did what they did not like, and took trouble for other people, and worked to feed their little brothers and sisters instead of caring only for their play. And, when she began to tell a story about a holy child in old times, who [died because he] would not worship idols, Tom could bear no more, and ran away and hid among the rocks.

Part Three

And, when Ellie came back, he was shy with her, because he fancied she looked down on him, and thought him a coward. And then he grew quite cross with her, because she was superior to him, and did what he could not do. And poor Ellie was quite surprised and sad; and at last Tom burst out crying; but he would not tell her what was really in his mind. And all the while he was eaten up with curiosity to know where Ellie went to; so that he began not to care for his playmates, or for the sea-palace, or anything else. But perhaps that made matters all the easier for him; for he grew so discontented with everything round him that he did not care to stay, and did not care where he went.

"Well," he said, at last, "I am so miserable here, **I'll go**; if only you will go with me?"

"Ah!" said Ellie, "I wish I might; but the worst of it is, that the fairy says that you must go alone if you go at all. Now don't poke that poor crab about, Tom" (for he was feeling very naughty and mischievous), "or the fairy will have to punish you."

Tom was very nearly saying, "I don't care if she does;" but he stopped himself in time. "I know what she wants me to do," he said, whining most dolefully. "She wants me to go after that horrid old Grimes. I don't like *him*, that's certain. And if I find him, he will turn me into a chimney-sweep again, I know. That's what I have been afraid of all along."

"No, he won't—I know as much as that. Nobody can turn water-babies into sweeps, or hurt them at all, as long as they are good."

Sailors and Seababies

"Ah," said naughty Tom, "I see what you want; you are persuading me all along to go, because you are tired of me, and want to get rid of me."

Little Ellie opened her eyes very wide at that, and they were all brimming over with tears. "Oh, Tom, Tom!" she said, very mournfully—and then she cried, "Oh, Tom! where are you?"

And Tom cried, "Oh, Ellie, where are you?" For neither of them could see each other—not the least. Little Ellie vanished quite away, and Tom heard her voice calling him, and growing smaller and smaller, and fainter and fainter, till all was silent.

Narration and Discussion

Why did Tom not "care for his playmates, or for the sea-palace," or want to hear the fairy's stories anymore?

Why do you think Ellie disappeared? Can Tom help her to come back?

Reading #22

Introduction

Mrs. Bedonebyasyoudid tells a very strange story, but it does convince Tom that doing just-as-you-like can lead to trouble.

Vocabulary

> **make his own bed and lie on it:** Refers to the old saying, "You have made your bed, and now you must lie on it."
>
> **her photographs did not merely represent light and shade, as ours do:** In Kingsley's time, even black-and-white photography was quite new and astonishing.
>
> **[jaw] harp:** a small musical instrument which is twanged against the teeth or lips
>
> **flapdoodle:** foolishness, nonsense
>
> **hippopotamus majors:** See note in **Reading #15**.

Reading

Part One

Who was frightened then but Tom? He swam up and down among the rocks, into all the halls and chambers, faster than ever he swam before, but could not find her. He shouted after her, but she did not answer; he asked all the other children, but they had not seen her; and at last he went up to the top of the water and began crying and screaming for Mrs. Bedonebyasyoudid—which perhaps was the best thing to do—for she came in a moment.

"Oh!" said Tom. "Oh, dear, oh dear! I have been naughty to Ellie, and I have killed her—I know I have killed her."

"Not quite that," said the fairy; "but I have sent her away home, and she will not come back again for I do not know how long."

And at that Tom cried so bitterly that the salt sea was swelled with his tears, and the tide was 3,954,620,819ths of an inch higher than it had been the day before; but perhaps that was owing to the waxing of the moon.

"How cruel of you to send Ellie away!" sobbed Tom. "However, I will find her again, if I go to the world's end to look for her."

The fairy did not slap Tom, and tell him to hold his tongue; but she took him on her lap very kindly, just as her sister would have done; and put him in mind how it was not her fault, because she was wound up inside, like watches, and could not help doing things whether she liked or not. And then she told him how he had been "in the nursery" long enough, and must go out now and see the world, if he intended ever to be a man; and how he must go all alone by himself, as everyone else that ever was born has to go, and see with his own eyes, and smell with his own nose, and **make his own bed and lie on it**, and burn his own fingers if he put them into the fire.

And then she told him how many fine things there were to be seen in the world, and what an odd, curious, pleasant, orderly, respectable, well-managed, and, on the whole, successful (as, indeed, might have been expected) sort of a place it was, if people would only be tolerably brave and honest and good in it; and then she told him not to be afraid of anything he met, for nothing would harm him if he remembered all his lessons, and did what he knew was right. And at last she comforted poor little Tom so much that he was quite eager to go, and wanted to set out that minute. "Only," he said, "if I might see Ellie once before I went!"

"Why do you want that?"

"Because—because I should be so much happier if I thought she had forgiven me."

And in the twinkling of an eye there stood Ellie, smiling, and looking so happy that Tom longed to kiss her; but was still afraid it would not be respectful, because she was a lady born.

Part Two

"I am going, Ellie!" said Tom. "I am going, if it is to the world's end. But I don't like going at all, and that's the truth."

"Pooh! pooh! pooh!" said the fairy. "You will like it very well indeed, you little rogue, and you know that at the bottom of your heart. But if you don't, I will make you like it. Come here, and see what happens to people who do only what is pleasant."

And she took out of one of her cupboards (she had all sorts of mysterious cupboards in the cracks of the rocks) the most wonderful waterproof book, full of such photographs as never were seen. For she had found out photography (and this is a fact) more than 13,598,000 years before anybody was born; and, what is more, **her photographs did not merely represent light and shade, as ours do**, but color also, and all colors, as you may see if you look at a blackcock's tail, or a butterfly's wing, or indeed most things that are or can be, so to speak. And therefore her photographs were very curious and famous, and the children looked with great delight for the opening of the book.

And on the title-page was written, "The History of the great and famous nation of the Doasyoulikes, who came away from the country of Hardwork, because they wanted to play on the **[jaw] harp** all day long."

In the first picture they saw these Doasyoulikes living in the land of Readymade, at the foot of the Happy-go-lucky Mountains, where **flapdoodle** grows wild *[omission]*. They lived very much such a life as those jolly old Greeks in Sicily, whom you may see painted on the ancient vases, and really there seemed to be great excuses for them, for they had no need to work *[omission]*. They were very fond of music, but it was too much trouble to learn the piano or the violin; and as for dancing, that would have been too great an exertion.

So they sat on ant-hills all day long, and played on the [jaw] harp; and, if the ants bit them, why they just got up and went to the next ant-hill, till they were bitten there likewise. And they sat under the flapdoodle-trees, and let the flapdoodle drop into their mouths; and under the vines, and squeezed the grape-juice down their throats; and, if any little pigs ran about ready roasted, crying, "Come and eat me," as was their fashion in that country, they waited till the pigs ran against their mouths, and then took a bite, and were content, just as so many oysters would have been.

They needed no weapons, for no enemies ever came near their land; and no tools, for everything was readymade to their hand; and the stern old fairy Necessity never came near them to hunt them up, and make them use their wits, or die. And so on, and so on, and so on, till there were never such comfortable, easy-going, happy-go-lucky people in the world.

"Well, that is a jolly life," said Tom.

"You think so?" said the fairy. "Do you see that great peaked mountain there behind," said the fairy, "with smoke coming out of its top?"

"Yes."

"And do you see all those ashes, and slag, and cinders lying about?"

"Yes."

"Then turn over the next five hundred years, and you will see what happens next."

And behold the mountain had blown up like a barrel of gunpowder, and then boiled over like a kettle; whereby one-third of the Doasyoulikes were blown into the air, and another third were smothered in ashes; so that there was only one-third left.

"You see," said the fairy, "what comes of living on a burning mountain."

"Oh, why did you not warn them?" said little Ellie.

"I did warn them all that I could. I let the smoke come out of the mountain; and wherever there is smoke there is fire. And I laid the ashes and cinders all about; and wherever there are cinders, cinders may be again. But they did not like to face facts, my dears, as very few people do." *[omission]*

And then she turned over the next five hundred years: and there were the remnant of the Doasyoulikes, doing as they liked, as before. They were too lazy to move away from the mountain; so they said, "If it has blown up once, that is all the more reason that it should not blow up again." And they were few in number: but they only said, "The more the merrier, but the fewer the better fare."

However, that was not quite true; for all the flapdoodle-trees were killed by the volcano, and they had eaten all the roast pigs, who, of course, could not be expected to have little ones. So they had to live very hard, on nuts and roots which they scratched out of the ground with sticks. Some of them talked of sowing corn, as their ancestors used to do, before they came into the land of Readymade; but they had forgotten how to make ploughs (they had forgotten even how to make [jaw] harps by this time), and had eaten all the seed-corn which they brought out of the land of Hardwork years since; and of course it was too much trouble to go away and find more. So they lived miserably on roots and nuts *[omission]*.

And she turned over the next five hundred years. And there they were all living up in trees, and making nests to keep off the rain. And underneath the trees lions were prowling about.

"Why," said Ellie, "the lions seem to have eaten a good many of them, for there are very few left now."

"Yes," said the fairy; "you see it was only the strongest and most active ones who could climb the trees, and so escape."

"But what great, hulking, broad-shouldered chaps they are," said Tom; "they are a rough lot as ever I saw."

"Yes, they are getting very strong now; for the ladies will not marry any but the very strongest and fiercest gentlemen, who can help them up the trees out of the lions' way."

[The story goes on, and the Doasyoulikes continue to devolve into something much less like human beings.]

Then the fairy turned over the next five hundred years. And they were fewer still.

"Why, there is one on the ground picking up roots," said Ellie, "and he cannot walk upright." No more he could; for in the same way that the shape of their feet had altered, the shape of their backs had altered also.

"Why," cried Tom, "I declare they are all apes."

"Something fearfully like it, poor creatures," said the fairy. "They are grown so [foolish] now, that they can hardly think: for none of them have used their wits for many hundred years." *[omission]*

And in the next five hundred years they were all dead and gone, by bad food and wild beasts and hunters *[omission]*. And that was the end of the great and jolly nation of the Doasyoulikes.

And, when Tom and Ellie came to the end of the book, they looked very sad and solemn; and they had good reason so to do, for they really fancied that the men were apes, and never thought, in their simplicity, of asking whether the creatures had **hippopotamus majors** in their brains or not; in which case, as you have been told already, they could not possibly have been apes, though they were more apish than the apes of all aperies.

"And where are they all now?" asked Ellie.

"Exactly where they ought to be, my dear."

Part Three

"Yes!" said the fairy, solemnly, half to herself, as she closed the wonderful book. "Folks say now that I can make beasts into men, by circumstances, and selection, and competition, and so forth. Well, perhaps they are right; and perhaps, again, they are wrong *[omission]*.

"But let them recollect this, that there are two sides to every question, and a downhill as well as an uphill road; and, if I can turn beasts into men, I can, by the same laws of circumstances, and selection, and competition, turn men into beasts. You were very near being turned into a beast once or twice, little Tom. Indeed, if you had not made up your mind to go on this journey, and see the world *[omission]*, I am not sure but that you would have ended as an eft in a pond."

"Oh, dear me!" said Tom; "sooner than that, and be all over slime, I'll go this minute, if it is to the world's end."

Narration and Discussion

It seems unlikely that humans, even lazy humans, would forget how to do all those things! But what might (more realistically) happen to people who will not try to learn or do hard things?

Do you remember the mayfly, earlier on, who said he intended to go out and see the world? Is there a difference between his travel intentions and Tom's?

For further thought: What is the hardest thing you have had to work at learning? Was the effort worthwhile?

For even further thought: Here is a bit more from Charlotte Mason's book *Ourselves*. Just as the good appetite Hunger has his "evil twin" named Gluttony, the helpful servant Rest has his dark side, named Sloth.

> Once Sloth is ruler in Mansoul, the person cannot wake up in the morning, dawdles over his dressing, comes down late for breakfast, hates a walk, can't bear games, dawdles over his [schoolwork], does not want to make boats or whistles, or collect stamps... [and] never does anything for anybody, not because he is unkind or ill-natured,

but because he will not take the trouble.

Poor fellow! he does not know that he is falling daily more and more under the power of a hard master. The less he exerts himself, the less he is able to exert himself, because the muscles, which Restlessness keeps firm and in good order, Sloth relaxes and weakens until it becomes a labour to raise the hand to the head or to drag one foot after another...But take courage, the escape is easy: Restlessness is on the alert to save you from Sloth in the beginning. Up and be doing, whether at work or play. (*Ourselves Book I*, p. 20)

Poetic Interlude #7

The famous biologist and zoologist Louis Agassiz was born in Switzerland in 1807, but later went to the United States and taught at Harvard University. In 1857, there was a great celebration for his fiftieth birthday, and his friend Henry Wadsworth Longfellow was asked to write a poem in his honour. Kingsley chose these lines from "The Fiftieth Birthday of Agassiz" to send Tom off on his journey.

And Nature, the old Nurse, took
The child upon her knee,
Saying, 'Here is a story book
Thy father hath written for thee.

'Come wander with me,' she said,
'Into regions yet untrod,
And read what is still unread
In the Manuscripts of God.'

And he wandered away and away
With Nature, the dear old Nurse,
Who sang to him night and day
The rhymes of the universe.

The Water-Babies

Reading #23

Introduction

Tom sets off on his journey to the Other-end-of-Nowhere. But he doesn't have a map or clear directions, as Mrs. Bedonebyasyoudid says it's better for him to figure out the way for himself.

Vocabulary

propeller: This type of ship was powered by a steam engine, and propelled by one or more large "screws" or propellers. It replaced an earlier type of steamboat, the paddle steamer, and it would still have been fairly new (and exciting) in Kingsley's day.

deep black widow's weeds: mourning clothes

King of the Herrings: probably the giant oarfish (the world's longest bony fish)

sprat: small fish

Gairfowl [or Garefowl]: the Great Auk, a flightless bird that became extinct by the middle of the nineteenth century

bedizened: gaudily dressed or decorated

People

Mother Carey: A figure representing the power of the sea, and especially its storms. Kingsley did not create this name himself; "Mother Carey" was known to sailors in the eighteenth and nineteenth centuries, and has been used in other works of literature such as the novel *Moby-Dick*. It is thought that her name might come from the Latin words *Mater cara*, "dear mother."

Reading

Part One

"Now," said Tom, "I am ready to be off, if it's to the world's end."

"Ah!" said the fairy, "that is a brave, good boy. But you must go farther than the world's end, if you want to find Mr. Grimes; for he is at the Other-end-of-Nowhere. You must go to Shiny Wall, and through the white gate that never was opened; and then you will come to Peacepool, and **Mother Carey's** Haven, where the good whales go when they die. And there Mother Carey will tell you the way to the Other-end-of-Nowhere, and there you will find Mr. Grimes."

"Oh, dear!" said Tom. "But I do not know my way to Shiny Wall, or where it is at all."

"Little boys must take the trouble to find out things for themselves, or they will never grow to be men; so that you must ask all the beasts in the sea and the birds in the air, and if you have been good to them, some of them will tell you the way to Shiny Wall."

"Well," said Tom, "it will be a long journey, so I had better start at once. Good-bye, Miss Ellie; you know I am getting [to be] a big boy, and I must go out and see the world."

"I know you must," said Ellie; "but you will not forget me, Tom. I shall wait here till you come." And she shook hands with him, and bade him good-bye. Tom longed very much again to kiss her; but he thought it would not be respectful, considering she was a lady born; so he promised not to forget her: but his little whirlabout of a head was so full of the notion of going out to see the world, that it forgot her in five minutes: however, though his head forgot her, I am glad to say his heart did not.

Part Two

So he asked all the beasts in the sea, and all the birds in the air, but none of them knew the way to Shiny Wall. For why? He was still too far down south.

Then he met a ship, far larger than he had ever seen—a gallant ocean-steamer, with a long cloud of smoke trailing behind; and he wondered how she went on without sails, and swam up to her to see. A school of dolphins were running races round and round her, going three feet for her one, and Tom asked them the way to Shiny Wall: but they did not know.

Then he tried to find out how she moved, and at last he saw her **[propeller]**, and was so delighted with it that he played under her quarter[deck] all day, till he nearly had his nose knocked off by the fans, and thought it time to move. Then he watched the sailors upon deck, and the ladies, with their bonnets and parasols: but none of them could see him, because their eyes were not opened—as, indeed, most people's eyes are not.

At last there came out into the quarter-gallery a very pretty lady, in **deep black widow's weeds**, and in her arms a baby. She leaned over the quarter-gallery, and looked back and back toward England far away; and as she looked she sang:

> Soft soft wind, from out the sweet south sliding,
>
> Waft thy silver cloud-webs athwart the summer sea;
>
> Thin thin threads of mist on dewy fingers twining
>
> Weave a veil of dappled gauze to shade my babe and me.
>
> Deep deep Love, within thine own abyss abiding,
>
> Pour Thyself abroad, O Lord, on earth and air and sea;

Worn weary hearts within Thy holy temple hiding,

Shield from sorrow, sin, and shame my helpless babe and me.

Her voice was so soft and low, and the music of the air so sweet, that Tom could have listened to it all day. But as she held the baby over the gallery rail, to show it the dolphins leaping and the water gurgling in the ship's wake, lo! and behold, the baby saw Tom. He was quite sure of that; for when their eyes met, the baby smiled and held out his hands; and Tom smiled and held out his hands too; and the baby kicked and leaped, as if it wanted to jump overboard to him.

"What do you see, my darling?" said the lady; and her eyes followed the baby's till she too caught sight of Tom, swimming about among the foam-beads below.

She gave a little shriek and start; and then she said, quite quietly,

"Babies in the sea? Well, perhaps it is the happiest place for them" *[omission for content]*.

And Tom turned away northward, sad and wondering, and watched the great steamer slide away into the dusk, and the lights on board peep out one by one, and die out again, and the long bar of smoke fade away into the evening mist, till all was out of sight.

Part Three

And he swam northward again, day after day, till at last he met the **King of the Herrings**, with a curry-comb growing out of his nose, and a **sprat** in his mouth for a cigar. Tom asked him the way to Shiny Wall; so he bolted his sprat head foremost, and said: "If I were you, young gentleman, I should go to the Allalonestone, and ask the last of the **Gairfowl**. She is of a very ancient clan, very nearly as ancient as my own; and knows a good deal which these modern upstarts don't, as ladies of old houses are likely to do."

Tom asked his way to her, and the King of the Herrings told him very kindly, for he was a courteous old gentleman of the old school, though he was horribly ugly, and strangely **bedizened** too *[omission]*. But just as Tom had thanked him and set off, he called after him: "Hi! I say, can you fly?"

"I never tried," says Tom. "Why?"

"Because, if you can, I should advise you to say nothing to the old lady about it. There; take a hint. Good-bye."

Narration and Discussion

Why do you think the woman and the baby could see Tom, when the others could not?

What do you think Tom will do if he finds Mr. Grimes?

Reading #24

Introduction

The Gairfowl is not a great deal of help; but Mother Carey's "chickens" agree to show Tom the way to Shiny Wall.

Vocabulary

marrocks, dovekies, razorbills: seabirds related to the great auk.

noblesse oblige: (French) Nobility is more than just entitlement; in other words, great privilege requires great responsibility.

deceased: dead. Tom thinks she is saying **diseased**.

petrels: storm petrels, also called "Mother Carey's Chickens"

Places

Jan Mayen's Land: an island in the Arctic Ocean

Reading

Part One

And away Tom went for seven days and seven nights due north-west, till he came to a great cod bank, the like of which he never saw before. The great cod lay below in tens of thousands, and gobbled shell-fish all day long; and the blue sharks roved above in hundreds, and gobbled them when they came up. So they ate, and ate, and ate each other, as they had done since the making of the world; for no man had come here yet to catch them, and find out how rich old Mother Carey is.

And there he saw the last of the Gairfowl, standing up on the Allalonestone, all alone. And a very grand old lady she was, full three feet high, and bolt upright, like some old Highland chieftainess. She had on a black velvet gown, and a white *[omission]* apron, and a very high bridge to her nose (which is a sure mark of high breeding), and a large pair of white spectacles on it, which made her look rather odd: but it was the ancient fashion of her house.

And instead of wings, she had two little feathery arms, with which she fanned herself, and complained of the dreadful heat; and she kept on crooning an old song to herself, which she learnt when she was a little baby-bird, long ago—

> Two little birds they sat on a stone,

> One swam away, and then there was one,
>   With a fal-lal-la-lady.
>
> The other swam after, and then there was none,
>   And so the poor stone was left all alone;
>   With a fal-lal-la-lady.

It was "flew" away, properly, and not "swam" away: but, as she could not fly, she had a right to alter it. However, it was a very fit song for her to sing, because she was a lady herself.

Tom came up to her very humbly, and made his bow; and the first thing she said was— "Have you wings? Can you fly?"

"Oh, dear, no, ma'am; I should not think of such a thing," said cunning little Tom.

"Then I shall have great pleasure in talking to you, my dear. It is quite refreshing nowadays to see anything without wings. They must all have wings, forsooth, now, every new upstart sort of bird, and fly. What can they want with flying, and raising themselves above their proper station in life? In the days of my ancestors no birds ever thought of having wings, and did very well without; and now they all laugh at me because I keep to the good old fashion. Why, the very **marrocks** and **dovekies** have got wings, the vulgar creatures, and poor little ones enough they are; and my own cousins too, the **razorbills**, who are gentlefolk born, and ought to know better than to ape their inferiors."

And so she was running on, while Tom tried to get in a word edgeways; and at last he did, when the old lady got out of breath, and began fanning herself again; and then he asked if she knew the way to Shiny Wall. This is what she said:

> Shiny Wall? Who should know better than I? We all came from Shiny Wall, thousands of years ago, when it was decently cold, and the climate was fit for gentlefolk; but now, what with the heat, and what with these vulgar-winged things who fly up and down and eat everything, so that gentlepeople's hunting is all spoilt, and one really cannot get one's living, or hardly venture off the rock for fear of being flown against by some creature that would not have dared to come within a mile of one a thousand years ago— What was I saying? Why, we have quite gone down in the world, my dear, and have nothing left but our honour. And I am the last of my family. A friend of mine and I came and settled on this rock when we were young, to be out of the way of low people. Once we were a great nation, and spread over all the Northern Isles. But men shot us so, and knocked us on the head, and took our eggs—why, if you will believe it, they say that on the coast of Labrador the sailors used to lay a plank from the rock on board the thing called their ship, and drive us along the plank by hundreds, till we tumbled down into the ship's waist in heaps; and then, I suppose, they ate us, the nasty fellows!

Sailors and Seababies

Well—but—what was I saying? At last, there were none of us left, except on the old Gairfowlskerry, just off the Iceland coast, up which no man could climb. Even there we had no peace; for one day, when I was quite a young girl, the land rocked, and the sea boiled, and the sky grew dark, and all the air was filled with smoke and dust, and down tumbled the old Gairfowlskerry into the sea.

The dovekies and marrocks, of course, all flew away; but we were too proud to do that. Some of us were dashed to pieces, and some drowned; and those who were left got away to Eldey, and the dovekies tell me they are all dead now, and that another Gairfowlskerry has risen out of the sea close to the old one, but that it is such a poor flat place that it is not safe to live on: and so here I am left alone.

This was the Gairfowl's story, and, strange as it may seem, it is every word of it true.

"If you only had had wings!" said Tom; "then you might all have flown away too."

"Yes, young gentleman: and if people are not gentlemen and ladies, and forget that **noblesse oblige**, they will find it as easy to get on in the world as other people who don't care what they do. Why, if I had not recollected that *noblesse oblige*, I should not have been all alone now." And the poor old lady sighed.

"How was that, ma'am?"

"Why, my dear, a gentleman came hither with me, and after we had been here some time, he wanted to marry—in fact, he actually proposed to me. Well, I can't blame him; I was young, and very handsome then, I don't deny: but, you see, I could not hear of such a thing, because he was my **deceased** sister's husband, you see?"

"Of course not, ma'am," said Tom; though, of course, he knew nothing about it. "She was very much **diseased**, I suppose?"

"You do not understand me, my dear. I mean, that being a lady, and with right and honourable feelings, as our house always has had, I felt it my duty to snub him, and howk him, and peck him continually, to keep him at his proper distance; and, to tell the truth, I once pecked him a little too hard, poor fellow, and he tumbled backwards off the rock, and—really, it was very unfortunate, but it was not my fault—a shark coming by saw him flapping, and snapped him up. And since then I have lived all alone—

with a fal-lal-la-lady.

"And soon I shall be gone, my little dear, and nobody will miss me; and then the poor stone will be left all alone."

"But, please, which is the way to Shiny Wall?" said Tom.

"Oh, you must go, my little dear—you must go. Let me see—I am sure—that is—really, my poor old brains are getting quite puzzled. Do you know, my little dear, I am afraid, if you want to know, you must ask some of these vulgar birds about, for I have quite forgotten."

And the poor old Gairfowl began to cry tears of pure oil; and Tom was quite sorry for her; and for himself too, for he was at his wit's end whom to ask.

Part Three

But by there came a flock of **petrels**, who are Mother Carey's own chickens; and Tom thought them much prettier than Lady Gairfowl, and so perhaps they were; for Mother Carey had had a great deal of fresh experience between the time that she invented the Gairfowl and the time that she invented them. They flitted along like a flock of black swallows, and hopped and skipped from wave to wave, lifting up their little feet behind them so daintily, and whistling to each other so tenderly, that Tom fell in love with them at once, and called them to know the way to Shiny Wall.

"Shiny Wall? Do you want Shiny Wall? Then come with us, and we will show you. We are Mother Carey's own chickens, and she sends us out over all the seas, to show the good birds the way home." Tom was delighted, and swam off to them, after he had made his bow to the Gairfowl. But she would not return his bow: but held herself bolt upright, and wept tears of oil as she sang:

>And so the poor stone was left all alone;

>With a fal-lal-la-lady.

[omission for length and content]

Part Four

And now Tom was all agog to start for Shiny Wall; but the petrels said not. They must go first to [the island of] **Allfowlsness**, and wait there for the great gathering of all the sea-birds, before they start for their summer breeding places far away in the Northern Isles; and there they would be sure to find some birds which were going to Shiny Wall: but where Allfowlsness was, he must promise never to tell, lest men should go there and shoot the birds, and stuff them, and put them into [dull] museums, instead of leaving them to play and breed and work in Mother Carey's water-garden, where they ought to be.

[omission for length and content]

And after a while the birds began to gather at Allfowlsness, in thousands and tens of thousands, blackening all the air: swans and brant geese, harlequins and eiders, harolds and garganeys, smews and gossanders, divers and loons, grebes and dovekies, auks and razorbills, gannets and petrels, skuas and terns, with gulls beyond all naming or numbering; and they paddled and washed and splashed and combed and brushed themselves on the sand, till the shore was white with feathers; and they quacked and clucked and gabbled and chattered and screamed and whooped as they talked over matters with their friends, and settled where they were to go and breed that summer, till you might have heard them ten miles off; and lucky it was for them that there was no one to hear them but the old keeper, who lived all alone upon the Ness, in a turf hut thatched with heather and fringed round with great stones slung across the roof by bent-ropes, lest the winter gales should blow the hut right away *[omission]*.

Then the petrels asked this bird and that whether they would take Tom to Shiny Wall: but one set was going to Sutherland, and one to the Shetlands, and one to Norway, and one to Spitzbergen, and one to Iceland, and one to Greenland: but none would go to Shiny Wall. So the good-natured petrels said that they would show him part of the way themselves, but they were only going as far as **Jan Mayen's Land**; and after that he must shift for himself.

And then all the birds rose up, and streamed away in long black lines, north, and north-east, and north-west, across the bright blue summer sky; and their cry was like ten thousand packs of hounds, and ten thousand peals of bells *[omission]*.

Narration and Discussion

Why does the gairfowl think it better not to have wings?

For further thought: What do you think about *noblesse oblige*? Compare this with Luke 12:48.

Creative narration: Imagine that the Gairfowl is still standing on the rock. Send someone to interview her and ask her opinion on the world today.

Reading #25

Introduction

After discovering a shipwreck, Tom acquires a "water-dog." The two of them get all the way to Shiny Wall, with the help of some birds, but there is no gate in sight. However, Tom discovers his own way in.

Vocabulary

    gale: wind storm

    right abaft: a sailing term meaning "at our stern," or "behind us." Kingsley may have been thinking of an old sea song that goes "Come, come, my brave boys, / the wind's right abaft."

    billows: waves

    new water-baby: Kingsley seems to break his own rule here, as he has said before that the water-babies are children who die from abuse or neglect; and others (like Ellie) go to the "beautiful place." However, as Kingsley would point out, this is a fairy tale, and it does not always have to be consistent.

molly-mock, molly: mollymawk, or sooty albatross; a large seabird

blubber: the fat of a sea mammal, especially a whale or seal

lubbers: short for "landlubbers," those unfamiliar with sailing

you won't earn your discharge from her: Kingsley is playing here with the idea of reincarnation. The old whalers who were "saucy and greedy" are now forced to live as seabirds, until Mother Carey decides they have "done their time."

a good plucked one: a brave boy

pack: pack ice; the sea ice cover in the Arctic

if you have pluck: if you are brave enough

here goes for a header: something like "here goes nothing"

Reading

Part One

And, as Tom and the petrels went north-eastward, it began to blow right hard *[omission]*. But [they] never cared, for the **gale** was **right abaft**, and away they went over the crests of the **billows**, as merry as so many flying-fish.

And at last they saw an ugly sight—the black side of a great ship, water-logged in the trough of the sea. Her funnel and her masts were overboard, and swayed and surged under her lee; her decks were swept as clean as a barn floor, and there was no living soul on board.

The petrels flew up to her, and wailed round her; for they were very sorry indeed, and also they expected to find some salt pork; and Tom scrambled on board of her and looked round, frightened and sad. And there, in a little cot, lashed tight under the bulwark, lay a baby fast asleep; the very same baby, Tom saw at once, which he had seen in the singing lady's arms. He went up to it, and wanted to wake it; but behold, from under the cot out jumped a little black and tan terrier dog, and began barking and snapping at Tom, and would not let him touch the cot.

Tom knew the dog's teeth could not hurt him: but at least it could shove him away, and did; and he and the dog fought and struggled, for he wanted to help the baby, and did not want to throw the poor dog overboard: but as they were struggling, [there came a tall green wave, which rolled in over the side of the ship, and swept them all into the sea].

"Oh, the baby, the baby!" screamed Tom: but the next moment he did not scream at all; for he saw the cot settling down through the green water, with the baby, smiling in it, fast asleep; and he saw the fairies come up from below, and carry baby and cradle gently down in their soft arms; and then he knew it was all right, and that there would be a **new water-baby** in St. Brendan's Isle.

And the poor little dog? Why, after he had kicked and coughed a little, he sneezed so hard, that he sneezed himself clean out of his skin, and turned into a water-dog, and jumped and danced round Tom, and ran over the crests of the waves, and snapped at the jelly-fish and the mackerel, and followed Tom the whole way to the Other-end-of-Nowhere.

Part Two

Then they went on again, till they began to see the peak of Jan Mayen's Land, standing up like a white sugar-loaf, two miles above the clouds. And there they fell in with a whole flock of **molly-mocks**, who were feeding on a dead whale.

"These are the fellows to show you the way," said Mother Carey's chickens; "we cannot help you farther north. We don't like to get among the ice pack, for fear it should nip our toes: but the **mollys** dare fly anywhere." So the petrels called to the mollys: but they were so busy and greedy, gobbling and pecking and spluttering and fighting over the **blubber**, that they did not take the least notice.

"Come, come," said the petrels, "you lazy greedy **lubbers**, this young gentleman is going to Mother Carey, and if you don't attend on him, **you won't earn your discharge from her**, you know."

"Greedy we are," says a great fat old molly, "but lazy we ain't; and, as for lubbers, we're no more lubbers than you. Let's have a look at the lad." And he flapped right into Tom's face, and stared at him in the most impudent way (for the mollys are audacious fellows, as all whalers know), and then asked him where he hailed from, and what land he sighted last. And, when Tom told him, he seemed pleased, and said he was **a good plucked one** to have got so far.

"Come along, lads," he said to the rest, "and give this little chap a cast over the pack, for Mother Carey's sake. We've eaten blubber enough for today, and we'll e'en work out a bit of our time by helping the lad." So the mollys took Tom up on their backs, and flew off with him, laughing and joking *[omission]*.

"Who are you, you jolly birds?" asked Tom.

"We are the spirits of the old Greenland skippers (as every sailor knows), who hunted here, right whales and horse-whales, full hundreds of years agone. But, because we were saucy and greedy, we were all turned into mollys, to eat whale's blubber all our days. But lubbers we are none, and could sail a ship now against any man in the North seas, though we don't hold with this new-fangled steam. And it's a shame of those black imps of petrels to call us so; but because they're her grace's pets, they think they may say anything they like."

[omission for length and content]

Part Three

And now they came to the edge of the **pack**, and beyond it they could see Shiny Wall looming, through mist, and snow, and storm. But the pack rolled horribly upon the swell, and the ice giants fought and roared, and leapt upon each other's backs, and ground each other to powder, so that Tom was afraid to venture among them, lest he should be ground to powder too *[omission]*. But the good mollys took Tom and his dog up, and flew with them safe over the pack and the roaring ice giants, and set them down at the foot of Shiny Wall.

"And where is the gate?" asked Tom.

"There is no gate," said the mollys.

"No gate?" cried Tom, aghast.

"None; never a crack of one, and that's the whole of the secret, as better fellows, lad, than you have found to their cost *[omission]*."

"What am I to do, then?"

"Dive under the floe, to be sure, **if you have pluck**."

"I've not come so far to turn now," said Tom; "so **here goes for a header**."

"A lucky voyage to you, lad," said the mollys; "we knew you were one of the right sort. So good-bye."

"Why don't you come too?" asked Tom.

But the mollys only wailed sadly, "We can't go yet, we can't go yet," and flew away over the pack. So Tom dived under [the ice], and went on in black darkness, at the bottom of the sea, for seven days and seven nights. And yet he was not a bit frightened. Why should he be? He was a brave English lad, whose business is to go out and see all the world.

Narration and Discussion

Do you think Tom has "pluck?"

What do you think of the mollys?

For further thought: Whalers become mollymocks, orphaned babies go to St. Brendan's Isle, and abandoned dogs become water-dogs. Did Charles Kingsley, who was a priest in the Church of England, believe that the Bible taught these things? (Probably not.) It seems that we have to go by the fairy tale rules, whether those take us to the Other-end-of-Nowhere, or to the Lone Islands.

> *The coracle went more and more quickly, and beautifully it rushed up the wave's side. For one split second they saw its shape and Reepicheep's on the very top. Then it vanished, and since that moment no one can truly claim to have seen Reepicheep the Mouse. But my belief is that he came safe to Aslan's country and is alive there to this day.* (C. S. Lewis, The Voyage of the Dawn Treader)

Reading #26

Introduction

Tom finally finds Mother Carey, who tells him that the way to the Other-end-of-Nowhere is…to go backwards.

Vocabulary

fathoms: One fathom is six feet long (1.8 m).

conjuring tricks: magic tricks

harpoon and lance them: kill them with spears

salpae: the plural form of **salp** or **salpa**, a kind of plankton, which are very small creatures that fish and whales like to eat

all the ills which flesh is heir to: The original Greek myth does not get as specific as Mother Carey (or Kingsley) does, and, while we agree with the undesirability of tight shoes and unpaid bills, we are not certain why potatoes are included among the world's evils. For everyone's sake, we have shortened the list a bit.

lucifers: matches

he set the Thames on fire: Again, that is not exactly the way the original story goes, but Mother Carey's version will do for now.

as if you saw it in a looking-glass: Perhaps this idea also interested Lewis Carroll. (Have you read *Through the Looking-Glass* yet?)

People

Julius Caesar: When Julius Caesar was being stabbed, he is said to have drawn his toga around his legs, so that he would be properly covered and "die decently."

Prometheus: Mentioned here and there in ***The Heroes***. One of the Titans (the original Greek gods), and associated with fire. His name literally means "Fore-thought."

Epimetheus: Another Titan, whose name means "After-thought" or "Hindsight."

Places

Mount Erebus: the second-highest volcano in Antarctica

Reading

Part One

And at last he saw the light, and clear clear water overhead; and up he came a thousand **fathoms**, among clouds of sea-moths, which fluttered round his head. There were moths with pink heads and wings and opal bodies, that flapped about slowly; moths with brown wings that flapped about quickly; yellow shrimps that hopped and skipped most quickly of all; and jellies of all the colours in the world, that neither hopped nor skipped, but only dawdled and yawned, and would not get out of his way.

The dog snapped at them till his jaws were tired; but Tom hardly minded them at all, he was so eager to get to the top of the water, and see the pool where the good whales go. And a very large pool it was, miles and miles across, though the air was so clear that the ice cliffs on the opposite side looked as if they were close at hand. All round it the ice cliffs rose, in walls and spires and battlements, and caves and bridges, and stones and galleries, in which the ice-fairies live, and drive away the storms and clouds, that Mother Carey's pool may lie calm from year's end to year's end.

And the sun acted [as a] policeman, and walked round outside every day, peeping just over the top of the ice wall, to see that all went right; and now and then he played **conjuring tricks**, or had an exhibition of fireworks, to amuse the ice-fairies. For he would make himself into four or five suns at once, or paint the sky with rings and crosses and crescents of white fire, and stick himself in the middle of them, and wink at the fairies; and I daresay they were very much amused; for anything's fun in the country.

And there the good whales lay, the happy sleepy beasts, upon the still oily sea. They were all right whales, you must know, and finners, and razorbacks, and bottlenoses, and spotted sea-unicorns with long ivory horns. But the sperm whales are such raging, ramping, roaring, rumbustious fellows, that, if Mother Carey let them in, there would be no more peace in Peacepool. So she packs them away in a great pond by themselves at the South Pole, two hundred and sixty-three miles south-south-east of **Mount Erebus**, the great volcano in the ice; and there they butt each other with their ugly noses, day and night from year's end to year's end.

But here there were only good quiet beasts, lying about like the black hulls of sloops, and blowing every now and then jets of white steam, or sculling round with their huge mouths open, for the sea-moths to swim down their throats. There were no threshers there to thresh their poor old backs, or swordfish to stab their stomachs, or sawfish to rip them up, or ice-sharks to bite lumps out of their sides, or whalers to **harpoon and lance them**. They were quite safe and happy there; and all they had to do was to wait quietly in Peacepool, till Mother Carey sent for them to make them out of old beasts into new.

Tom swam up to the nearest whale, and asked the way to Mother Carey.

"There she sits in the middle," said the whale. Tom looked; but he could see nothing in the middle of the pool, but one peaked iceberg; and he said so.

"That's Mother Carey," said the whale, "as you will find when you get to her. There she sits making old beasts into new all the year round."

"How does she do that?"

"That's her concern, not mine," said the old whale; and yawned so wide (for he was very large) that there swam into his mouth 943 sea-moths, 13,846 jelly-fish no bigger than pins' heads, a string of **salpae** nine yards long, and forty-three little ice-crabs, who gave each other a parting pinch all round, tucked their legs under their stomachs, and determined to die decently, like **Julius Caesar**.

"I suppose," said Tom, "she cuts up a great whale like you into a whole shoal of porpoises?" At which the old whale laughed so violently that he coughed up all the creatures; who swam away again very thankful at having escaped out of that terrible whalebone net of his, from which *[omission]* no traveler returns; and Tom went on to the iceberg, wondering.

Part Two

And, when he came near it, it took the form of the grandest old lady he had ever seen—a white marble lady, sitting on a white marble throne. And from the foot of the throne there swum away, out and out into the sea, millions of new-born creatures, of more shapes and colours than man ever dreamed. And they were Mother Carey's children, whom she makes out of the sea-water all day long.

He expected, of course—like some grown people who ought to know better—to find her snipping, piecing, fitting, stitching, cobbling, basting, filing, planing, hammering, turning, polishing, moulding, measuring, chiseling, clipping, and so forth, as men do when they go to work to make anything.

But, instead of that, she sat quite still with her chin upon her hand, looking down into the sea with two great grand blue eyes, as blue as the sea itself. Her hair was as white as the snow—for she was very very old—in fact, as old as anything which you are likely to come across, except the difference between right and wrong. And, when she saw Tom, she looked at him very kindly.

"What do you want, my little man? It is long since I have seen a water-baby here." Tom told her his errand, and asked the way to the Other-end-of-Nowhere.

"You ought to know yourself, for you have been there already."

"Have I, ma'am? I'm sure I forget all about it."

"Then look at me." And, as Tom looked into her great blue eyes, he recollected the way perfectly. Now, was not that strange?

"Thank you, ma'am," said Tom. "Then I won't trouble your ladyship anymore; I hear you are very busy."

"I am never more busy than I am now," she said, without stirring a finger.

"I heard, ma'am, that you were always making new beasts out of old."

"So people fancy. But I am not going to trouble myself to make things, my little dear. I sit here and make them make themselves."

"You are a clever fairy, indeed," thought Tom. And he was quite right.

[omission for length]

"And now, my pretty little man," said Mother Carey, "you are sure you know the way to the Other-end-of-Nowhere?" Tom thought; and behold, he had forgotten it utterly.

"That is because you took your eyes off me." Tom looked at her again, and recollected; and then looked away, and forgot in an instant.

"But what am I to do, ma'am? For I can't keep looking at you when I am somewhere else."

"You must do without me, as most people have to do, for nine-hundred-and ninety-nine-thousandths of their lives; and look at the dog instead; for he knows the way well enough, and will not forget it. Besides, you may meet some very [odd] people there, who will not let you pass without this passport of mine, which you must hang round your neck and take care of; and, of course, as the dog will always go behind you, you must go the whole way backward."

"Backward!" cried Tom. "Then I shall not be able to see my way."

"On the contrary, if you look forward, you will not see a step before you, and be certain to go wrong; but, if you look behind you, and watch carefully whatever you have passed, and especially keep your eye on the dog, who goes by instinct, and therefore can't go wrong, then you will know what is coming next, as plainly **as if you saw it in a looking-glass**."

Tom was very much astonished: but he obeyed her, for he had learnt always to believe what the fairies told him.

Part Three: An Old Story In the Story

"So it is, my dear child," said Mother Carey; "and I will tell you a story, which will show you that I am perfectly right, as it is my custom to be.

"Once on a time, there were two brothers. One was called **Prometheus**, because he always looked before him, and boasted that he was wise beforehand. The other was called **Epimetheus**, because he always looked behind him, and did not boast at all; but said humbly *[omission]* that he had sooner prophesy after the event.

"Well, Prometheus was a very clever fellow, of course, and invented all sorts of wonderful things. But, unfortunately, when they were set to work, to work was just what they would not do: wherefore very little has come of them, and very little is left of them; and now nobody knows what they were, save a few archaeological old gentlemen who scratch in [strange] corners.

"But Epimetheus was a very slow fellow, certainly, and men called him a clod, and a muff, and a milksop, and a slowcoach, and a bloke, and a boodle, and so forth. And very little he did, for many years: but what he did, he never had to do over again.

"And what happened at last? There came to the two brothers the most beautiful creature that ever was seen, Pandora by name; which means 'All the gifts of the gods.' But because she had a strange box in her hand, this fanciful, forecasting, suspicious, prudential, theoretical, deductive, prophesying Prometheus, who was always settling what was going to happen, would have nothing to do with pretty Pandora and her box.

"But Epimetheus took her and it, as he took everything that came; and married her for better for worse, as every man ought, whenever he has even the chance of a good wife. And they opened the box between them, of course, to see what was inside: for, else, of what possible use could it have been to them?

"And out flew **all the ills which flesh is heir to**; all the children of the four great Bogies [which are] Self-will, Ignorance, Fear, and Dirt. [Things like measles, unpaid bills, wars, potatoes, bad doctors, and shoes that pinch your feet.] And, worst of all, Naughty Boys and Girls.

"But one thing remained at the bottom of the box, and that was, Hope.

"So Epimetheus got a great deal of trouble, as most men do in this world; but he got the three best things in the world into the bargain—a good wife, and experience, and hope.

"[Now, we have not forgotten Prometheus.] Prometheus kept on looking before him so far ahead, that as he was running about with a box of **lucifers** *[matches]* (which were the only useful things he ever invented, and do as much harm as good), he trod on his own nose, and tumbled down *[omission]*; whereby **he set the Thames on fire;** and they have hardly put it out again yet. So he had to be chained to the top of a mountain, with a vulture by him to give him a peck whenever he stirred.

"But *[omission]* old Epimetheus went working and grubbing on, with the help of his wife Pandora, always looking behind him to see what had happened, till he really learnt to know now and then what would happen next; and understood so well which side his bread was buttered, and which way the cat jumped, that he began to make things which would work, and go on working, too; till at last he grew very rich and fat, and people thought twice before they meddled with him *[omission]*.

"And his children are the men of science, who get good lasting work done in the world; but the children of Prometheus are *[omission]* the noisy, windy people, who go telling silly folk what will happen, instead of looking to see what has happened already."

[Tom thought that was a good story. But what happened when he tried to go backwards?]

Part Four

He was very sorely tried; for though, by keeping the dog to heels (or rather to toes, for he had to walk backward), he could see pretty well which way the dog was hunting, yet it was much slower work to go backwards than to go forwards. But, what was more trying still, no sooner had he got out of Peacepool, than there came running to him [all sorts of prophets and fortune-tellers], all bawling and screaming at him, "Look ahead, only look ahead; and we will show you what man never saw before, and right away to the end of the world!"

But I am proud to say that Tom was such a little dogged, hard, gnarly, foursquare brick of an English boy, that he never turned his head round once all the way from Peacepool to the Other-end-of-Nowhere; but [he] kept his eye on the dog, and let him pick out the scent, hot or cold, straight or crooked, wet or dry, up hill or down dale; by which means he never made a single mistake, and saw all the wonderful and hitherto by-no-mortal-man-imagined things which it is my duty to relate to you in the next chapter.

Narration and Discussion

Well, we weren't expecting a whole Greek myth in the middle of *The Water-Babies*, were we? Why is it important, according to Mother Carey, to keep looking backwards? How can that help us, like Epimetheus, to know (at least "now and then") what might happen next?

Creative narration: Kingsley's version of Pandora's box is not too serious—or at least we should say that he used his imagination to embellish it a bit. If you were to draw such a box (and you don't hate potatoes), what would you put in it? (Don't forget to add some Hope at the bottom.)

Poetic Interlude #8

To begin the last chapter, Kingsley chose the beginning and ending stanzas of Longfellow's poem "Children." [This is included in AO's Year Five collection of poems.]

Come to me, O ye children!
For I hear you at your play;
And the questions that perplexed me
Have vanished quite away.

Ye open the Eastern windows,
That look towards the sun,
Where thoughts are singing swallows,
And the brooks of morning run.

For what are all our contrivings
And the wisdom of our books,
When compared with your caresses,
And the gladness of your looks?

Ye are better than all the ballads
That ever were sung or said;
For ye are living poems,
And all the rest are dead.

The Water-Babies

Reading #27

Introduction

Tom's travels now get him into some seriously strange places.

Vocabulary

world-pap: We might translate this as "the biscuit dough that shapes the earth."

foul: disgusting, polluted

gruel: thin oatmeal porridge (something Kingsley considers one of the world's evils)

silt: sandy stuff

stupid: boring, dull, without purpose

slops, messes, tuck: these are all words referring to food. If you have been to camp, you might have eaten in the "mess hall," and bought snacks at the "tuck shop."

gastrocnemius muscle: at the back of the leg

Places

Polupragmosyne: This is very close to a Greek word meaning "meddlesome," which the people there certainly are.

Reading

Prologue

Here begins the never-to-be-too-much-studied account of the nine-hundred-and-ninety-ninth part of the wonderful things which Tom saw on his journey to the Other-end-of-Nowhere; which all good little children are requested to read; that, if ever they get to the Other-end-of-Nowhere, as they may very probably do, they may not burst out laughing, or try to run away, or do any other silly vulgar thing which may offend Mrs. Bedonebyasyoudid.

Part One

Now, as soon as Tom had left Peacepool, he came to the white lap of the great sea-mother, ten thousand fathoms deep; where she makes **world-pap** all day long, for the steam-giants to knead, and the fire-giants to bake, till it has risen and hardened into mountain-loaves and island-cakes. And there Tom was very near being kneaded up in the world-pap, and turned into a fossil water-baby; which would have astonished the Geological Society of New Zealand some hundreds of thousands of years hence.

For, as he walked along in the silence of the sea-twilight, on the soft white ocean floor, he was aware of a hissing, and a roaring, and a thumping, and a pumping, as of all the steam-engines in the world at once. And, when he came near, the water grew boiling-hot; not that that hurt him in the least: but it also grew as **foul** as **gruel**; and every moment he stumbled over dead shells, and fish, and sharks, and seals, and whales, which had been killed by the hot water.

And at last he came to the great sea-serpent himself, lying dead at the bottom; and as he was too thick to scramble over, Tom had to walk round him three-quarters of a mile and more, which put him out of his path sadly; and, when he had got round, he came to the place called Stop. And there he stopped, and just in time.

For he was on the edge of a vast hole in the bottom of the sea, up which was rushing and roaring clear steam enough to work all the engines in the world at once; so clear, indeed, that it was quite light at moments; and Tom could see almost up to the top of the water above, and down below into the pit for nobody knows how far.

But, as soon as he bent his head over the edge, he got such a rap on the nose from pebbles, that he jumped back again; for the steam, as it rushed up, rasped away the sides of the hole, and hurled it up into the sea in a shower of mud and gravel and ashes; and then it spread all around, and sank again, and covered in the dead fish so fast, that before Tom had stood there five minutes he was buried in **silt** up to his ankles, and began to be afraid that he should have been buried alive.

[omission for length]

But, all of a sudden, somebody shut off the steam below, and the hole was left empty in an instant; and then down rushed the water into the hole in a whirlpool, [and in went Tom as well]. And, when he got to the bottom, he swam till he was washed on shore safe upon the Other-end-of-Nowhere; and he found it, to his surprise, as most other people do, much more like This-End-of-Somewhere than he had been in the habit of expecting.

Part Two

First he went through Waste-paper-land, where all the **stupid** books lie in heaps, up hill and down dale, like leaves in a winter wood; and there he saw people digging and grubbing among them, to make worse books out of bad ones *[omission]*; and a very good trade they drove thereby, especially among children.

Then he went by the sea of **slops**, to the mountain of **messes**, and the territory of **tuck**, where the ground was very sticky, for it was all made of bad toffee *[omission]*, and full of deep cracks and holes choked with wind-fallen fruit, and green gooseberries, and sloes, and [crabapples], and hips and haws, and all the nasty things which little children will eat, if they can get them. But the fairies hide them out of the way in that country as fast as they can, and very hard work they have, and of very little use it is. For as fast as they hide away the old trash, foolish and wicked people make fresh trash full of lime and poisonous paints, and actually go and steal receipts out of old Madame Science's big book to invent poisons for little children, and sell them at *[omission]* fairs and tuck-shops. Very well. Let them go on *[omission]*. But the Fairy with the birch-rod will catch them all in time, and make them begin at one corner of their shops, and eat their way out at the other; by which time they will have got such stomach-aches as will cure them of poisoning little children.

Next he saw all the little people in the world, writing all the little books in the world, about all the other little people in the world; probably because they had no great people to write about: and if the names of the books were not *Squeeky*, nor the *Pump-lighter*, nor the *Narrow Narrow World*, nor the *Hills of the Chattermuch*, nor the *Children's Twaddeday*, why then they were something else. And all the rest of the little people in the world read the books, and thought themselves each as good as the President; and perhaps they were right, for everyone knows his own business best. But Tom thought he would sooner have a jolly good fairy tale, about Jack the Giant-killer or Beauty and the Beast, which taught him something that he didn't know already.

[omission]

Part Three

Then came Tom to the Island of **Polupragmosyne** *[omission]*, [where] everyone knows his neighbour's business better than his own; and a very noisy place it is, as might be expected, considering that all the inhabitants are *[omission]* always making wry mouths, and crying that the fairies' grapes were sour. Tom saw ploughs drawing horses, nails driving hammers, birds' nests taking boys, books making authors, bulls keeping china-shops, and monkeys shaving cats *[omission]*; and, in short, every one set to do something which he had not learnt, because in what he had learnt, or pretended to learn, he had failed.

[omission]

When he got into the middle of the town, they all set on him at once, to show him his way; or rather, to show him that he did not know his way; for as for asking him what way he wanted to go, no one ever thought of that.

But one pulled him hither, and another poked him thither, and a third cried— "You mustn't go west, I tell you; it is destruction to go west."

"But I am not going west, as you may see," said Tom.

And another, "The east lies here, my dear; I assure you this is the east."

"But I don't want to go east," said Tom.

"Well, then, at all events, whichever way you are going, you are going wrong," cried they all with one voice—which was the only thing which they ever agreed about; and all pointed at once to all the thirty-and-two points of the compass, till Tom thought all the sign-posts in England had got together, and fallen fighting.

And whether he would have ever escaped out of the town, it is hard to say, if the dog had not taken it into his head that they were going to pull his master in pieces, and tackled them so sharply about the **gastrocnemius muscle**, that he gave them some business of their own to think of at last; and while they were rubbing their bitten calves, Tom and the dog got safe away.

[omission for length]

Narration and Discussion

Would you rather read a good fairy tale, or something like *Narrow Narrow World*? (Kingsley obviously hopes you will choose the first.) What are your favourite books that are *not* "little books…about all the other little people in the world?"

> *Something was crawling. Worse still, something was coming out. Edmund or Lucy or you would have recognized it at once, but Eustace had read none of the right books…[his books] had a lot to say about exports and imports and governments and rains, but they were weak on dragons.* (C. S. Lewis, **The Voyage of the Dawn-Treader**)

Kingsley wrote, "When he got into the middle of the town, they all set on him at once, to show him his way; or rather, to show him that he did not know his way; for as for asking him what way he wanted to go, no one ever thought of that." Have you ever been told a lot of different things to do, or not to do, by people who mean well but who, perhaps, forget to ask what it is you are trying to do in the first place? In this story, there was not much left to do but run. Can you think of any other ways to deal with a situation like that?

For further thought: Tom finds that the Other-end-of-Nowhere is "much more like This-End-of-Somewhere than he had been in the habit of expecting." Why might that be? How can we perhaps keep our part of This-End-of-Somewhere from turning into the Other-end-of-Nowhere?

Reading #28

Introduction

While traveling through the Other-end-of-Nowhere, Tom meets a most peculiar giant, who gives him one good piece of advice.

Vocabulary

hearsay: something you hear that cannot be proved; a rumor

fugleman: drill sergeant; one who shows the others what to do

remarked: noticed

made a truce: made peace

pick his brains: ask questions to find out what a person knows about something

tact: the ability to say or do the right thing without making people angry

Do the duty which lies nearest you, and catch the first beetle you come across: A variation on a quote by Thomas Carlyle (from his book *Sartor Resartus*): "Do the duty which lies nearest to thee, which thou knowest to be a duty! The second duty will already have become clearer."

Reading

Part One

Then came Tom to the great land of **Hearsay**, in which are no less than thirty and odd kings, beside half a dozen Republics, and perhaps more *[omission]*. And there he fell in with a deep, dark, deadly, and destructive war, waged by the princes and potentates of those parts, both spiritual and temporal, against what do you think? One thing I am sure of. That unless I told you, you would never know; nor how they waged that war either; for all their strategy and art military consisted in the safe and easy process of stopping their ears and screaming, "Oh, don't tell us!" and then running away.

So when Tom came into that land, he found them all, high and low, man, woman, and child, running for their lives day and night continually, and entreating not to be told they didn't know what: only the land being an island, and they having a dislike to the water (being a musty lot for the most part), they ran round and round the shore forever, which (as the island was exactly of the same circumference as the planet on which we have the honour of living) was hard work, especially to those who had business to look after.

But before them, as bandmaster and **fugleman**, ran a gentleman shearing a pig; the melodious strains of which animal led them forever, if not to conquest, still to flight; and kept up their spirits mightily with the thought that they would at least have the pig's wool for their pains.

And running after them, day and night, came such a poor, lean, seedy, hard-worked old giant, as ought to have been [treated well], and had a good dinner given him, and a good wife found him, and been set to play with little children; and then he would have been a very presentable old fellow after all; for he had a heart, though it was considerably overgrown with brains. He was made up principally of fish bones and parchment, put together with wire and Canada balsam; and smelt strongly of spirits, though he never drank anything but water *[omission]*. He had a great pair of spectacles on his nose, and a butterfly-net in one hand, and a geological hammer in the other; and was hung all over with pockets, full of collecting boxes, bottles, microscopes, telescopes, barometers, ordnance maps, scalpels, forceps, photographic apparatus, and all other tackle for finding out everything about everything, and a little more too. And, most strange of all, he was running not forwards but backwards, as fast as he could.

Away all the good folks ran from him, except Tom, who stood his ground and dodged between his legs; and the giant, when he had passed him, looked down, and cried, as if he was quite pleased and comforted,— "What? who are you? And you actually don't run away, like all the rest?" But he had to take his spectacles off, Tom **remarked**, in order to see him plainly.

Part Two

Tom told him who he was; and the giant pulled out a bottle and a cork instantly, to collect him with. But Tom was too sharp for that, and dodged between his legs and in front of him; and then the giant could not see him at all.

"No, no, no!" said Tom, "I've not been round the world, and through the world, and up to Mother Carey's haven, besides being caught in a net and called a Holothurian and a Cephalopod, to be bottled up by any old giant like you."

And when the giant understood what a great traveler Tom had been, he **made a truce** with him at once, and would have kept him there to this day to **pick his brains**, so delighted was he at finding any one to tell him what he did not know before.

"Ah, you lucky little dog!" said he at last, quite simply—for he was the simplest, pleasantest, honestest, kindliest old *[omission]* giant that ever turned the world upside down without intending it— "ah, you lucky little dog! If I had only been where you have been, to see what you have seen!"

"Well," said Tom, "if you want to do that, you had best put your head under water for a few hours, as I did, and turn into a water-baby, or some other baby, and then you might have a chance."

"Turn into a baby, eh? If I could do that, and know what was happening to me for but one hour, I should know everything then, and be at rest. But I can't; I can't be a little child again; and I suppose if I could, it would be no use, because then I should know nothing about what was happening to me. Ah, you lucky little dog!" said the poor old giant.

"But why do you run after all these poor people?" said Tom, who liked the giant very much.

"My dear, it's they that have been running after me *[omission]* for hundreds and hundreds of years, throwing stones at me till they have knocked off my spectacles fifty times, and calling me [all kinds of names]—and hunting me round and round—though catch me they can't, for every time I go over the same ground, I go the faster, and grow the bigger. While all I want is to be friends with them, and to tell them something to their advantage: only somehow they are so strangely afraid of hearing it. But, I suppose I am not a man of the world, and have no **tact**."

"But why don't you turn round and tell them so?"

"Because I can't. You see, I must go backwards, if I am to go at all."

"But why don't you stop, and let them come up to you?"

"Why, my dear, only think. If I did, all the butterflies and cockyolybirds would fly past me, and then I should catch no more new species, and should grow rusty and mouldy, and die. And I don't intend to do that, my dear; for I have a destiny before me, they say: though what it is I don't know, and don't care."

"Don't care?" said Tom.

"No. **Do the duty which lies nearest you, and catch the first beetle you come across**, is my motto; and I have thriven by it for some hundred years. Now I must go on. Dear me, while I have been talking to you, at least nine new species have escaped me."

[omission]

So the giant ran round after the people, and the people ran round after the giant, and they are running unto this day for aught I know, or do not know; and will run till either he, or they, or both, turn into little children [omission].

Narration and Discussion

The giant seems to be a sort of scientist, with all his microscopes and cameras and everything. Why do the people run away from him? (The name of the country, **Hearsay**, might be a clue.)

What do you think of his advice to Tom?

Reading #29

Introduction

Kingsley has a few things to say about education here, plus a great deal of nonsense about talking turnips.

Vocabulary

Tomtoddy: tadpole, young frog

ringing little pigs: putting rings in their noses

mangold wurzel: a vegetable

taken up: arrested

upstairs, downstairs, in my lady's chamber: Refers to the nursery rhyme "Goosey Goosey Gander"

binding heavy burdens and grievous to be borne: Matthew 23:4

People

Captain Gulliver: the main character of Jonathan Swift's book *Gulliver's Travels*

Roger Ascham: an English scholar of the 16th century, known for his theories of education (he was also the tutor of Queen Elizabeth I)

King Edward the Sixth: the son of King Henry the Eighth, and brother of Elizabeth.

Places

Isle of Laputa: an (imaginary) flying island in *Gulliver's Travels*

Aldershot on a field-day: Aldershot is a town in Hampshire, England, famous for its army training camp.

Reading

Part One

Then Tom came to a very famous island, which was called, in the days of the great traveler **Captain Gulliver**, the **Isle of Laputa**. But Mrs. Bedonebyasyoudid has named it over again the Isle of **Tomtoddies**, all heads and no bodies.

And when Tom came near it, he heard such a grumbling and grunting and growling and wailing and weeping and whining that he thought people must be **ringing little pigs**, or cropping puppies' ears *[omission]*; but when he came nearer still, he began to hear words among the noise; which was the Tomtoddies' song which they sing morning and evening, and all night too *[omission]*—

"I can't learn my lessons: the examiner's coming!"

And that was the only song which they knew.

When Tom got on shore the first thing he saw was a great pillar, on one side of which was inscribed, "Playthings not allowed here"; at which he was so shocked that he would not stay to see what was written on the other side.

Then he looked round for the people of the island: but instead of men, women, and children, he found nothing but turnips and radishes, beet and **mangold wurzel**, without a single green leaf among them, and half of them burst and decayed, with toadstools growing out of them. Those which were left began crying to Tom, in half a dozen different languages at once, and all of them badly spoken, "I can't learn my lesson; do come and help me!"

And one cried, "Can you show me how to extract this square root?"

And another, "Can you tell me the distance between [alpha] Lyrae and [beta] Camelopardis?"

And another, "What is the latitude and longitude of Snooksville, in Noman's County, Oregon, U.S.?"

And another, "What was the name of Mutius Scaevola's thirteenth cousin's grandmother's maid's cat?"

And another, "How long would it take a school-inspector of average activity to tumble head over heels from London to York?"

And another, "Can you tell me the name of a place that nobody ever heard of, where nothing ever happened, in a country which has not been discovered yet?" *[omission]* And so on, and so on, and so on *[omission]*.

"And what good on earth will it do you if I did tell you?" quoth Tom.

Well, they didn't know that: all they knew was the examiner was coming.

Part Two

Then Tom stumbled on the hugest and softest nimblecomequick turnip you ever saw *[omission]*, and it cried to him, "Can you tell me anything at all about anything you like?"

"About what?" says Tom.

"About anything you like; for as fast as I learn things I forget them again. So my mamma says that my intellect is not adapted for methodic science, and says that I must go in for general information." Tom told him that he did not know General Information, nor any officers in the army; only he had a friend once that went for a drummer: but he could tell him a great many strange things which he had seen in his travels.

So he told him prettily enough, while the poor turnip listened very carefully; and the more he listened, the more he forgot, and the more water ran out of him. Tom thought he was crying: but it was only his poor brains running away, from being worked so hard; and as Tom talked, the unhappy turnip streamed down all over with juice, and split and shrank till nothing was left of him but rind and water; whereat Tom ran away in a fright, for he thought he might be **taken up** for killing the turnip.

But, on the contrary, the turnip's parents were highly delighted, and considered him a saint and a martyr, and put up a long inscription over his tomb about his wonderful talents, early development, and unparalleled precocity.

[omission]

Sailors and Seababies

Tom was so puzzled and frightened with all he saw, that he was longing to ask the meaning of it; and at last he stumbled over a respectable old [walking] stick lying half covered with earth. But a very stout and worthy stick it was, for it belonged to good **Roger Ascham** in old time, and had carved on its head [a picture of] **King Edward the Sixth,** with the Bible in his hand.

"You see," said the stick, "there were as pretty little children once as you could wish to see, and might have been so still if they had been only left to grow up like human beings, and then handed over to me; but their foolish fathers and mothers, instead of letting them pick flowers, and make dirt-pies, and get birds' nests, and dance round the gooseberry bush, as little children should, kept them always at lessons, working, working, working, learning week-day lessons all week-days, and Sunday lessons all Sunday, and weekly examinations every Saturday, and monthly examinations every month, and yearly examinations every year, everything seven times over, as if once was not enough, and enough as good as a feast—till their brains grew big, and their bodies grew small, and they were all changed into turnips, with little but water inside; and still their foolish parents actually pick the leaves off them as fast as they grow, lest they should have anything green about them."

"Ah!" said Tom, "if dear Mrs. Doasyouwouldbedoneby knew of it she would send them a lot of tops, and balls, and marbles, and ninepins, and make them all as jolly as sand-boys."

"It would be no use," said the stick. "They can't play now, if they tried. Don't you see how their legs have turned to roots and grown into the ground, by never taking any exercise, but sapping and moping always in the same place? But here comes the Examiner-of-all-Examiners. So you had better get away, I warn you, or he will examine you and your dog into the bargain *[omission]*. There is no escaping out of his hands, for his nose is nine thousand miles long, and can go down chimneys, and through keyholes, **upstairs, downstairs, in my lady's chamber,** examining all little boys, and the little boys' tutors likewise. But when he is thrashed—so Mrs. Bedonebyasyoudid has promised me—I shall have the thrashing of him: and if I don't lay it on with a will it's a pity."

Part Three

Tom went off, but rather slowly and surlily; for he was somewhat minded to face this same Examiner-of-all-Examiners, who came striding among the poor turnips, **binding heavy burdens and grievous to be borne**, and laying them on little children's shoulders *[omission]*.

But when he got near, he looked so big and burly and dictatorial, and shouted so loud to Tom, to come and be examined, that Tom ran for his life, and the dog too. And really it was time; for the poor turnips, in their hurry and fright, crammed themselves so fast to be ready for the Examiner, that they burst and popped by dozens all round him, till the place sounded like **Aldershot on a field-day**, and Tom thought he should be blown into the air, dog and all.

As he went down to the shore he passed the poor turnip's new tomb. But Mrs. Bedonebyasyoudid had taken away the epitaph about talents and precocity and development, and put up one of her own instead which Tom thought much more sensible:—

>Instruction sore long time I bore,
>>And cramming was in vain;
>Till heaven did please my woes to ease
>>With water on the brain.

So Tom jumped into the sea, and swam on his way, singing:—

>Farewell, Tomtoddies all; I thank my stars
>>That nought I know save those three royal r's:
>Reading and 'riting sure, with 'rithmetic,
>>Will help a lad of sense through thin and thick.

[Omitted for length and content: Tom's journeys to the land of Oldwivesfabledom and Leaveheavenalone]

Narration and Discussion

Do you have examinations in your school or homeschool? Are they anything like those of the turnips?

Kingsley wrote that "If dear Mrs. Doasyouwouldbedoneby knew of it she would send them a lot of tops, and balls, and marbles, and ninepins, and make them all as jolly as sand-boys." He also says that children should "pick flowers, and make dirt-pies, and get birds' nests, and dance round the gooseberry bush." But the walking-stick responds, "It would be no use…They can't play now, if they tried." Why is having the chance to play, and do these other things, so important?

For further thought: Tom leaves the island of Tomtoddies with a song about how the "royal r's" are quite enough for "a lad of sense." Considering what he has seen of the overstuffed turnips, this might be a very reasonable response. But does that mean we should not study history, geography, science, and the rest?

For even further thought: Kingsley has pointed out several times that it is foolish not to "look backwards," and he also speaks of how important "men of science" can be to the world. Is there another way to go about this?

Sailors and Seababies

Reading #30

Introduction

Tom finally finds Mr. Grimes, who is in a very sad state (and can't even make his pipe work). Mrs. Bedonebyasyoudid also joins in this rescue attempt.

Vocabulary

> **truncheon:** a short, heavy stick carried by a police officer; a billy club
>
> **naviculae:** the plural of **navicula**, a single-celled organism shaped like a boat (which is where it gets its name).
>
> **Mother Carey's pass:** Do you remember? Mother Carey had given Tom a "passport" to wear around his neck.
>
> **he was always in a position of stable equilibrium:** he could always manage to balance himself
>
> **brass blunderbuss charged up to the muzzle with slugs:** an old-fashioned kind of gun, and apparently loaded
>
> **porter:** doorkeeper
>
> **just like Punch:** in old English puppet shows
>
> **attend:** pay attention
>
> **atomy:** body
>
> **small shot:** pellets from a gun
>
> **I'm beat now:** Do you remember how Tom felt b-e-a-t, beat?
>
> **ticket-of-leave:** paper allowing him to leave the prison

Places

> **[Mount] Etna:** a famous volcano in Sicily

Reading

Part One

And at last, after innumerable adventures, each more wonderful than the last, he saw before him a huge building. Tom walked towards [it], wondering what it was, and having a strange fancy that he might find Mr. Grimes inside it; till he saw running toward him, and shouting "Stop!" three or four people, who, when they came nearer, were nothing else than policemen's **truncheons**, running along without legs or arms.

Tom was not astonished. He was long past that. Besides, he had seen the **naviculae** in the water move nobody knows how, a hundred times, without arms or legs, or anything to stand in their stead. Neither was he frightened; for he had been doing no harm. So he stopped; and, when the foremost truncheon came up and asked his business, he showed **Mother Carey's pass**; and the truncheon looked at it in the oddest fashion; for he had one eye in the middle of his upper end, so that when he looked at anything, being quite stiff, he had to slope himself, and poke himself, till it was a wonder why he did not tumble over; but, being quite full of the spirit of justice (as all policemen, and their truncheons, ought to be), **he was always in a position of stable equilibrium**, whichever way he put himself.

"All right—pass on," said he at last. And then he added: "I had better go with you, young man." And Tom had no objection, for such company was both respectable and safe; so the truncheon coiled its [strap] neatly round its handle, to prevent tripping itself up—for [it] had got loose in running—and marched on by Tom's side.

"Why have you no policeman to carry you?" asked Tom, after a while.

"Because we are not like those clumsy-made truncheons in the land-world, which cannot go without having a whole man to carry them about. We do our own work for ourselves; and do it very well, though I say it who should not."

"Then why have you a [strap] to your handle?" asked Tom.

"To hang ourselves up by, of course, when we are off duty."

Tom had got his answer, and had no more to say, till they came up to the great iron door of the prison. And there the truncheon knocked twice, with its own head.

Part Two

A wicket in the door opened, and out looked a tremendous old **brass blunderbuss charged up to the muzzle with slugs**, who was the **porter**; and Tom started back a little at the sight of him.

"What case is this?" he asked in a deep voice, out of his broad bell mouth.

"If you please, sir, it is no case; only a young gentleman from her ladyship, who wants to see Grimes, the master-sweep."

"Grimes?" said the blunderbuss. And he pulled in his muzzle, perhaps to look over his prison-lists.

"Grimes is up chimney No. 345," he said from inside. "So the young gentleman had better go on to the roof." Tom looked up at the enormous wall, which seemed at least ninety miles high, and wondered how he should ever get up; but, when he hinted that to the truncheon, it settled the matter in a moment. For it whisked round, and gave him such a shove behind as sent him up to the roof in no time, with his little dog under his arm.

Sailors and Seababies

And there he walked along the leads, till he met another truncheon, and told him his errand.

"Very good," it said. "Come along: but it will be of no use. He is the most unremorseful, hard-hearted, foul-mouthed fellow I have in charge; and thinks about nothing but beer and pipes, which are not allowed here, of course."

So they walked along over the leads, and very sooty they were, and Tom thought the chimneys must want sweeping very much. But he was surprised to see that the soot did not stick to his feet, or dirty them in the least. Neither did the live coals, which were lying about in plenty, burn him, [as he was a water-baby].

[omission]

At last they came to chimney No. 345. Out of the top of it, his head and shoulders just showing, stuck poor Mr. Grimes, so sooty, and bleared, and ugly, that Tom could hardly bear to look at him. And in his mouth was a pipe; but it was not alight; though he was [trying to draw smoke from it] with all his might.

"Attention, Mr. Grimes," said the truncheon, "here is a gentleman come to see you." But Mr. Grimes only said bad words; and kept grumbling, "My pipe won't draw. My pipe won't draw."

"Keep a civil tongue, and attend!" said the truncheon; and popped up **just like Punch**, hitting Grimes such a crack over the head with itself, that his brains rattled inside like a dried walnut in its shell. He tried to get his hands out, and rub the place: but he could not, for they were stuck fast in the chimney. Now he was forced to **attend**.

"Hey!" he said, "why, it's Tom! I suppose you have come here to laugh at me, you spiteful little **atomy**?" Tom assured him he had not, but only wanted to help him.

"I don't want anything except beer, and that I can't get; and a light to this bothering pipe, and that I can't get either."

"I'll get you one," said Tom; and he took up a live coal (there were plenty lying about) and put it to Grimes' pipe: but it went out instantly.

"It's no use," said the **truncheon**, leaning itself up against the chimney and looking on. "I tell you, it is no use. His heart is so cold that it freezes everything that comes near him. You will see that presently, plain enough."

"Oh, of course, it's my fault. Everything's always my fault," said Grimes. "Now don't go to hit me again" (for the truncheon started upright, and looked very wicked); "you know, if my arms were only free, you daren't hit me then." The truncheon leant back against the chimney, and took no notice of the personal insult, like a well-trained policeman as it was, though he was ready enough to avenge any transgression against morality or order.

"But can't I help you in any other way? Can't I help you to get out of this chimney?" said Tom.

"No," interposed the truncheon; "he has come to the place where everybody must help themselves; and he will find it out, I hope, before he has done with me."

Part Three

"Oh, yes," said Grimes, "of course it's me. Did I ask to be brought here into the prison? Did I ask to be set to sweep your foul chimneys? Did I ask to have lighted straw put under me to make me go up? Did I ask to stick fast in the very first chimney of all, because it was so shamefully clogged up with soot? Did I ask to stay here—I don't know how long—a hundred years, I do believe, and never get my pipe, nor my beer, nor nothing fit for a beast, let alone a man?"

"No," answered a solemn voice behind. "No more did Tom, when you behaved to him in the very same way."

It was Mrs. Bedonebyasyoudid. And, when the truncheon saw her, it started bolt upright—Attention!—and made such a low bow, that if it had not been full of the spirit of justice, it must have trembled on its end, and probably hurt its one eye. And Tom made his bow too.

"Oh, ma'am," he said, "don't think about me; that's all past and gone, and good times and bad times and all times pass over. But may not I help poor Mr. Grimes? Mayn't I try and get some of these bricks away, that he may move his arms?"

"You may try, of course," she said. So Tom pulled and tugged at the bricks: but he could not move one. And then he tried to wipe Mr. Grimes' face: but the soot would not come off.

"Oh, dear!" he said. "I have come all this way, through all these terrible places, to help you, and now I am of no use at all."

"You had best leave me alone," said Grimes; "you are a good-natured forgiving little chap, and that's truth; but you'd best be off. The hail's coming on soon, and it will beat the eyes out of your little head."

"What hail?"

"Why, hail that falls every evening here; and, till it comes close to me, it's like so much warm rain: but then it turns to hail over my head, and knocks me about like **small shot.**"

"That hail will never come any more," said the strange lady. "I have told you before what it was. It was your mother's tears, those which she shed when she prayed for you by her bedside; but your cold heart froze it into hail. But she is gone to heaven now, and will weep no more for her graceless son."

Then Grimes was silent awhile; and then he looked very sad. "So my old mother's gone, and I never there to speak to her! Ah! a good woman she was, and might have been a happy one, in her little school there in Vendale, if it hadn't been for me and my bad ways."

"Did she keep the school in Vendale?" asked Tom. And then he told Grimes all the story of his going to her house, and how she could not abide the sight of a chimney-sweep, and then how kind she was, and how he turned into a water-baby.

"Ah!" said Grimes, "good reason she had to hate the sight of a chimney-sweep. I ran away from her and took up with the sweeps, and never let her know where I was, nor sent her a penny to help her, and now it's too late—too late!" said Mr. Grimes.

And he began crying and blubbering like a great baby, till his pipe dropped out of his mouth, and broke all to bits. "Oh, dear, if I was but a little chap in Vendale again, to see the clear beck, and the apple-orchard, and the yew-hedge, how different I would go on! But it's too late now. So you go along, you kind little chap, and don't stand to look at a man crying, that's old enough to be your father, and never feared the face of man, nor of worse neither. But **I'm beat now**, and beat I must be. I've made my bed, and I must lie on it. Foul I would be, and foul I am, as an Irishwoman said to me once; and little I heeded it. It's all my own fault; but it's too late." And he cried so bitterly that Tom began crying too.

"Never too late," said the fairy, in such a strange soft new voice that Tom looked up at her; and she was so beautiful for the moment, that Tom half fancied she was her sister.

No more was it too late. For, as poor Grimes cried and blubbered on, his own tears did what his mother's could not do, and Tom's could not do, and nobody's on earth could do for him; for they washed the soot off his face and off his clothes; and then they washed the mortar away from between the bricks; and the chimney crumbled down; and Grimes began to get out of it.

Up jumped the truncheon, and was going to hit him on the crown a tremendous thump, and drive him down again like a cork into a bottle. But the strange lady put it aside. "Will you obey me if I give you a chance?"

"As you please, ma'am. You're stronger than me—that I know too well, and wiser than me, I know too well also. And, as for being my own master, I've fared ill enough with that as yet. So whatever your ladyship pleases to order me; for I'm beat, and that's the truth."

"Be it so then—you may come out. But remember, disobey me again, and into a worse place still you go."

"I beg pardon, ma'am, but I never disobeyed you that I know of. I never had the honour of setting eyes upon you till I came to these ugly quarters."

"Never saw me? Who said to you, Those that will be foul, foul they will be?"

Grimes looked up; and Tom looked up too; for the voice was that of the Irishwoman who met them the day that they went out together to Harthover. "I gave you your warning then: but you gave it yourself a thousand times before and since. Every bad word that you said—every cruel and mean thing that you did—every time that you got tipsy—every day that you went dirty—you were disobeying me, whether you knew it or not."

"If I'd only known, ma'am—"

"You knew well enough that you were disobeying something, though you did not know it was me. But come out and take your chance. Perhaps it may be your last."

So Grimes stepped out of the chimney, and really, if it had not been for the scars on his face, he looked as clean and respectable as a master-sweep need look.

"Take him away," said she to the truncheon, "and give him his **ticket-of-leave**."

"And what is he to do, ma'am?"

"Get him to sweep out the crater of **Etna**; he will find some very steady men working out their time there, who will teach him his business: but mind, if that crater gets choked again, and there is an earthquake in consequence, bring them all to me, and I shall investigate the case very severely."

So the truncheon marched off Mr. Grimes, looking as meek as a drowned worm. And for aught I know, or do not know, he is sweeping the crater of Etna to this very day.

Narration and Discussion

Why were Grimes' own tears the only ones that could melt away the soot and the chimney?

Was Tom's mission successful?

Reading #31

Introduction

"Your work here is done," says the fairy to Tom. But what is next for him?

Vocabulary

keep your eye single: stay focused on the important things (Matthew 6:22)

dog days: the hottest days of the year

Reading

Part One

"And now," said the fairy to Tom, "your work here is done. You may as well go back again."

"I should be glad enough to go," said Tom, "but how am I to get up that great hole again, now the steam has stopped blowing?"

"I will take you up the backstairs. But I must bandage your eyes first; for I never allow anybody to see those backstairs of mine."

[omission for length]

So she tied the bandage on his eyes with one hand, and with the other she took it off. "Now," she said, "you are safe up the stairs." Tom opened his eyes very wide, and his mouth too; for he had not, as he thought, moved a single step. But, when he looked round him, there could be no doubt that he was safe up the backstairs, whatsoever they may be, which no man is going to tell you, for the plain reason that no man knows.

The first thing which Tom saw was the black cedars, high and sharp against the rosy dawn; and St. Brendan's Isle reflected double in the still broad silver sea. The wind sang softly in the cedars, and the water sang among the caves; the sea-birds sang as they streamed out into the ocean, and the land-birds as they built among the boughs; and the air was so full of song that it stirred St. Brendan and his hermits, as they slumbered in the shade; and they moved their good old lips, and sang their morning hymn amid their dreams. But among all the songs one came across the water more sweet and clear than all; for it was the song of a young girl's voice.

And what was the song which she sang?

Ah, my little man, I am too old to sing that song, and you too young to understand it. But have patience, and **keep your eye single**, and your hands clean, and you will learn some day to sing it yourself, without needing any man to teach you.

Part Two

And as Tom neared the island, there sat upon a rock the most graceful creature that ever was seen, looking down, with her chin upon her hand, and paddling with her feet in the water. And when they came to her she looked up, and behold it was Ellie.

"Oh, Miss Ellie," said he, "how you are grown!"

"Oh, Tom," said she, "how you are grown too!" And no wonder; they were both quite grown up—he into a tall man, and she into a beautiful woman.

"Perhaps I may be grown," she said. "I have had time enough; for I have been sitting here waiting for you many a hundred years, till I thought you were never coming."

"Many a hundred years?" thought Tom; but he had seen so much in his travels that he had quite given up being astonished; and, indeed, he could think of nothing but Ellie. So he stood and looked at Ellie, and Ellie looked at him; and they liked the employment so much that they stood and looked for seven years more, and neither spoke nor stirred.

Part Three

At last they heard the fairy say: "Attention, children. Are you never going to look at me again?"

"We have been looking at you all this while," they said. And so they thought they had been.

"Then look at me once more," said she. They looked—and both of them cried out at once, "Oh, who are you, after all?"

"You are our dear Mrs. Doasyouwouldbedoneby."

"No, you are good Mrs. Bedonebyasyoudid; but you are grown quite beautiful now!"

"To you," said the fairy, "but look again."

"You are Mother Carey," said Tom, in a very low, solemn voice; for he had found out something which made him very happy, and yet frightened him more than all that he had ever seen.

"But you are grown quite young again."

"To you," said the fairy. "Look again."

"You are the Irishwoman who met me the day I went to Harthover!"

And when they looked she was neither of them, and yet all of them at once.

"My name is written in my eyes, if you have eyes to see it there." And they looked into her great, deep, soft eyes, and they changed again and again into every hue, as the light changes in a diamond.

"Now read my name," said she, at last. And her eyes flashed, for one moment, clear, white, blazing light: but the children could not read her name; for they were dazzled, and hid their faces in their hands.

"Not yet, young things, not yet," said she, smiling; and then she turned to Ellie. "You may take him home with you now on Sundays, Ellie. He has won his spurs in the great battle, and become fit to go with you and be a man; because he has done the thing he did not like."

So Tom went home with Ellie on Sundays, and sometimes on week-days, too; and he is now a great man of science, and can plan railroads, and steam-engines, and electric telegraphs, and rifled guns, and so forth; and knows everything about everything, except why a hen's egg don't turn into a crocodile, and two or three other little things which no one will know till the coming of the Cocqcigrues.

And all this from what he learnt when he was a water-baby, underneath the sea.

And of course Tom married Ellie?

My dear child, what a silly notion! Don't you know that no one ever marries in a fairy tale, under the rank of a prince or a princess?

And Tom's dog?

Oh, you may see him any clear night in July; for the old Dog Star was so worn out by the last three hot summers that there have been no **dog days** since; so that they had to take him down and put Tom's dog up in his place. Therefore, as new brooms sweep clean, we may hope for some warm weather this year. And that is the end of my story.

Moral

And now, my dear little man, what should we learn from this parable?

We should learn thirty-seven or thirty-nine things, I am not exactly sure which; but one thing, at least, we may learn, and that is this—when we see efts in the pond, never to throw stones at them, or catch them with crooked pins, or put them into vivariums with sticklebacks, that the sticklebacks may prick them in their poor little stomachs, and make them jump out of the glass into somebody's work-box, and so come to a bad end.

For these efts are nothing else but water-babies who are [foolish] and dirty, and will not learn their lessons and keep themselves clean; and, therefore (as comparative anatomists will tell you fifty years hence, though they are not learned enough to tell you now), their skulls grow fat, their jaws grow out, and their brains grow small, and their tails grow long, and they lose all their ribs (which I am sure you would not like to do), and their skins grow dirty and spotted, and they never get into the clear rivers, much less into the great wide sea, but hang about in dirty ponds, and live in the mud, and eat worms, as they deserve to do.

But that is no reason why you should ill-use them; but only why you should pity them and be kind to them, and hope that someday they will wake up, and be ashamed of their nasty, dirty, lazy, [foolish] life, and try to amend, and become something better once more.

For, perhaps, if they do so, then after 379,423 years, nine months, thirteen days, two hours, and twenty-one minutes (for aught that appears to the contrary), if they work very hard and wash very hard all that time, their brains may grow bigger, and their jaws grow smaller, and their ribs come back, and their tails wither off, and they will turn into water-babies again, and perhaps after that into land-babies; and after that perhaps into grown men.

You know they won't?

Very well, I daresay you know best. But you see, some folks have a great liking for those poor little efts. They never did anybody any harm, or could if they tried; and their only fault is, that they do no good—any more than some thousands of their betters. But what with ducks, and what with pike, and what with sticklebacks, and what with water-beetles, and what with naughty boys, they are "sae sair hadden doun," as the Scotsmen say, that it is a wonder how they live; and some folks can't help hoping, with good Bishop Butler, that they may have another chance, to make things fair and even, somewhere, somewhen, somehow.

Meanwhile, do you learn your lessons, and thank God that you have plenty of cold water to wash in; and wash in it too. And then, if my story is not true, something better is; and if I am not quite right, still you will be, as long as you stick to hard work and cold water. But remember always, as I told you at first, that this is all a fairy tale, and only fun and pretense: and, therefore, you are not to believe a word of it, even if it is true.

Narration and Discussion

Have you learned thirty-seven or thirty-nine things from this story?

Kingsley says, "And then, if my story is not true, something better is." What might that be?

Entirely Optional Exam Questions for *The Water-Babies*

Tell what you remember about one of these stories:

1. How Tom became a water-baby

2. About Tom and the sea-toffees

3. About something Tom saw in the Other-end-of-Nowhere

4. How Tom tried to help Mr. Grimes

Bibliography

Abberley, Will. "Animal Cunning: Deceptive Nature and Truthful Science in Charles Kingsley's Natural Theology." Victorian Studies, vol. 58, no. 1, 2015, pp. 34–56. JSTOR, https://doi.org/10.2979/victorianstudies.58.1.02. Accessed 4 July 2024.

Arnold, Matthew. "The Forsaken Merman." Retrieved from Poets.org. https://www.poetryfoundation.org/poems/43589/the-forsaken-merman

Ballard, J. G. "J. G. Ballard." In *The Pleasure of Reading*. Edited by Antonia Fraser. Bloomsbury Paperbacks, an Imprint of Bloomsbury Publishing PLC, 2015.

Buckley, Andrew. "Bilbo's Last Song: The Power of Fairy Stories." *Coffee With Keats* substack. June 29, 2024.
https://coffeewithkeats.substack.com/p/bilbos-last-song

Bulfinch, Thomas. *Bulfinch's Mythology Illustrated*. Avenel, 1979.

Calmgrove. "Kingsley's riddle." Calmgrove: Exploring the world of ideas through books. September 16, 2021.
https://calmgrove.wordpress.com/2021/09/16/wb/

Esolen, Anthony M. *Ten Ways to Destroy the Imagination of Your Child*. Wilmington, DE: ISI Books, 2010.

Glass, Karen. *Know and Tell: The Art of Narration*. N.p., 2018.

Glass, Karen. *Much May Be Done With Sparrows*. N.p., 2024.

Hamilton, Edith. *Mythology*. New York, NY: Back Bay Books / Little, Brown and Company, 1998. (First published 1942.)

Hawthorne, Nathaniel. *Tanglewood Tales*. Boston: Ticknor, Reed, and Fields, 1853.

"Jo." "*The Water-Babies*, Charles Kingsley/Looe, Cornwall." *Return of a Native: Landscapes of Literature, Art and Song*. 2024.
https://returnofanative.com/stories/the-water-babies-charles-kingsley/

Kingsley, Charles. *Glaucus, or, The Wonders of the Shore*. Cambridge/London: Macmillan and Co., 1859.

Bibliography

Kingsley, Charles. *Madam How and Lady Why, or, First Lessons in Earth Lore for Children.* New York: The Macmillan Company, 1901.

Lehmann, R. C. (1904). Living books in the teaching of history. *Parents' Review*, 15, 1, 25-32

Lewis, C. S. *The Abolition of Man.* New York, N.Y. The Macmillan Company, 1947.

Lewis, C. S. *Prince Caspian.* London: Geoffrey Bles, 1951.

Lewis, C. S. *The Magician's Nephew.* London: The Bodley Head, 1955.

Lewis, C. S. *Voyage of the Dawn Treader.* London: Geoffrey Bles, 1955.

Mason, Charlotte M. *Home Education.* Vol. 1 of *The Original Home Schooling Series.* Wheaton, IL: Tyndale House, 1989. Originally published 1935 by Kegan Paul, Trench, Trubner and Co., Ltd. (London). Page references are to the 1989 edition.

Mason, Charlotte M. *Ourselves.* Vol. 4 of *The Original Home Schooling Series.* Wheaton, IL: Tyndale House, 1989. Originally published 1905 by Kegan Paul, Trench, Trubner and Co., Ltd. (London). Page references are to the 1989 edition.

Mason, Charlotte M. *Parents and Children.* Vol. 2 of *The Original Home Schooling Series.* Wheaton, IL: Tyndale House, 1989. Originally published 1904 by Kegan Paul, Trench, Trubner and Co., Ltd. (London). Page references are to the 1989 edition.

Mason, Charlotte M. *A Philosophy of Education.* Vol. 6 of *The Original Home Schooling Series.* Wheaton, IL: Tyndale House, 1989. Originally published 1925 as *An Essay Towards a Philosophy of Education* by Kegan Paul, Trench, Trubner and Co., Ltd. (London). Page references are to the 1989 edition.

Neill, Anna. "Marvelous Plasticity and the Fortunes of Species in *The Water Babies*." Philosophy and Literature 38.1 (April, 2014) Retrieved from KU ScholarWorks. https://kuscholarworks.kul.edu

"One Hippopotami Lyrics." *Lyrics.com.* STANDS4 LLC, 2024. Web. 4 Jul 2024. https://www.lyrics.com/lyric/570619/Allan+Sherman/One+Hippopotami.

Turley, Steven R. *Beauty Matters: Creating a High Aesthetic in School Culture.* N.p., 2018.

"The Wire." *Star Trek: Deep Space Nine*, Season 2, Ep. 22, Paramount Pictures, 1994.

Finally, I need to give credit to Julien Miquel, @YouTubeJulien, whose how-to-pronounce-names videos were invaluable in preparing these notes.

www.ingramcontent.com/pod-product-compliance
Lightning Source LLC
LaVergne TN
LVHW061344060426
835512LV00012B/2559